THE
LAST LEAF

STUART LUTZ

THE
LAST LEAF

VOICES OF HISTORY'S
LAST-KNOWN SURVIVORS

 Prometheus Books

59 John Glenn Drive
Amherst, New York 14228–2119

Published 2010 by Prometheus Books

Inquiries should be addressed to
Prometheus Books
59 John Glenn Drive
Amherst, New York 14228–2119
VOICE: 716–691–0133
FAX: 716–691–0137
WWW.PROMETHEUSBOOKS.COM

14 13 12 11 10   5 4 3 2 1

Library of Congress Cataloging-in-Publication Data

Lutz, Stuart.
    The last leaf : voices of history's last-known survivors / by Stuart Lutz.
        p. cm.
    ISBN 978–1–61614–162–2 (cloth : alk. paper)
    1. Biography—20th century. 2. United States—Biography.

CT220 .L88 2010
920.073—dc22

                                                                    2009047150

Printed in the United States of America on acid-free paper

To Sara,
who traveled many of the miles in the book,

and to Aidan,
with whom I hope to share these stories one day

Contents

Foreword   11
  Bernard Edelman

A Letter of Thanks   15

"The Last Leaf"   17
  Oliver Wendell Holmes

Introduction   21

PART 1: WITNESSES TO GREAT HISTORY

Civil War Widows   29
  Gertrude Grubb Janeway: The Last Union Widow   30
  Maudie Celia Hopkins:
      The Final Confederate Widow   39
  Alberta Martin: The Next-to-Last
      Confederate Widow   45
Thomas Brewer: The Last Participant in the
  Scopes Monkey Trial of 1925   51

7

Frank Buckles: The Last American World War I Soldier   59
John Coolidge: The Last Person Alive to Live
    in the White House in the 1920s   70
Ruth Dyk: The Final Suffragette to March for
    Women's Rights before the Nineteenth Amendment   77
John Finn: The Last Medal of Honor Recipient
    for Heroic Actions on Pearl Harbor Day   84
Robert Myers: The Final Man from the Committee
    That Created Social Security   94
George Putnam Jr.: The Last Person Still Alive
    to Have Flown with Amelia Earhart   101
Boyce Price: One of the Final Two Officers to Work
    in President Franklin D. Roosevelt's
    Secret White House Map Room   109
Budd Schulberg: The Last Man to Write
    with F. Scott Fitzgerald   119
Norman Vaughan: The Final Explorer to Accompany
    Admiral Byrd to the Antarctic in 1929   127
McKinley Wooden: The Last Living Soldier to Serve with
    Harry S. Truman in Battery D during World War I   135

PART 2: SURVIVORS

Rose Freedman: The Final Survivor of the
    1911 Triangle Shirtwaist Factory Fire   143
John Fulton: One of the Last-Surviving Ground Crew
    from the *Hindenburg* Explosion   151
Frank Holmgren: The Final Survivor of the USS *Juneau*   159
Charles Lindberg: The Last Iwo Jima Flag Raiser   167
Cora Luchetti: One of the Final People to Remember
    the 1906 San Francisco Earthquake   178
Barbara Anderson McDermott: The Last Passenger
    of the Sunken *Lusitania*   183

Robie Mortin: The Final Witness to the Infamous
    1923 Rosewood Race Riots in Florida   194
Esther Raab: One of the Last Escapees of the
    Nazi Death Camp Sobibor   204
David Stoliar: The Only Survivor of the *Struma* Sinking   219
Thomas Torresson Jr.: One of the Last Survivors of the
    Morro Castle Passenger Ship, Which Burned in 1934   226
Adella Wotherspoon: The Final Survivor of the
    1904 *General Slocum* Fire on the East River   236

PART 3: WITNESSES TO TECHNOLOGICAL INNOVATION

Arthur Burks: The Last Major Designer of the ENIAC,
    the First Electronic General-Purpose Computer   249
Pem Farnsworth: The Final Witness to the
    First Electronic Television Broadcast in 1927   259
Robert Halgrim: The Last Man Alive to
    Work with Thomas Edison   268
Harry Mills: The Final Person to Hear the
    First Commercial Radio Broadcast   279
Jerry Minter: One of the Last People to Have Known
    Edwin Armstrong, the Creator of FM Radio   288
Albert Wattenberg: One of the Final Physicists Present
    at the First Controlled Nuclear Reaction   295

PART 4: ATHLETES AND ENTERTAINERS

Slim Bryant: The Final Musician to Play with
    Country Music Star Jimmie Rodgers   305
George R. Gibson: The Final Player on an NFL Team
    That Folded during the Great Depression   312

Kitty Carlisle Hart: The Last Starring Actress
    from a Marx Brothers Movie   319
Paul Hopkins: The Last Living Pitcher to Give Up
    a Home Run to Babe Ruth in His
    Historic 1927 Season   325
Robert Lockwood Jr.: The Final Musician to
    Play with Blues Legend Robert Johnson   331
Hal Prieste: The Last Participant in the
    1920 Antwerp Olympics   341
Doris Eaton Travis: The Last of the Original
    Ziegfeld Follies Performers   348
Dorothy Young: Harry Houdini's Final Stage Assistant   361

Afterword   369

Foreword

Bernard Edelman

I once read about a newspaper reporter in Washington State who selected a name at random from the county telephone directory every week. He dialed the number, asked for the person, and told him or her he wanted to write a story about them. "Me?" often came the reply. "Whaddaya want to write about me? Nothing interesting or special about my life."

The reporter persisted. He set up an interview, visited the skeptical citizen, and invariably plumbed a life, probing into whatever piqued his interest, composing a well-illustrated feature piece of substance. He did this for years, so obviously he struck a chord with the readers of his paper.

In *The Last Leaf*, Stuart Lutz has worked a variation of this. In a ten-year sojourn, he has managed to find, meet, speak with, and compile the reminiscences and recollections of individuals who are, in effect, footnotes to history. They are, for the most part, the final survivors—the Last Men and Women Standing, one might say—who witnessed or experienced

Bernard Edelman is the editor of *Dear America: Letters Home from Vietnam* and the author of the oral history *Centenarians: The Story of the 20th Century by the Americans Who Lived It*.

events of historical, technological, or social significance in the turbulent and tempestuous twentieth century. As you read this, most of the people you will meet in this volume have gone to their final rest. But the smorgasbord of stories Mr. Lutz has collected offers tantalizing glimpses into some of the seminal events and personalities of the century past.

The youngest interviewee in *The Last Leaf* is in his ninth decade. More than a few hit the century mark. Their stories concern events and personalities that are "ancient history" to most of us. But their memories and their reflections, in a global sense, remind us of where we came from; "ancient history," it turns out, is not so ancient after all.

In the realm of conflict in a century marred by bloodshed and the deaths of millions, you'll meet John Finn, who relives the Japanese attack on Pearl Harbor. Lieutenant Finn is the last-surviving recipient of the Medal of Honor—fifteen were awarded—from that apocalyptic foray. Perhaps you will glean an understanding of what a hero really is: not someone who hits a baseball very far, or throws a football for lots of yards, or drives a souped-up car very fast and wins races. Lieutenant Finn did none of these things. Rather, he rallied stunned comrades into defending the battered naval base. "I was hit about twenty times," he recalls. "My left arm wouldn't work anymore; I had some broken bones and was also shot in my left foot. Some of the worst pain came from the tiny shrapnel no one could see and the doctor really had to search to find. I refused medical attention, even though I was ordered to sick bay. It wasn't until 2:00 the next morning that I went. When I got there, everyone there was seriously wounded, so I went home to make sure my wife was all right; a few hours later, I went back to sick bay. I was hospitalized from December 8 to December 24." And, he adds, "I really didn't think much about what I had done."

You'll see Harry Truman—*Captain* Harry Truman—

through the eyes of McKinley Wooden, the last man to serve with him in Battery D, 129th Field Artillery, during World War I. You'll get insights into President Truman's predecessor, Franklin Delano Roosevelt, through Boyce Price's stories of the top-secret Map Room in the White House. You'll applaud Esther Raab and her comrades who manage to escape from the brutal German concentration camp Sobibor.

In the arena of technological wizardry in a century of astonishing progress, you'll get an appreciation of Thomas Alva Edison from Robert Halgrim, the inventor's longtime personal assistant. "Look around you," Mr. Halgrim tells Stuart Lutz. "Edison is present in many things we see today, from cement sidewalks to tubes for television images. He invented 1,087 different things . . . [yet m]any young people have no idea who he was or how he influenced . . . radio, CDs, the computer, the VCR, air-conditioning, and having cold milk for breakfast. It's all due to electricity. Just think about it. The [invention of the] lightbulb brought about so many things."

Considering the computer, the fulcrum of the Age of Information, you'll spend time with Dr. Arthur Burks, the last major designer of the Electronic Numerical Integrator And Computer, the forerunner of today's ubiquitous desktops and laptops.

In an age of social reform, you'll meet Ruth Dyk, the last of the suffragettes whose agitation for women's right to vote culminated in the passage of the Nineteenth Amendment. "There was a unified spirit of working together for the cause," she relates. "I was only eleven or so when I first started marching in 1912. There were a number of parades in Boston, and my mother used to take me to the ones on Beacon Hill, by the Massachusetts State House." But there were "people lined up on the streets protesting us. I guess they were afraid of us upsetting the balance and giving women some political power. Making women equal with men." And when the Nineteenth

Amendment was ratified, "Oh, we were excited, glad, delighted," she says. "We all had the feeling we finally succeeded in what we had tried to do for so long." Ironically, Ruth Dyk didn't get to vote in the presidential elections the following year: she had not yet turned twenty-one.

You'll escape with Rose Freedman from the Triangle Shirtwaist Factory fire, which claimed the lives of 146 young immigrant women and led to legislation advancing the rights of workers. You'll be present with Robert Myers, one of the architects of Social Security who served as the chief actuarial officer for the Social Security Administration from 1947 through 1970. President Roosevelt made Social Security one of the landmarks of his administration—and one of the most important and far-reaching pieces of social legislation in the twentieth century.

In the world of entertainment, you'll go back to the early days of the blues with Robert Lockwood Jr., a musician mentored by the legendary Robert Johnson; and Paul Hopkins, a onetime pitcher for the lowly Washington Senators, the last living hurler to surrender a home run—a grand slam, actually—to the Sultan of Swat, Babe Ruth.

The Last Leaf really has no beginning and no end. You can pick out someone whose story might interest you and read it. You might then read the next story, or skip a hundred pages. In the modern rush-rush world, where we connect in cyberspace with others across the globe and access information in an instant on the most esoteric of subjects, it is refreshing to recall a slower time, when momentous events riveted the world on radio and in newsprint—and when "24/7" were just two numbers.

A Letter of Thanks

*I*t took more than a decade to compile *The Last Leaf*. I owe many, many people a note—or, more accurately, a long letter—of thanks.

My first round of thank-yous is extended to the nearly forty "Last Leaves" themselves. They graciously opened their homes and their antique memories for me. They answered my questions, provided pictures and original memorabilia for me to photograph, and corrected their own chapters. I hope that in some small way I can return their multitude of favors with this book, and that I have accurately transcribed their tales.

Often, when I visited the Last Leaves, they had caretakers present during my interviews. Usually these were children or spouses who sat through the retelling of old tales one more time. The helpers, however, also included home health aides or neighbors. I know of a couple of helpers who drove more than an hour to attend my interview. I give my thanks for their time and effort.

I must thank my friends and family who alerted me to news stories about final survivors. For example, Mrs. Alberta

Martin, believed to be the last Confederate widow, died in 2004. Soon after Mrs. Martin's death, Mrs. Maudie Hopkins announced that she was now the final Confederate widow, and this story was carried in the media. My e-mail box was filled by my friends, who thought of me when they saw articles about Mrs. Hopkins.

I thank two published writers who gave me a great deal of assistance and encouragement, Judith Lindbergh and Lady Borton.

I have to remember my fellow authors in the Writers Support Circle that I attend every Thursday night. They have critiqued chapters and given me encouragement.

My mother, Arlene, spent days reading every single word, and her eagle-eyed editing improved the book. I also have to thank her for my inherent love of history. My father, Kenneth, lent some much-needed technical assistance, such as explaining nuclear fission and the superheterodyne receiver (which I still don't completely understand, even now). And special thanks also to Donna Lutz and Keith Shafritz.

A final thank you goes to my wife, Sara, for her endless support on this project. She accompanied me on many road trips described in the book, from Elba, Alabama, to Fort Myers, Florida, to Camden, New Jersey. And when I had to leave home for a few days to interview a Last Leaf, she understood.

"The Last Leaf"

Oliver Wendell Holmes

I saw him once before,
As he passed by the door,
   And again
The pavement stones resound,
As he totters o'er the ground
   With his cane.

They say that in his prime,
Ere the pruning-knife of Time
   Cut him down,
Not a better man was found
By the Crier on his round
   Through the town.

But now he walks the streets,
And he looks at all he meets
   Sad and wan,
And he shakes his feeble head,
That it seems as if he said,
   "They are gone."

The mossy marbles rest
On the lips that he has prest
        In their bloom,
And the names he loves to hear
Have been carved for many a year
        On the tomb.

My grandmamma has said—
Poor old lady, she is dead
        Long ago—
That he had a Roman nose,
And his cheek was like a rose
        In the snow.

But now his nose is thin,
And it rests upon his chin
        Like a staff,
And a crook is in his back,
And a melancholy crack
        In his laugh.

I know it is a sin
For me to sit and grin
        At him here;
But the old three-cornered hat,
And the breeches, and all that,
        Are so queer!

And if I should live to be
The last leaf upon the tree
        In the spring,
Let them smile, as I do now,
At the forsaken old bough
        Where I cling . . .

A handwritten copy of Holmes's "The Last Leaf"
photo courtesy Stuart Lutz

Introduction

It was one of those blistering days in Charleston, South Carolina, that children raised in the North are unprepared for. One early afternoon my parents took me on a historical walking tour of the classic city. I could not wait for it to end so I could find sweet shade and—Dad willing—an ice cream cone.

The tour guide pointed to an old building. There were no remarkable architectural features about it, nor was it historically significant itself. The guide, in his molasses drawl, informed us, "That building there is our home for Confederate widows. And I am proud to report that we still have a couple of them alive."

"But how can that be?" I whispered to my mother. I knew the bloody Civil War had ended 125 years earlier, and people could not live that long.

"I don't know. Ask the tour guide," she suggested. So I did.

"You see," he explained with a friendly laugh, "some of the Confederate veterans were old men when they married very young women long after the war ended. The old soldiers died. Now those once-young ladies are old Confederate widows, and they live here." I was amazed to learn a few women married to a Johnny Reb were still alive. This was my first step on my Last Leaf journey to interview the final survivors of historically important events. I never imagined then that I would one day meet the last three Civil War widows in their Southern homes.

As a boy, my great-grandparents Bill and Emma, who were wed for seventy-seven years, visited occasionally. To impress me, Bill, who was then in his early eighties, rode my bicycle up a side street and then climbed a mulberry tree, creating some anxious moments when he had difficulty descending. ("No, officer, it's not exactly a cat stuck up in the tree.") After Bill returned to terra firma, we went into the kitchen for a snack. My father, pointing to his octogenarian grandparents, said, "My grandparents were born before the Wright brothers flew." Born before flight? I couldn't imagine it. I was, after all, raised in a time when skies were cluttered by glittering airplanes.

I sat, transfixed by their stories of growing up in czarist Russia, boarding an immigrant ship steaming toward golden America, and seeing an airplane for the first time. Emma proudly recounted how she voted for the first time in 1920, although she had already been married for four years.

My father retrieved a framed picture from the next room. The family photograph shows five people arranged on a green sofa. "See," he said, pointing to the red-headed baby on his lap. "That's you and me." He moved his finger to the left. "That's my mother, your grandmother. And sitting next to her is your great-grandfather." He motioned to my great-grandfather sitting across the round kitchen table. "And that's"—he said with extra emphasis—"your great-great-grandmother. She was born in 1872, when Ulysses Grant was president. That's a five-generation photograph. You're really lucky because very few people have a picture like this."

photo courtesy Stuart Lutz

Much like seeing the Confederate widows' home in South Carolina, I was mesmerized by this family experience. This was the second step on my Last Leaf journey.

As a boy, I flipped through military history books. One author wrote about "Last Man Clubs." They were formed when a group of former comrades-in-arms would chip in a few dollars each and purchase an expensive bottle of wine or champagne. The unopened bottle was kept in a safe place. The veterans would meet for annual dinners and note which fellows had died during the previous year. It was the solemn task of the final Last Man Club member to drink a silent toast to his deceased friends with the liquor. This book passage was the third step on my Last Leaf journey.

I watched little television as a child, but one of my favorite programs featured the nomadic Charles Kuralt on Sunday mornings. He created segments about common Americans who had extraordinary stories or had the experience of witnessing unusual events. I never saw one that failed to fascinate. Kuralt's segments were the fourth step in my Last Leaf journey. I wanted to create a work chronicling American life, much as Kuralt had done. All I needed was a unique idea.

When a significant event occurs, many people are often privy to it, and we read accounts in the newspaper the next day— "Journalism is the first draft of history." Death's scythe slowly removes the eyewitnesses and participants until there is but one left. The Last Leaf. When that final person passes away, no one can challenge our thinking about that particular occurrence. No witness can give a new perspective to old events or recount anecdotes no one else knows. Once this Last Leaf dies, the story enters a new realm, one occupied by academic historians fighting over the meanings of the event and ignoring the larger and often more interesting narrative. For example, I learned in college about the deadly Triangle Shirtwaist Factory fire in 1911. More than 140 immigrant women were killed because the escape doors had been bolted shut, and many women died jumping to the sidewalk in an attempt to escape. I never knew there were any survivors, because the educational emphasis was on the significance and the aftermath of the event, not the actual tale of the blaze.

This book's goal is to fill in those gaps by recording the stories of the Last Leaves. I believe it is important to capture the tales of these last witnesses to history before, as one of the final survivors of the most murderous Nazi death camp eloquently stated, "we are all gone." This book gives us a last chance to hear how a seventeen-year-old worker escaped the tragic Triangle Shirtwaist Factory fire by illogically fleeing upstairs as her coworkers jumped to their deaths. It gives us the chance to understand why a young woman married an old Civil War veteran, leaving her as the last widow 140 years after the start of the conflict. It gives us the opportunity to recount how a young Marine scaled Iwo Jima's viciously defended Mount Suribachi to plant Old Glory on its volcanic peak.

This book covers nearly all types of human endeavors, sufferings, and accomplishments. Some stories are light, such as those of the boy who plucked the jury names out of a hat at the famous Scopes Monkey Trial, or the final pitcher to surrender a home run to Babe Ruth in his record-setting 1927 season. Other tales are tragic, such as those of the only passenger of the torpedoed *Struma* plucked out of the Black Sea or the last survivor of a cruel race riot in Florida. Still other stories relate to human achievement, such as those of the last witness to the first electronic television broadcast, one of the final physicists at the first controlled nuclear chain reaction, and the last explorer to accompany Admiral Richard Byrd to the Antarctic.

Some of the chapters recount events and personalities largely forgotten in the foggy American consciousness, such as the deadly *General Slocum* fire and the influential yet unremembered inventor of FM radio, Edwin Armstrong. A few tales recall events that still influence the country today, such as the Scopes Monkey Trial, the woman suffrage movement, and the development of the first electronic general-purpose computer.

In writing this book, I learned one unexpected lesson that revealed itself only after many interviews. When I called a ninety-eight-year-old suffragette to schedule a meeting, she told me that she needed to review her busy schedule to see when she could fit me in. I watched a centenarian Olympian perform his daily stretching exercises. I met with a nonagenarian Oscar winner who insists that he loves working every day. I heard from a 101-year-old woman who graduated college at age eighty-eight with a degree in (what else?) history; she is now working on her master's degree. I went to the home of Harry Houdini's last stage assistant, who lives alone and runs up her steps at a pace I would not attempt. I watched my octogenarian great-grandfather cycling as a boy. I discovered that a commonality to nearly all the Last Leaves is they remain active and that they have something to look forward to every day. You can forget diets and miracle medicines; activity is the answer to Ponce de León's quest.

I traveled to seventeen states to conduct in-person interviews with these remarkable men and women, from tiny Lexa, Arkansas, to collegiate Hanover, New Hampshire; from sunny West Palm Beach, Florida, to Urbana, Illinois. This count does not include those states I only drove through, such as Mississippi and Georgia. After ten years of interviews, it is my great honor to present to you the remarkable Last Leaves.

If you know of the final survivor of a historically significant event whose tales should be included in *The Last Leaf, Volume II*, please e-mail me at TheLastLeaf@aol.com. Kindly include your contact information and a brief description of the person to be profiled.

Part 1
Witnesses to Great History

Civil War Widows

The death toll of the Civil War is difficult to fathom. From 1861 to 1865 there were approximately 620,000 deaths, roughly 2 percent of the entire population of the United States. By today's standards, that translates into approximately 6 million deaths, or the loss of the entire population of Indiana. The three days of the Battle of Gettysburg, the war's most famous clash, resulted in approximately 50,000 American casualties, almost the same number of American lives lost throughout the lengthy Vietnam conflict.

Despite the rampant destruction and death, millions of soldiers who fought in the butternut or blue survived the horrors, returned to their homes, and married. While the veterans have long since passed away, there remain three women who hold unique perspectives on the Civil War and its aftermath. They are the last-surviving Civil War widows, and, 140 years after the start of the war, they tell an amazing tale. One is Union and two are Confederate, although all three are Southerners.

The three Civil War widows were young women when they married their octogenarian suitors, and although this age gap might seem strange to Americans today, such marriages were not uncommon decades ago, for one simple reason. The women came from destitute Southern families, in regions devastated by the farm depression of the 1920s. At that time, a Civil War pension was one of the few steady incomes available to rural families. An impoverished girl might marry a much older veteran, in part to be his caretaker. In return, the young lady was often granted her husband's reliable pension after his death.

GERTRUDE GRUBB JANEWAY
The Last Union Widow
"We really loved each other. And love don't forget."

Mrs. Gertrude Grubb Janeway, the last Union widow, resides in the small town of Blaine, Tennessee, not far from Knoxville. She was born in July 1909, forty-four years after the conclusion of the Civil War. In 1927, at the age of eighteen, she married eighty-one-year-old John Janeway, a Union army veteran who, at age eighteen, was forcibly enlisted in early 1864. On July 31, 1864, Janeway was captured near Chattahoochee, Georgia, after a skirmish between General William Sherman's cavalry and the Confederates. Paroled in Savannah, Georgia, on November 30, 1864, Janeway then reported to a prisoner of war camp in Maryland on December 10.[1] His capture ended his Civil War service, but the country's obligation to his widow, Gertrude Janeway, continued nearly 140 years after his service.

Mrs. Janeway's closest relative, nephew Duel Grubb, dutifully visits her every Saturday afternoon. She resides in a little log cabin with a rusting roof, rough-hewn walls, and piles of scrap on the front porch. The last Union widow, an elderly woman, lays in a hospital bed, partially raised so she is half sitting, in the far right corner of the small room; the room has a

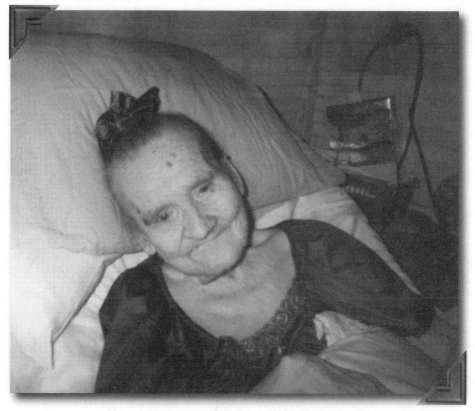

Mrs. Janeway at the time of the interview
photo by Stuart Lutz

new tile floor, two televisions, a solitary lightbulb hanging from the ceiling, and an old wood-burning stove. Mr. Grubb introduces his aunt, and she eagerly replies, "I've been expecting you" in a melodic and delightful drawl. Mrs. Janeway, who recently celebrated her ninetieth birthday, wears a blue dress with a matching blue ribbon in her gray hair, which is pulled straight back. She has kind and deep blue eyes.

Mrs. Janeway is eager to talk about her childhood. "When I was a young 'un, I's born and raised in the country 'bout two miles from here." She waves her finger to an imaginary spot

Mrs. Janeway's nineteenth-century cabin
photo by Stuart Lutz

beyond the cabin. "The doctor didn't get there in time, so two old people had to do the work." She pauses, then shakes her left fist and continues emphatically: "Grubb was my family name. My mama was Hattie Grubb, my daddy was Tom Grubb; they worked on the farm all the time. They raised an awful good garden. We couldn't buy [food]. We had no money to buy it. We had to raise it or starve. We had some apple trees that really helped us out. Mama would gather 'em for breakfast. I had just one good dress to wear to school. I was the oldest of four, with three brothers. My father died in 1922; my mother died in 1939. I lived with my brother Rueben 'til he died in 1989." She stops, then summarizes with, "We was just as poor as we could be."

She knows a little about her husband's Civil War service, beginning with his 1864 enlistment as an eighteen-year-old.

Mr. and Mrs. Janeway about 1927
photo reprinted by permission of the *Knoxville News Sentinel*

"John lived up the road a little piece, towards New Corinth [Tennessee]. He had just shelled up a bushel of corn to get ground. As he was heading to the mill, a bunch of soldiers came 'long and they all stopped. One of them said to him, 'You look like a stout young man. How 'bout getting up with us and joining the army?' He looked around, wondering how he'd get the meal back home, but decided to join anyway. When he joined the army, he gave them the fake name of January so that his mama and daddy couldn't find him." Her gaze turns to the large oval portrait of her and her husband, hanging on the rough-hewn wall. "His mama and daddy worried about him. But his father said that the Lord'll make a man of him."

Mrs. Janeway says that her husband rarely spoke of his Civil War days. "Not hardly ever, unless I asked about it. Sometimes he'd answer me and sometimes he wouldn't. He wasn't stuck up a bit, but when he talked about it, he talked just like you and me talk." She waves her left hand back and forth between us. "But sometimes he'd say, 'Honey, don't ask me so many questions. I don't want to talk about it.' He did tell me one story of when he laid down during a fight, and when he stood up, he saw a bullet had gone through his hat brim. He was later captured at Atlanta and served to the end of the war."

She discusses her eighty-one-year-old groom, whom she married as an eighteen-year-old bride in 1927. "After the army, he came back to here, got a wife, and went to California 'til she died. Then he came back here again as an old man, where he still knew a few people. He was surprised that Mama, who he knew from their youth, was still alive, so he called on her. He came four times to talk to her 'fore asking permission to see me. So my family went to church and he came to see my mother. He asked her for permission to see me. Mother told him, 'She's old enough. Ask her.' So he turned right around and asked me, right there in the middle of church! I was only fifteen, so we went together three years on account of my age. Then my man got the license. We was married in the middle of a big road 'bout half a mile from here: no one but me and my man and the squire, and another man that drove us up there. He was the one who also got the preacher. By the time we was done, every door and window had peeping faces. My man said, 'I do.' He treated me as good as a baby, he never gave me a short word. Once he scolded me and I cried, but he apologized." She gazes again at the portrait on the wall, then points to it with great pride. The hand-tinted picture shows a seated young Mrs. Janeway wearing a large hat, her feet unable to reach the floor; she sits beside an elderly man. "We had that [photograph] taken in Knoxville, about 1927. It's the only picture of us together." Just below the portrait is a color picture of a white tombstone.

Mrs. Janeway proudly points to a number of framed certificates on the wall. One is a recent letter from the governor of Tennessee, congratulating her on her ninetieth birthday. It makes no mention of her Civil War widow status. Another certificate is from the Daughters of Union Veterans, who honor her for her unique standing.

"We really loved each other. And love don't forget. I really do miss him. We had ten years of good times. I wish it had lasted twenty or forty years." She says this mournfully, even though she has been a widow for sixty-two years.

After her husband died, Mrs. Janeway did not work—she explains that her right hand cannot shut—but she did receive her husband's Civil War pension. She removes her right arm from under the blanket to show her deformed hand, then quickly puts it back under the covers.

Eastern Tennessee was one of the most sectionally divided areas during the Civil War. Although the state left the Union to join the Confederacy, few residents of this poor area could afford slaves; the region's poverty created some Unionist sympathy. President Andrew Johnson, the Democratic successor to the Republican president Abraham Lincoln, grew up in Greeneville, about sixty miles east of Mrs. Janeway's home. As a child, however, she never saw any simmering emotions from the Civil War. She adds, "I never really traveled much beyond the country here anyway."

Mrs. Janeway discusses her ancient cabin. "Lord, I can't tell you how old [the cabin] is. It was here when I was a little girl, and I remember it as a child. Lord, I guess it was 'bout five years after we was married that we bought this. We had to save up five dollars a month until we had enough to get it."

Mr. Grubb drives to the New Corinth Church to show me Mr. Janeway's grave. As we travel past the cow pastures littered with hay rolls and slatted tobacco barns, he offers additional information on his aunt. "We made an application for a medical aide to see Gertrude, and on the form, we wrote that she was a Civil War widow. Well, that seemed a bit extraordinary to the hospital clerk, who called a reporter. But you have to understand one thing about Gertrude. She lives a very simple life and really doesn't want for anything. We got her Supplementary Security Income in 1981, only because of the health insurance. She has offers from people to pay her property taxes, which doesn't amount to much, but she declines it because she doesn't believe in that. She didn't even have electricity in the cabin until 1984. She only got that air conditioner in the past couple of years, and one of the televisions was donated by her mailman." After a pause, Mr. Grubb continues appreciatively, "Because of Gertrude's deformed hand, she probably never would have married if it hadn't been for Mr. Janeway."

At the country churchyard, Mr. Grubb points down the road. "We figure that's where Mr. Janeway was enlisted into the army." Then, turning around to look at the small building, he continues, "This is where Mr. Janeway and Gertrude first met, so it's kinda fitting that they will be buried here together.

Mr. Janeway's tombstone
photo by Stuart Lutz

Gertrude and Rueben used to walk eight to ten miles to church each way every Sunday, even though she couldn't walk very well. Gertrude will be buried next to Rueben. She figures that Mr. Janeway has been here long enough on his own, and now there's no room to bury her next to her husband."

Mr. Janeway's gravestone has the incorrect last name "January" carved on it. There is an engraved patriotic shield, followed by "Co. B 14th Ill. Cav." It is the same tombstone shown in the photograph by Mrs. Janeway's bed. The Grubb family does not know where Mr. Janeway's first wife is buried in California, and Mr. Grubb admits, "We really don't even know where to start looking."

Mr. Grubb chuckles, then tells another story. "Well, somehow the military got wind that she was the last Union widow, so some important general wanted to fly down here and present her with some silly award. Gertrude declined that offer. You know, if it weren't for that newspaper interview last year, no one would know of her and she would have died quietly without any fanfare. Maybe just a small obituary in the local newspaper."

Mr. Grubb says his aunt has no desire to meet Mrs. Alberta Martin, who was at the time believed to be the last Confederate widow. "Her people really wanted to meet Gertrude, but Gertrude just wasn't interested in being some puppet for their cause. Besides, after all, we won the war." He speaks this statement in a distinctive Southern accent. He further explains that Mrs. Janeway has turned down all requests for personal appearances at various Civil War events throughout the country.

Gertrude Grubb Janeway died on January 17, 2003, at the age of ninety-three.

MAUDIE CELIA HOPKINS
The Final Confederate Widow

"He was a clean, respectable man—no nasty tramp. I called him 'Mr. Cantrell' a lot, but 'Bill' if I needed him to do something for me."

In 1996 Alberta Martin of Elba, Alabama, crowned herself as the last living widow of a Confederate soldier. When she died in 2004, she was given a full Confederate funeral. A few weeks

Mrs. Hopkins at the time of the interview
photo by Stuart Lutz

after Martin's death, the *Washington Times* broke the story that another Confederate widow, Maudie Celia Hopkins, was still living, in Lexa, Arkansas.

Glenn Railsback is a genial, middle-aged Arkansas resident with a great interest in Civil War history. He has conducted a great deal of research on Maudie Hopkins and her first husband, William M. Cantrell, a Confederate soldier. According to his findings, Cantrell was born on March 15, 1847, in Wise County, Virginia. William joined an obscure Confederate regiment of the Virginia Infantry raised by J. M. French. The five-foot-four Cantrell, who was assigned to Company A of French's battalion, is described in his war record as having a fair complexion and black hair. Although his unit was based in Virginia, most of the men in the company were from Pike County, Kentucky. After a skirmish in Pike County, the sixteen-year-old Cantrell was captured on April 15, 1863, held in Cincinnati, and returned to the Confederacy in exchange for Union prisoners in May 1863. In 1868 the young veteran Cantrell married Matilda McFall in Kentucky, with whom he later moved to Arkansas. Sometime thereafter he moved to Colorado and was listed as a justice of the peace in a census in the early 1900s. Matilda died in 1929, and Cantrell later appeared in the 1930 census, listed as a widower in Baxter County, Arkansas.

At the time of our meeting, Mrs. Hopkins is eighty-nine and still living alone in a cozy, well-maintained white house on a corner lot in Lexa; she lives hundreds of miles from the most famous Civil War battlefields, such as Shiloh, Antietam, and Gettysburg. Three flags are arranged on her coffee table: the Arkansas state flag, the United States flag, and the Stars and Bars. Mrs. Hopkins has a head full of thick white curls, and she wears a bright blue shirt with a gold United Daughters of the Confederacy pin on her right lapel. "I can hear well," she explains in her surprisingly fast drawl, "but I can't walk too good."

David O. Dodd Chapter 212
and
Arkansas Division
𝕌nite🄳 🄳aughters of the Confederacy ®

Invite you to a reception honoring

Maudie Acklin Cantrell Hopkins
Widow of
William M. Cantrell
Co. A, French's Battalion, C.S.A.

Phillips County Museum
623 Pecan Street
Helena, Arkansas

Saturday, August 21, 2004
Two o'clock in the afternoon

R.S.V.P.
870-535-8147

Invitation to the United Daughters of the Confederacy reception for Mrs. Hopkins
photo by Stuart Lutz

Mr. and Mrs. Cantrell, perhaps on their wedding day
photo courtesy Phoebe Jane Cox

She begins with her childhood. "I was born on December 7, 1914, in Baxter County. My birth name was Maudie Acklin. I grew up there too. My mommy and daddy had a bunch of kids, all I can tell you, so many kids—ten in all. My daddy worked with lumber, but he quit and farmed patches and did things like that. We stripped cane and made molasses out of it. The times were so hard back then, we couldn't get money hardly for nothing. I wore my shoes so long that they were all worn out. We put them together with baling wire. We didn't have no money."

She married William Cantrell, then an eighty-seven-year-old former rebel, when she was nineteen, on February 2, 1934. She recounts how she met her first husband. "I got out of my home when I was young and cleaned houses. I was cleaning the house of a woman who lived not far from Mr. Cantrell when he came over and said, 'I want you to clean my house.' And a bidding war started. She was giving me ten dollars, and he offered twelve dollars. I just wanted a new pair of shoes, so I cleaned his house. It took two days. At the end of the second day, he proposed. 'Why don't we get married?' he said. I asked him for some time to think about it, but he already had the license and the JP [justice of the peace] ready. 'We are going to get married tonight,' he said, so we did. Two neighbors, a man and woman, were there. They were the witnesses, and they stayed all night. My family wasn't there, for they lived up in the hills, but they were pleased about it.

"Once we were married, I went and housed with him in a little town called Advance, and my family all came over to our house. He liked them and they liked him. He was a clean, respectable man—no nasty tramp. I called him 'Mr. Cantrell' a lot, but 'Bill' if I needed him to do something for me. A lot of people laughed about [the marriage], but I paid no attention. In one ear and out the other." She makes this motion with her hands. "We made a garden, peaches and apples, plenty of fruit and vegetables. We raised chickens. A couple gave me some hogs before marriage, so we had meat. And we sold a yearling or two for money."

The old veteran rarely spoke about the Civil War. "I know that during the war his supporters that went around his legs were eaten by lice. He didn't have much to eat. He went into people's houses to get food, even widowed women. He destroyed their stuff. The Civil War was terrible." Mr. Cantrell also found out that his Civil War pension was erratic. "I know the poor man got twenty-five dollars every two or three months for his pension. There was one whole year where he got nothing. The Northern veterans got eighty dollars a month.[2] It was hard on him, but things were cheaper then."

Mrs. Hopkins recounts one religious incident with her husband. "Not long after the marriage, I went to get baptized by the water mill. Mr. Cantrell hitched up the team and wagon 'cause he didn't want me to get wet. Well, the preacher dunked me and I couldn't get my breath good. Mr. Cantrell walked in full-dressed with a towel and dried off my head. He helped me back up to the wagon, put me on the spring seat, and returned home."

Three years later, in February 1937, Mr. Cantrell was riding a mule to pick up the mail when a hog cut in front of his mount, which threw him to the ground. He was bedridden following his accident, during which time Mrs. Hopkins spoon-fed him and tried to nurse him back to health. He succumbed to his injuries on February 12, 1937. His twenty-two-year-old widow inherited his house and two hundred acres in Advance, Arkansas. "After Mr. Cantrell died," she explains, "I had to go out and work. I took care of elderly people and cleaned houses. I moved out of the Cantrell house around 1942, but my children lived there for a short time. I've lived in Phillips County for the past half century." The young widow remarried shortly thereafter and had three children with her second husband. In all, Mrs. Hopkins has had four husbands, and she has outlived them all. Yet she has never been eligible for a Confederate pension from her first marriage. Arkansas revised its Civil War pension laws to discourage young women from marrying older men solely for their pension checks; qualified widows had to be born prior to 1870, "unless she be the widow of such soldier or sailor by his first marriage."[3]

"Being the last Confederate widow, it's all right," she concludes. "I enjoy all the new people, and I've learned a lot of things I hadn't known. I feel important, I guess." Six weeks after our meeting, the United Daughters of the Confederacy honored Hopkins with a reception in Helena.

Maudie Celia Hopkins died on August 17, 2008, at the age of ninety-three.

ALBERTA MARTIN
The Next-to-Last Confederate Widow
*"It's far better to be an old man's darling
than a young man's slave."*

Although Alberta Martin was not the final Confederate widow, she died believing she was the last link to the Lost Cause. Unlike Mrs. Hopkins, who lived quietly in Arkansas, Mrs. Martin spent the last decade of her life centered on her role as a Confederate widow, and the country, during her lifetime, accepted her as the last widow of a Southern soldier. Thus, Mrs. Martin's tale is worthy of inclusion.

In 1996 Alberta Martin of Elba, Alabama, announced that she believed she was the last living widow of a Confederate soldier. Born in 1906 as Alberta Stewart, at twenty-one years old she had married the eighty-one-year-old Confederate veteran William Jasper Martin in December 1927. The soldier was born in 1845 in Macon County, Georgia.[4]

I meet with Dr. Kenneth Chancey, a local dentist who is Mrs. Martin's power-of-attorney, in Elba's courthouse square. He gives a brief biography of Mrs. Martin: "She was married first to a man named Howard Farrow, with whom she had a son named Harold. Well, her first husband was soon after

Mrs. Martin at the time of the interview
photo by Jay Hare

killed in a car crash, leaving her with a young son to care for. Now, as for William Martin, the Confederate veteran, he had already been married twice before. And it was now 1927, the middle of some pretty bad times down here. Young Alberta met Mr. Martin while talking over a fence. He was coming back from the local store where he and a bunch of other fellows played dominoes. Now, you have to understand something. It wasn't love quite like what we see in Hollywood. It was more out of economic necessity. She had a young child, and he had a desirable pension. And so it was more like a partnership. Anyway, Mr. Martin died in the summer of 1932, and she was eligible to collect the widow's pension. A short time later, however, she married the older Mr. Martin's grandson [from one of his previous marriages], Charlie Martin, making her ineligible to collect the Civil War widow's pension. Charlie died in 1983 after fifty years of marriage, and since he was a World War II vet, she collected his war pension. Mrs. Martin just never figured that she was still eligible for the Civil War pension after all these years. Now she lives with her son William Jr. He's the son of the Confederate veteran. We estimate there are about three hundred True Sons of the Confederacy still alive, and we believe him to be the youngest," he says in a satisfied tone.[5]

"I found Mrs. Martin a few years ago. I am a proud member of the Sons of Confederate Veterans, and we found out that there was supposedly a Confederate widow living around here. So I volunteered to drive over to Mrs. Martin's and investigate her claim, which turned out to be true. The state of Alabama stopped paying Confederate pensions in 1986, when the last-known widow died. Anyway, a state senator, Dwight Adams from Enterprise, and myself campaigned to get Mrs. Martin's rightful pension, and the legislature passed it. Now, since she was eligible since 1983, we're fighting to get those thirteen extra years of her pension paid to her. And there's one more rule when interviewing her. No asking about her pension, please. It's the source of some jealousy around here because it's very generous and we don't want any trouble. There was a man in New Jersey who read that Mrs. Martin couldn't afford an air conditioner until the state legislature passed a bill to give her a pension. He sent a check for $350 to buy her one."

Dr. Chancey adds that Mrs. Martin has traveled extensively around the South, and that she just returned that weekend from a Civil War event in Mobile. "There was one event in Virginia where she got a five-minute standing ovation."

He drives down a narrow lane and pulls into a driveway next to a house painted robin's-egg blue. He raps on the metal screen door, then yells, "Miss Martin!" as we enter the small house. A very large Confederate flag hangs on one wall of the living room. A man who appears to be about ninety is sitting in an armchair. Dr. Chancey introduces Mrs. Martin's son William, the youngest True Son of the Confederacy.

Mrs. Martin's small home is a shrine to her Southern status. On an adjacent wall are nearly a dozen framed pictures and documents. The most prominent image is a famous photograph of General Robert E. Lee, and nearby is a very old portrait of William Jasper Martin. Mrs. Martin's shrine also includes a 1996 letter from Governor George Wallace, the Varina Davis award (named after the Confederate First Lady), a proclamation from the Alabama Legislature, and documents from the Sons of Confederate Veterans, the League of the South, and the Daughters of the Confederacy.

Mrs. Martin enters the room. "It's nice to meet you," she says in a gorgeous accent. Pointing to Dr. Chancey, she adds, "He's never gotten lost yet coming here." She begins her tale by describing her early life in rural Alabama: "Oh, it was pretty bad times is all I can say. I lost my mother in 1918 when I was twelve, then times got worse than ever. Daddy drove around from one farm to another doing work."

She quickly moves on to her marriage. "I met Mr. Martin—I always called him Mr. Martin—by talking to him over a fence. I was just tired of living in that house with my siblings, and they expecting me to clean up after them. So Mr. Martin asked if I'd be his wife and I agreed. My daddy agreed too. [Mr. Martin] got fifty dollars a month from the state, and that was a lot of money then. But he had a very short temper and he guarded me. He was jealous of other young men looking at me, including his own grandson." After a moment, she adds, "And he never liked to talk about the war."

She explains the very large difference in age between her and her second husband. "It's not hard to understand," she drawls. "I wanted to get away from home, and I had a little boy to take care of. There's an old saying, 'It's far better to be an old man's darling than a young man's slave.'"

As for being one of the last Civil War widows, she relishes the fame her unique status has given her. "It's exciting. And it gets more exciting. As time goes by, more people want to meet me. It's exciting being in all those newspapers and magazines. If I could have known how famous I'd become earlier, I would have remembered more!" she jokes. "It's just been in the last few years. It seems like the younger generation is more into the Civil War than the real old people. Maybe it's because people my age are something new to the younger people. Or that the older generation is closer to the war. But I'm happy to see the younger generation carrying it on."

She gently mocks the mail that she receives. "The lady at the post office complains about it. She says she gets mail just addressed to 'The Last Confederate Widow,' without my name on it. I guess I get four or five pieces a day, mostly autograph requests. And most of the mail is Northern. When the publicity goes up, I get lots more letters." One such occurrence was in 1997, when Mrs. Martin met Daisy Anderson, the next-to-last Union widow, at a small ceremony at Gettysburg. There, the ancient widows shook hands and placed roses on a soldier's grave.[6]

Mrs. Martin expresses a strong opinion on the controversial topic of flying the Confederate flag on public property, such as the South Carolina State House: "I think it is very nice. I think it shows the proper respect." She also has high praise for Civil War reenactors, the Daughters of the Confederacy, and the Sons of Confederate Veterans. "I think they do a wonderful thing, I sure do. They are fighting for their country and love their country. And one day, I believe we're gonna have a black president. The blacks now go to school and get lots of education. They're as smart as white people."

Dr. Chancey takes photographs of us, then adds, "You might want to send her a copy. We are going to donate everything she has on being the last Confederate widow to the local historical society when she passes on. And write your name and the date on the back." Mrs. Martin chirps, "If you put the picture of me in the garden, it'll scare away the rabbits!"

Alberta Martin died on May 31, 2004, at age ninety-seven. She lay in state in the Alabama State House before she was given a full Confederate funeral.

NOTES

1. Information on John Janeway comes from his service records, courtesy of the National Archives.

2. As the Civil War cost the federal government tens of thousands of lives and millions of dollars, pensions to Confederate soldiers or their widows were refused.

3. Index to Arkansas Confederate Pension Applications, Arkansas Department of Public Welfare.

4. Phillip Rawls, "Last Living Widow of Civil War Veteran Dies at Age 97," Associated Press, May 31, 2004, http://www.dixiescv .org/last-widow.html (accessed July 26, 2009).

5. True Sons of the Confederacy are men whose fathers were Confederate soldiers.

6. "Alberta Martin, 97, Confederate Widow, Dies," *New York Times*, June 1, 2004.

THOMAS BREWER
The Last Participant in the
Scopes Monkey Trial of 1925
"There I am!"

Long before the O. J. Simpson murder trial, there were two other "Trials of the Century." One was the Lindbergh baby kidnapping case, in which Bruno Hauptmann was convicted and subsequently executed. The other occurred in the Tennessee hamlet of Dayton during 1925 in the famous Scopes Monkey Trial, which sought to punish the teaching of evolution in schools. The Scopes case saw the most famous trial lawyer in American history, Clarence Darrow, take on William Jennings Bryan, perhaps the foremost orator of his day and a three-time presidential candidate. One reason the case has remained well known is its fictionalization in the popular movie *Inherit the Wind*. More than seventy-five years later, the trial that pitted religious belief against science still reverberates in American society. Thomas Brewer of Chattanooga is the last-surviving participant in the trial.

The roots of the Scopes Monkey Trial start sixty years earlier, when Charles Darwin published his controversial book *On the Origin of Species*, theorizing that modern-day humans and apes descended from a common ancestor through evolution, a concept also known as the "survival of the fittest." This theory opposed the biblical story of Creation.

In the aftermath of World War I, some people believed that Germany's attempt to prove that it was the fittest nation had caused that horrific war.[1] Thus, anti-evolutionism was popular in the 1920s. In early 1925 the Tennessee legislature passed the Butler Bill, which prohibited teachers from instructing "any theory that denies the story of the Divine Creation of man taught in the Bible, and to teach instead that man has descended from a lower order of animals."[2] The fine for a conviction was between one hundred and five hundred dollars.

Mr. Brewer at the time of the interview
photo by Stuart Lutz

The American Civil Liberties Union wanted to test the constitutionality of this case, and it looked for a teacher who was willing to be charged. Local Dayton civic leaders thought the small town was ideal for such a case, for it would draw tourists and boost the local economy. Dayton science teacher and football coach John Scopes reluctantly agreed to participate, and he was arrested for teaching evolution on May 7, 1925.[3] Scopes, who was in on the idea of a trial, found the sheriff to arrest him.[4] He was indicted, and the trial was slated for the summer.

William Jennings Bryan, a deeply religious man, volunteered to come to Dayton to be the chief prosecutor, hoping to stem what he saw as the evil of evolution.[5] He arrived in Dayton by train to a hero's welcome. Upon hearing of Bryan's participation, Clarence Darrow decided to be the defense counsel because he disagreed with the religious point of view.[6]

The Scopes trial began on Friday, July 10, 1925. The jury was selected by four-year-old Tommy Brewer, who pulled their names out of a hat. Born in 1920 in Dayton, he lived with his

**A signed photograph of
Clarence Darrow**

photo courtesy Stuart Lutz

family next door to the courthouse. Mr. Brewer remembers his participation in that historic trial. "Well, [the court officers] wanted the [Rhea County] sheriff to get someone under five years old so there was no trickery," he explains in a soft Southern voice. "We were good friends with the sheriff, so he came down to the house. My mother agreed to let me do it. I can remember when I was taken to the courthouse and put on a corner of the judge's desk. They had a hat there with all the names rolled up and put in there. I pulled them out one at a time and handed it to him. When I was done, I got down and went back home. The only time I was in the courtroom was when I picked the jury."

He pauses, then adds, "You know, they had a newsreel at that time in the courtroom. There's a silent movie of me picking the names out. I remember when I was very young, my

**Thomas Brewer as a boy,
a few years after
the Scopes Monkey Trial**
photo courtesy Tommye Brewer Nail

mother took me to the movies and I saw myself on the big screen picking out the jury. For decades, I looked for that movie but could never find it."

Mr. Brewer stands up and walks into another room. He snaps on the television and pushes in a videotape. It is a program entitled "Monkey Trial," which had aired on a documentary series called *The American Experience*. Mr. Brewer had positioned the tape to start with four-year-old Tommy picking the jury names. When he sees his image on the screen, Mr. Brewer calls excitedly, "There I am!" The blond-haired boy is wearing a sailor's suit; he swings his legs on the top of the judge's desk. The child clutches a large black hat on his lap and holds a slip of paper in his right hand. We watch the few precious seconds of the silent black-and-white film several times. At its conclusion, Mr. Brewer chuckles. "I had shoulder-length blond hair, and my mother let it grow. I looked like a

Thomas Brewer as a sailor during World War II
photo courtesy Tommye Brewer Nail

little girl. She didn't cut it off until I started school. But I'm really glad that the movie has been found. I was thrilled to death when I saw it again [after decades of searching for it]—I couldn't believe my eyes. When I saw that the program was going to be on television, I watched it that night and I just couldn't believe it."

Mr. Brewer has a few other memories of the trial. "I do remember a lot of people in the courtyard. There was a man in a wheelchair selling popcorn. He didn't have any legs and he had two big handles to power the wheelchair. And two brothers and a sister built a stand in our yard. I would go over there and get some money because they were selling Cokes. That's a lot for a four-year-old to remember."

The trial lasted eight sweltering days, as Darrow and Bryan verbally dueled over religion and evolution, and their place in education.[7] The audience in the packed courthouse emphatically favored Bryan. On the last day of the trial, the defense team—in a daring move—called Bryan as an expert witness on the Bible. Foolishly, Bryan accepted the challenge, and Darrow humiliated him by showing Bryan's surprising lack of biblical knowledge.[8] Both sides sought a conviction: The prosecution wanted to prove that Tennessee had the right to control its school curriculum, and the defense team wanted a basis for an appeal to higher courts.[9] After a nine-minute deliberation, the jury returned with the desired guilty verdict; Judge John T. Raulston fined the twenty-four-year-old Scopes the minimum of one hundred dollars.[10] A few days after the trial, an ailing Bryan died.

Mr. Brewer never met John Scopes, "but they made a movie called *Inherit the Wind*. When they showed that at the drive-in theater in Dayton, they sent me tickets to it. And I believe Scopes was there at that time." When he was a teenager living in Dayton, Mr. Brewer remembers that the trial, now a decade past, was still the talk of the town. "Today, in the [Dayton] courthouse," he volunteers, "they have a museum there in the basement. On display are the drugstore tables and chairs where the participants dreamed up the trial. That's where it all started."

Mr. Brewer's coffee table has a giant, highly decorated Bible placed next to a thick scrapbook entitled "Monkey Trial." He reaches over to his "Monkey Trial" album and thumbs through it. It holds a few letters from people across the country requesting his autograph. He shows off his personal stationery, which has a monkey printed in the corner. He sees no contradictions in having a Bible next to his Scopes scrapbook. He puts his hand, the one that chose the jury, on the scrapbook. "I lived through this," he answers, then moves his hand to the Bible, "and I believe in this. I read the Bible every day."

As the last-surviving participant of the legendary trial, Mr. Brewer is a guest of honor at the annual celebration of the trial, which is held in the same Dayton courtroom where the Scopes case was tried and is sponsored by Bryan College, a local school. He views the reenactment of the trial and attends a dinner at the remembrance. The participants in the event include descendants of Bryan and the other prosecutors. One year, the reenactment showed the selection of the jury, and Mr. Brewer met the young actor who played Tommy Brewer. Dayton's civic leaders, who welcomed the economic boost the trial would bring, could not have imagined that the effects of the trial would continue into the twenty-first century.

Reflecting on the relevance of the Scopes trial in his life, he casually states, "It really makes me feel good, but it's not that important."

Thomas Brewer died on August 16, 2003, at age eighty-two.

NOTES

1. Don Nardo, *The Scopes Trial* (San Diego, CA: Lucent Books, 1997), 22.
2. Ibid., 25.
3. Ibid., 27.
4. Ibid., 29.
5. Ibid., 33.
6. Ibid., 35.

7. Paul K. Conkin, *When All the Gods Trembled* (Lanham, MD: Rowman & Littlefield, 1998), 87–91.

8. Ibid., 96.

9. Ibid., 87.

10. Ibid., 97.

FRANK BUCKLES
The Last American World War I Soldier
"I was just a soldier doing his job."

The final American link to one of the greatest twentieth-century holocausts lives at the end of a half-mile-long country road in Charles Town, West Virginia. It is the same small town where John Brown was hanged for seizing Harpers Ferry just before the Civil War. Frank Buckles survives ninety years after the Armistice that ended the Great War. Of the more than 4 million Americans who served in World War I, he is the final doughboy.

US involvement in World War I lasted roughly thirteen months; the first United States soldiers arrived in Europe in October 1917, and the war ended in November 1918. In a little over a year, 117,000 Americans died in the conflict.[1] By comparison, the Vietnam Veterans Memorial in Washington, DC, contains the names of 58,000 men and women who died

A pass to the April 2, 1917, session of Congress, at which President Woodrow Wilson asked Congress to declare war.
It is signed by Vice President Thomas Marshall.
photo courtesy Stuart Lutz

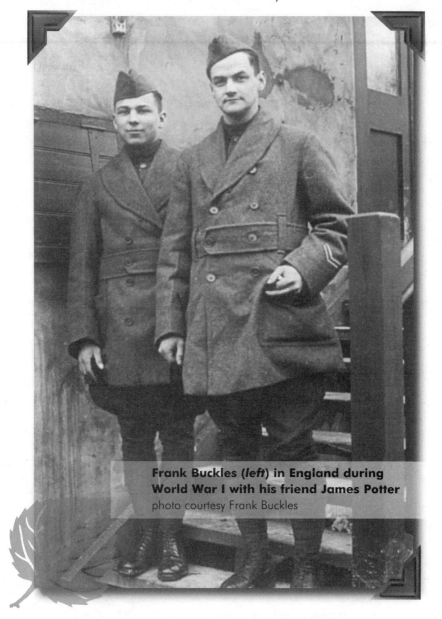

Frank Buckles (*left*) in England during World War I with his friend James Potter
photo courtesy Frank Buckles

**Frank Buckles in 1917
just after his enlistment**
photo courtesy Frank Buckles

Frank Buckles as a young soldier
photo courtesy Frank Buckles

in that war; this is only half of the deaths suffered in the country's brief World War I experience.

Mr. Buckles lives on a three-hundred-acre farm his family established in 1769. His ancient farmhouse, which has a library full of military and local history books, is decorated with classic American furniture. Wearing dark blue pants and a light blue cardigan, he sits on an armchair in his sunroom overlooking the placid countryside. The walls are crowded with photographs, bookshelves, and awards.

Frank Buckles was born on February 1, 1901, in Harrison County, Missouri. As a boy, his grandfather told him stories about his own grandfather, who had served in the American Revolution. "My parents were farmers. We were farmers for generations," he explains in an occasionally halting voice. "When I first met General [John] Pershing, he asked me where I was born. I told him Harrison County and he replied, 'That's just forty miles as the crow flies from where I was born in Linn County.'"

Mr. Buckles was a voracious reader as a child. Because he followed world events in the newspaper, he was aware of the Great War raging in Europe. As a teenager, he visited the nearby military base with his family. "We drove there in a car. Not many of them around then. Nobody had a driver's license," he chuckles.

Mr. Buckles was a schoolboy when Congress declared war on April 2, 1917. He was visiting a state fair in Wichita, Kansas, when he heard the news, so he tried to enlist, even though he had just turned sixteen. "I went to a recruiter and gave my age as eighteen. The Marine sergeant said I had to be twenty-one. I went to the navy and they rejected me because of my flat feet. I realized I had to go elsewhere and I took a train to Oklahoma City. I had the same bad result with the Marines and the navy. I tried with the army and the captain said he had to see a birth certificate. I told him that Missouri did not require birth certificates and my birth was recorded in the family Bible. He accepted that explanation and sent me to Fort Logan in Colorado to be sworn in. In the army, I had a choice of my branch of service. I took the advice of an old sergeant who said, 'If you want to get to France in a hurry, join the ambulance service. The military is begging for soldiers in that area.' I was sworn in on August 14, 1917, and then was sent to Fort Riley, Kansas, for training in trench retrieval and ambulance service. I was part of the First Fort Riley Causal Detachment—'casual' meaning 'unassigned.'" The last doughboy points to a large sepia photograph on his wall; it is almost three feet long but not very high. It shows dozens of young

Frank Buckles in 1920 on his way to visit General John Pershing in Oklahoma
photo courtesy Frank Buckles

faces in his regiment. Frank Buckles, wearing a hat, stands in the top row with his arms crossed. "That's the hat I wore during World War I," he explains as he points to a green wool cap nearby.

The cap Frank Buckles wore in World War I
photo by Stuart Lutz

He continues, "I went overseas in December on the *Carpathia*. Some of the ship's officers and crew took part in the *Titanic* rescue just a few years before." Throughout the interview, the 107-year-old man is in constant motion, crossing and uncrossing his legs.

One reason for the American entrance into World War I was the unlimited German U-boat activity in the Atlantic. "I wasn't a bit nervous about submarines. We sailed from Halifax, Nova Scotia, to Glasgow and then I arrived at camp in Winchester, England. I expected to be there a week until I was sent to France. I don't know how long I was in Winchester. I rode my first motorcycle there.

"Finally, Americans began to go to France. I asked to see the colonel in charge of the camp. I told him I enlisted to go to France. I liked England, but I was ready to move on. He replied that he also wanted to get to France, but we had to go when the government told us to go. I was always an independent person and I thought about how I could get to France.

"So I began to plan. Troops were marching out of camp to

go to France. I arranged to wait until it was dark and then I would fall in the back of a line of soldiers moving out. There were no Jeeps then—we hoofed it. The first night I planned to go with three other soldiers, I had a rare nighttime assignment and I missed them. They went on to France but were caught. A month later, I saw them back in camp. They were court-martialed and given two months of work."

Mr. Buckles discusses how he arrived in France: "An American lieutenant was left behind from his attachment to a signal corps unit. He needed an escort to accompany him across the channel and I got the job. I was attached to him and I took him to Southampton, where he would embark. We crossed the

The cup Frank Buckles used when imprisoned by the Japanese during World War II
photo by Stuart Lutz

The award presented to Frank Buckles in 2008 by Secretary of the Army Pete Geren
photo by Stuart Lutz

channel. There, the lieutenant took me by the wrist and asked me to write a letter to President [Woodrow] Wilson and General Pershing. This officer wanted me to be his keeper [servant]. We reported to headquarters in Paris. I wanted to see the city, but I couldn't leave the lieutenant. We took in the Eiffel Tower and Notre Dame. I had several assignments with the ambulance and streetcars, but I never really got close to the front.

"I had been in France for some time and I asked for a vacation and was granted one. I wanted to go to the Bay of Arcachon and I went with a sergeant to the town of Arles. We were the only Americans in the town, and we were celebrities. We had taken six cartons of Lucky Strikes with us and we used them as cash. We were eventually ready to go back to Paris, but we decided to go to Biarritz in Spain instead. We stayed at the Ritz Carlton. We had some troubles at a bar there since they didn't want soldiers there.

"When we returned to Paris, we were AWOL [absent without leave] and we thought that would require a court-martial of some sort. I was turned over to a young lieutenant and I told him the whole story of going to Spain and he thought it was fine."

Immediately after the war, Corporal Buckles was assigned the task of guarding German prisoners of war. "We were on a train and stopped a number of times. There were just 35 guards and 650 prisoners and no bathroom on the train. The first time in Germany, we stopped at the equivalent of a Red Cross and I got a cup of coffee. I thanked the man who was pouring—a distinguished-looking gentleman—in German. He reached below the table and pulled out a loaf of potato bread for me and I found a piece of bologna."

Mr. Buckles returned to a very different America than the one he left. "I came back in 1920. The parades were long over. I was discharged from the camp in Colorado. The American public forgot about the war quickly, and veterans were disappointed in the attitude of the people. Most Americans couldn't give a damn. There were now thousands of men returning to the business world. I had to figure out what to do. My father wanted me to return to school, so I went to business school in Oklahoma City. I got a job in the post office at night, but I also worked for the White Star Lines in Toronto."

Mr. Buckles returned to Europe for business, as well as traveling to Latin America and South America. Eventually he accepted an assignment with a steamship company in the Philippines. "The United States government claimed the Philippines was the safest place in the Far East. Then the Japanese invaded it. Anyone who made a serious study of the Japanese and knew how they approached war could see what they were going to do." The civilian Mr. Buckles was taken prisoner and held for three years and two months. "They saw no difference between the military and civilians," he says casually. "The first consideration of a prisoner is getting food. It's a slow death otherwise. I made a deal with the Japanese to get rice and beans. The Japanese have a very different idea of food from us. They can live on what Americans would starve to death on. On February 23, 1945, we were released by the Eleventh Airborne. It was a most remarkable rescue since all twenty-two hundred men, women, and children survived. The army had anticipated 10 to 20 percent deaths." Mr. Buckles points to a beat-up cup on his daybed. "I still have the cup I used during my imprisonment."

After the war, his company wanted him to return to Asia, but he declined. "My family was landowners. I wanted to get back to my roots." A decade after his release, Mr. Buckles bought his West Virginia farm. It was founded by a Buckles ancestor who came to West Virginia just before the American

A recent picture of Frank Buckles
photo courtesy David J. DeJonge © 2007

Revolution. "We have been here for over a half century. I gave up driving tractors and cars when I turned 102."

A few days before our interview, Mr. Buckles met then-president George W. Bush at the White House for a ceremony commemorating the doughboy's unique status. Of the president, Mr. Buckles says, "He is much more presentable in person than what the papers make him out to be. It was great to meet him personally. I liked the person, but not necessarily the things he stands for." During the ceremony, Secretary of the Army Pete Geren presented him with a medal on behalf of a grateful nation.

While in the nation's capital, Mr. Buckles visited the recently unveiled World War II monument. He notes that there is no national World War I monument in Washington. "What can I say? It is not for me to make decisions about a national memorial. We have gone this long without it." Washington, DC, does have a monument to its residents of the city who fought in World War I, but it is small and decaying. "My first reaction is that it was a bandstand that needed a paint job and some landscaping," he muses. Also during his trip to Washington, a photographer took his portrait, which will hang in the Pentagon.

Mr. Buckles is not surprised that he is the last man left of the 4 million who served in World War I. He does not require a walker or glasses. He sits beside a bucket of small dumbbells and explains that he lifts weights every day to remain fit. About his service in the war, he concludes, "I was just another soldier doing his job."

NOTE

1. "Fact Sheet: America's Wars," United States Department of Veterans Affairs, November 2008, http://www1.va.gov/opa/fact/amwars.asp (accessed May 18, 2009).

JOHN COOLIDGE
The Last Person Alive to Live
in the White House in the 1920s

"[I]t was very antiquated; the plumbing and heating were bad, and there was open wiring."

Calvin Coolidge had the most unusual inauguration of any president. On the night of August 2, 1923, President Warren G. Harding died in San Francisco. A transcontinental telephone call was placed to Vice President Calvin Coolidge, who had no telephone at his rural home in Plymouth Notch, Vermont. The nearest phone was several miles away. Some local men who took the call at 2:00 a.m. drove to the Coolidge

**Young John Coolidge (*far right*)
with his presidential family**
photo courtesy the Library of Congress

John Coolidge with his college roommate
public domain

house to alert the vice president that he was now president. Calvin's father, a justice of the peace, swore in his son in the family living room at 2:47 a.m., the only time a father ever inaugurated his son.

John Coolidge, the son of President Coolidge, was born in 1906; he is the last-surviving person to have lived in the White House in the 1920s, when the historic building was in decrepit condition. He lives in rustic Plymouth Notch, Vermont, just a few hundred feet from the house where his grandfather swore in his father. From a distance, one can see the Coolidge Home-

Mr. Coolidge, later in life
photo courtesy the
Calvin Coolidge Memorial Foundation, Inc.

stead nestled into a small valley; this area is more comfortable with horsepower than fossil fuels. Mr. Coolidge, who has a thin face reminiscent of his father's, vividly remembers the day he learned he was now "First Son": "I was sixteen and spending the summer of 1923 at a citizens' military camp for young men in Fort Devens, Massachusetts. I went to set an example for boys throughout the country. But I didn't enjoy it. It was a leftover camp from World War I; it was not in good shape, and it was hot and dusty. Mostly we just marched around. Well, on my first full morning there, the day after my arrival, I was lined up for breakfast. An army captain, who was in charge, asked me if I saw the morning newspaper. I hadn't, so he told me about the death of President Harding."

As the son of the president, John was accorded special protection as a student. "When my father was first inaugurated in 1923, I was a high school student at Mercerburg Academy in Pennsylvania. I was not allowed off campus except on Saturday afternoons to see movies downtown. I graduated from there in May 1924, then enrolled in Massachusetts' Amherst College in the autumn of 1924. While there, I was given a bodyguard, Colonel Edmund Starling. Starling was the second in command in the Secret Service, but he was unhappy with the job of protecting a college student. A couple of months later, I was assigned an agent in his early thirties named Russell Conway Wood, from near Richmond, Virginia. 'Woody' was my roommate until my parents left the White House in March 1929. I started dating a young Mount Holyoke student, so Woody accompanied me on my trips to the local women's college."

John did return to the White House for holidays, such as Christmas and Easter. "I only have general memories, no favorite one in particular. It was certainly an interesting house, and old too. But it was very antiquated; the plumbing and heating were bad, and there was open wiring. There were no built-in closets, just wardrobes. The rooms were very large, and the bedrooms too. My father and mother put in extra bedrooms, for there were not many guest rooms. I had a piano in my bedroom that is now in the reception center here in Plymouth. There was the Lincoln bed. My mother crocheted a coverlet for it, and the last time I inquired, her coverlet is still in the White House, though no longer covering the bed. I remember going to the top floor and seeing the charred timbers from the British burning during the War of 1812. Fortunately, [President Harry S.] Truman had it all changed, and it needed it!" The White House was renovated by Truman in the 1940s. "I was living in New Haven then and the man in charge of the White House restoration was from New Haven also. He knew I lived there, so he saved some things for me as mementos. The last time I was there was during the Nixon administration. He had a dinner for the duke and duchess of Windsor, so my wife and I attended. I haven't been back since."

Mr. Coolidge has an interesting anecdote about formal life at the White House. When visiting, he informed his father at breakfast that he wouldn't dress formally for dinner that night, as was the usual practice, because he was planning to attend a tea dance after dinner. His father sternly reprimanded him, "You will remember that you are dining at the table of the president of the United States and you will present yourself at the appointed hour properly clothed."[1]

Shortly after the Republicans renominated President Coolidge, nicknamed "Silent Cal," in 1924, the president was devastated by a personal tragedy. John and Calvin Jr., the younger of the president's two sons, played a sibling tennis match. Calvin, who did not wear socks with his shoes, developed a blister; subsequently, an infection set in. He died of blood poisoning at age sixteen, overwhelming the president with grief. Although Coolidge was reelected in 1924, the loss of his son affected him deeply throughout his second term. He declined to run again in 1928 and died in 1933. Mr. Coolidge relates a story about his brother and father: "My brother had a serious operation as a boy and was working in a tobacco field in Massachusetts. One of the other kids who was working with him teased my brother that '[i]f my father were president, I wouldn't be working here!' And my brother quickly retorted, 'Well, if your father were my father, you would!'" Mr. Coolidge gives a hearty laugh.

After Mr. Coolidge graduated from Amherst in 1928, he worked for the New Haven Railroad for two decades. He had no political ambitions. "I'd seen enough of politics and it didn't intrigue me. And it didn't pay well! Remember also that my father-in-law was Connecticut governor John Trumbull."

He gives a tour of his marvelous living room, which is off-limits when the public tours the Coolidge Homestead. As in most traditional New England homes, the room features a central fireplace, and the walls are covered with shelves holding generations of books. Mr. Coolidge points out engravings of his parents hung over the mantle. He also exhibits a small black elephant with white tusks. "That was my father's. The Republican Party gave it to him," he explains. On the opposite wall is an ancient document appointing a Coolidge ancestor as Revolutionary War soldier. Mr. Coolidge proudly points to a frame on the wall containing the draft of an unrehearsed speech his father gave in the early 1930s after Vermont was severely flooded. The reserved president, who would pass away soon after, praised the land of Vermont and its people:

> I could not look upon the peaks of Ascutney, Killington, Mansfield and Equinox without being moved in a way that no other scene could move me. It was here that I first saw the light of day; here I received my bride; here my dead lie pillowed on the loving breast of our everlasting hills. I love Vermont because of her hills and valleys, her scenery and invigorating climate, but most of all, because of her indomitable

people. They are a race of pioneers who have almost beg-
gared themselves to serve others. If the spirit of liberty
should vanish in other parts of the union and support of our
institutions should languish, it could all be replenished from
the generous store held by the people of this brave little state
of Vermont.

Finally, Mr. Coolidge locates a small card containing some
inspiring words of his father. It is entitled "Nothing in the
world can take the place of PERSISTENCE" and states:
"Talent will not; nothing is more common than unsuccessful
men with talent. Genius will not; unrewarded genius is almost
a proverb. Education will not; the world is full of educated
derelicts . . ."

*On May 31, 2000, John Coolidge died at age ninety-three. He
was buried in the family plot, with his parents and his brother,
near his Vermont home.*

NOTE

1. "John Coolidge, Guardian of President's Legacy, Dies at 93,"
New York Times, June 4, 2000.

RUTH DYK
The Final Suffragette to March for Women's Rights
before the Nineteenth Amendment
*"Suffragettes expected to do much more
than has been accomplished."*

"The rights of the citizens of the United States to vote shall not
be denied or abridged by the United States or by any state on
account of sex." The long-sought Nineteenth Amendment to
the Constitution, finally ratified on August 18, 1920, gave all
women the vote.

Ruth Dyk is likely the last living suffragette to have
marched for her voting rights before 1920. She lives in
Rochester, New York, just a few miles from the home of the
most famous suffragist, Susan B. Anthony. She also resides not
far from the small New York town of Seneca Falls, where, in
1848, Lucretia Mott and Elizabeth Cady Stanton presided
over a two-day convention that for the first time raised the
issue of a woman's right to vote. The conference issued the
Seneca Falls Declaration, which was signed by sixty-eight
female attendees and thirty-two male participants. The revolutionary statement argued in part:

> [A]ll men and women are created equal. . . . [We] demand
> the equal station to which [women] are entitled. . . . He has
> never permitted her to exercise her inalienable right to the
> elective franchise. . . . He has made her, if married, in the eye
> of the law, civilly dead. . . . He has taken from her all right
> in property, even to the wages she earns. . . . Resolved, That
> woman is man's equal . . . it is the duty of the women of this
> country to secure to themselves their sacred right to the elec-
> tive franchise.[1]

The seven-decade struggle to obtain equal suffrage produced women who would become nationally prominent, such

A Susan B. Anthony signed receipt for attending a suffragette conference
photo courtesy Stuart Lutz

as Victoria Woodhull, the first woman to run for president; the gifted orator and organizer Lucy Stone; and the movement's most dedicated leader, Susan B. Anthony, who was arrested in 1872 for attempting to vote.

The suffrage movement had some successes over the years. In 1869 Anthony and Stanton formed the National Woman Suffrage Association, while Lucy Stone created the American Woman Suffrage Association. That same year, Wyoming, while still a territory, granted women the franchise as a way to encourage them to move to that harsh land. By 1911, however, only six states had equal suffrage, and the movement appeared defunct. All of the early suffragettes went to their graves without ever voting.

In the 1910s, however, the energetic British suffrage movement reinvigorated the lethargic American women, and women in Great Britain were granted the right to vote in 1918. Upper-class ladies in America took to the streets, donning purple sashes and carrying "Votes for Women" signs. Additional impetus for granting equal suffrage came from World

War I, when many women patriotically worked factory jobs.

In May 1919 Congress approved the Nineteenth Amendment, and a mere fourteen months later Tennessee became the thirty-sixth state to ratify it, thereby providing the last vote needed to amend the Constitution. A nation of women voted in the 1920 presidential election, though Mrs. Dyk was unable to participate. "Even though I turned eighteen in March of 1920," she explains, "I could not vote in that election because I had to be twenty-one."

Ruth Dyk as an infant
photo courtesy
Judge Timothy B. Dyk

Mrs. Dyk was born on March 25, 1901, in Portland, Maine. "My father was a lawyer there, but he died when I was three. My mother was Anne Smith Belcher. She graduated from Wellesley College, class of 1890. Wellesley is one of the finest women's colleges in the country. But back then it was unusual for women to go to college. But once she started in the suffrage movement, she just kept on going. After my father died, she moved us to Massachusetts to be with her family. We lived in Newtown Circle. I was brought up by women, my mother and grandmother, and I'm very much in favor of having equality."

She eagerly shares her memories of her own teenage involvement in the suffrage movement. "I guess you could say that at a young age, I started in the movement. I remember going to the homes of my mother's friends to discuss the progress and raising money." She emphasizes her answers with open-handed jabs in the air. "There was a unified spirit of working together for the cause. I was only eleven or so when I first started marching in 1912. There were a number of

The young Ruth Dyk with her mother and family
photo courtesy Judge Timothy B. Dyk

Mrs. Dyk at the time of the interview
photo by Stuart Lutz

parades in Boston, and my mother used to take me to the ones on Beacon Hill, by the Massachusetts State House. We walked up and down the hill with the others. We had banners and speeches, and my mother and I went often."

Shaking her head in disbelief, she also remembers demonstrations by people who were opposed to woman suffrage. "People lined up on the streets protesting us. I guess they were afraid of us upsetting the balance and giving women some political power. Making women more equal with men. But it's just not right to exclude people from the political process. But when the Nineteenth Amendment was passed," she looks up proudly, "oh, we were excited, glad, delighted. We all had the feeling we finally succeeded in what we had tried to do for so long. But I have the same feelings when I voted for the first time as I did the other day when I voted in the New York State [presidential] primary. I feel anxious, and I worry that I am going to pull the wrong lever and vote for a Republican instead of a Democrat!" She giggles.

Mrs. Dyk graduated from Wellesley College in 1923 and received a master's degree from Simmons College in 1924. She continued to study psychology and economics at the University of California, and later attended Columbia University's School of Social Work. "I call myself a social scientist and I have always been interested in women's work," she explains of her professional life. "I worked at Yale doing research on delinquent children, but mostly on the mothers. Psychologists studied the children, whereas I studied the mothers."

"If I were younger," she laughs at this statement, "I would work in a place with coeducation and where women were equal with men. But I found little sex discrimination in my own career. See, we were all part of the same thing. I did their work and they did mine, in part."

This suffragette still believes that women have much work to do to become equal to men. "Suffragettes expected to do much more than has been accomplished. We have not done enough to equalize pay and jobs with men. I am disappointed that women have not had a larger share in the working place. I think women, and you can read this in any article"—she points to the current *Newsweek* laying on her coffee table— "are not paid equally for the same work. The man gets more than the woman. Women don't get supervising jobs. We need more men staying home and taking care of children," she charges. "It is my hope it will change. But I am disappointed women haven't made more progress. Being a suffragette was all about the place of women." After a pause, she adds, "There's not much I can do now except give money."

She holds little hope of America electing a female president. "It will be a long time," she sighs with a resigned tone. "It's hard enough for women to even get in the Senate. Just look at the tough time Mrs. Clinton is having [in the New York Senate race]. People just want a man." During her 2000 Senate campaign, candidate Hillary Rodham Clinton visited Mrs. Dyk and received the suffragette's blessing.

My mother has a large collection of suffragette material, and I share some of it with Mrs. Dyk. She extends her arms to grasp the binders in eager anticipation of holding the history. She reviews various paper items emblazoned with "Votes for Women" and comments on the pieces she has never seen. After viewing a picture of Anthony and Stanton, she remarks, "Stanton was much more attractive looking than Anthony. Anthony just seemed so homely."

Yet she claims not to be the last suffragette. "I'm not sure if I am *the* last one. After all, the suffragette movement's ideals and ideas are about women, their positions in politics and business. After all, you can't separate the women's movement from the suffragette movement, or politics and business. I approved of the Equal Rights Amendment. It was the natural successor to our movement."

Ruth Dyk died at age ninety-nine on November 18, 2000. Appropriately, it was eighty years to the month since all American women were granted the right to choose their leaders for the first time.

NOTE

1. Jay Crosby and Erik Bruun, eds., *Our Nation's Archive: The History of the United States in Documents* (New York: Black Dog & Leventhal, 1999), 295–97.

JOHN FINN
The Last Medal of Honor Recipient
for Heroic Actions on Pearl Harbor Day
*"I saw a plane overhead with the
big old dirty red meatballs underneath."*

"I would rather have that Medal [of Honor] than be president of the United States."
—President Harry S. Truman

"I'd give my immortal soul for that medal."
—General George S. Patton

After the September 11, 2001, terrorist strikes, many news stories compared those incidents to the Japanese sneak attack at Pearl Harbor, Hawaii, on December 7, 1941. Pearl Harbor conjures up images of burning battleships and a somber President Franklin D. Roosevelt speaking gravely to Congress, requesting a declaration of war. The military awarded fifteen Medals of Honor, the country's highest and most prestigious commendation, for heroic actions on Pearl Harbor Day. Only five of the recipients survived the Japanese attack, and Lieutenant John Finn is now the only living one.[1]

The tensions that led to the December 7, 1941, attack began many years earlier. In 1898 the United States annexed the Hawaiian Islands and made Pearl Harbor a major navy base. The military dredged the harbor, allowing the largest ships to dock.[2] During the 1930s an imperialistic and militaristic Japan colonized many East Asian countries, including China. Japan needed natural resources not found on its own islands, and its Asian expansion went unchecked for many years. In 1939 the navy expanded the dry dock facilities at Pearl Harbor, and the following year the navy's Pacific Fleet made Pearl Harbor its base. Japan thought that the Americans,

The Kaneohe monument at Pearl Harbor
photo by Stuart Lutz

United States Navy

FORD ISLAND

Patrol Squadron 21

Theodore W. Croft, AOM1c

KANEOHE NAVAL AIR STATION

Headquarters, Naval Air Station

Stanley D. Dosick, Sea1c

Patrol Squadron 11

John D. Buckley, AOM3c	James H. Robinson, Sea2c
Clarence M. Formoe, AMM1c	Joseph G. Smartt, Ens
Rodney S. Foss, Ens	Luther D. Weaver, Sea1c
Milburn A. Manning, AMM3c	

Patrol Squadron 12

Walter S. Brown, AMM2c	Carl W. Otterstetter, Sea2c
Lee Fox, Jr., Ens	Robert K. Porterfield, AMM3c
Daniel T. Griffin, AMM1c	Robert W. Uhlmann, Ens
George W. Ingram, Sea2c	Raphael A. Watson, AMM1c
Charles Lawrence, AMM2c	

Patrol Squadron 14

Laxton G. Newman, AMM3c

PEARL HARBOR NAVAL HOSPITAL

Arthur W. Russett, PhM1c

NAVAL MOBILE HOSPITAL #2

John H. Thuman, PhM3c

based in Hawaii, would stymie its Asian conquests, and the Japanese military believed that the best way to prevent an American challenge to its expansionism was to launch a surprise attack against the Pacific Fleet.[3]

On October 18, 1941, the militaristic Hideki Tojo became

prime minister of Japan. A month later, United States Army and Navy commanders in the Pacific received warnings about a possible Japanese attack, although they believed the target was elsewhere, such as the American bases in the Philippines or Malaysia. As a result, the Pearl Harbor commanders did not make preparations for an assault, instead continuing their

The USS *Arizona* lies just below the shallow waters
photo by Stuart Lutz

peacetime training exercises.[4] At the time of the strike, ninety-four vessels were docked at Pearl Harbor. Fortunately for the Americans, their valuable aircraft carriers were at sea and were thus unharmed by the attack.[5]

The attacking Japanese fleet was composed of six aircraft

The famous USS *Arizona* monument at Pearl Harbor
photo by Stuart Lutz

carriers, two battleships, and three cruisers.[6] The plan was to launch aircraft to sink the American warships moored in one small area. The Japanese planes, consisting of fighters, dive-bombers, and torpedo bombers, struck in two waves on the morning of December 7. The first airplanes hit at 7:55 a.m. Hawaiian time, and the second wave at 8:50 a.m. The Japanese used torpedoes specially designed for shallow water, which succeeded in devastating the battleships. The battleship *Arizona* was sunk in nine minutes and the *Oklahoma* rolled over on its side. The *Nevada* purposely ran aground to avoid sinking. The *California* and the *West Virginia* sank where they had been docked, and the *Utah* capsized. The *Maryland*, the *Pennsylvania*, and the *Tennessee*, while not capsized, suffered significant damage.[7] Nearly every American military plane in the area was destroyed.[8] American casualties were heavy: 2,403 were killed, including 1,177 sailors on the *Arizona*;

**Lieutenant Finn wearing
the Medal of Honor**
US Naval Historical Center photograph

1,176 were wounded.[9] The next day Roosevelt, in a speech in which he referred to December 7, 1941, as "a date which will live in infamy," asked Congress to declare war on Japan.

Lieutenant Finn, who is also the country's oldest-living Medal of Honor recipient, was born on July 24, 1909, in Los Angeles. "I had always wanted to go to the Naval Academy, but I couldn't. But I really wanted to join the navy and see the world. So a couple of weeks before my seventeenth birthday in 1926, I went down and enlisted. I was originally a gunner's mate. I grew up with a machine gun in my hand. I served in

The USS *Arizona* burning at Pearl Harbor
photo courtesy the United States Navy

the navy throughout the 1930s. In 1941 I was shipped to Kaneohe Naval Air Station on Oahu, which is about fifteen miles east of Pearl Harbor. I was the chief ordnance officer of a thirty-man crew. On Pearl Harbor Day, the first place the Japanese attacked was Kaneohe. They got to us about five minutes before they hit Pearl Harbor.

"Just before the attack, I was in bed but I wasn't asleep!" he says slyly. "The barracks we were living in were brand new, and that morning my neighbor's wife was doing some landscaping when she heard something. She banged on my front door, and I put on a pair of dungarees. I didn't even have on a pair of shoes, nor did I have on a uniform. Anyway, she said I was needed down at the hangar. See, the base held [amphibious patrol bomber] PBY planes, and they were housed down by the water. But I was still unaware of the attack at this point. So my neighbor and I got into my car and drove twenty miles an hour, which was the base speed limit. At first I thought the airplane noises were mock attacks. And then I heard machine gun fire, which was very strange since I was the ordnance officer. Then I saw a plane overhead with the big old dirty red meatballs underneath. It looked like the red paint had been mixed with mud. And he was so low I thought for certain he was going to hit one of the buildings. I said to my neighbor, who was named Ed Sullivan from New Jersey, 'This is the real McCoy, the real Japs!'

"So I threw my car into second, barreled to the hangar, and almost hit a couple of sailors coming from the mess hall who were unaware of what was going on. I parked my car, flipped off the engine, and had about a 125-yard dash to the hangar. Some of our planes were already smoking, and so were some cars. The Japanese used lots of incendiary ammo, and the American planes were all lined up and filled with gas. I think about two thousand gallons each. The tanks were in the wings and they just went up in flames. The planes just melted into a pile. Two and a half hours later, after the attack was done, you'd spot a propeller sticking up here, a wing there.

"By the time I got to the hangar, our soldiers already had two machine guns out and were shooting back at the Japs. But the biggest problem was that we didn't have the proper gun mounts for them. All the real mounts were riveted onto the melted planes. All we had to use that morning was a practice mount we used to show the recruits how to use and load a gun. Every time the Japanese would send another wave of planes, I'd go out there and use that practice platform to shoot at the planes. For two and a half hours!"

Soon Lieutenant Finn realized a larger problem was brewing. "Our planes weren't usually kept in the hangars. They were only put in there for maintenance. And some of our planes had antisubmarine duty. The hangars had five-hundred-pound depth charges. All dynamite. And they didn't have a thick metal coat. So if the Japs hit one of the hangars and exploded them, well, that wouldn't be good. So one of the most important things I did that day was order the men to take out the charges. It was a good thing, because the Japanese burned down one of the three hangars."

The sailor made preparations for a return attack. "I knew we needed more protection in case they returned. So I found the metalsmith on the base and ordered him to make machine gun platforms. Well, between the time the attack ended and that night, they made thirty-four mounts out of anything they could find. And we went through the plane wreckage and retrieved all the guns that were not burned.

"I was hit about twenty times. My left arm wouldn't work anymore, I had some broken bones and was also shot in my left foot. Some of the worst pain came from the tiny shrapnel no one could see and the doctor really had to search to find. But I refused medical attention, even though I was ordered to sick bay. It wasn't until 2:00 the next morning that I went. But when I got there, everyone there was seriously wounded, so I went home to make sure my wife was all right, and a few hours later I went back to sick bay. I was hospitalized from December 8 to December 24.

"I really didn't think much about what I had done. Many months later—it was in September 1942—I was called into my commanding officer's office. He told me I was going to be awarded the Medal of Honor. I was very appreciative of that, and I just asked him if he could make certain my wife would be there. The award ceremony was very simple and held right in Pearl Harbor. It was aboard the deck of the USS *Enterprise*, which was under construction. So just before the ceremony started, they turned off all the equipment. Admiral [Chester] Nimitz gave me the award. He hung it around my neck. And a minute after it was over, the construction noise began right up again. But I was happy it was Nimitz over Roosevelt. I refused to go to Washington to have the president give it to me. Even though he was my commander in chief, I opposed his third term. Although the presentation is generally made by the president, it can be awarded by others under some circumstances. I just either lucked out by being at Kaneohe or I was really unlucky by being there."

Lieutenant Finn's Medal of Honor citation states:

For extraordinary heroism distinguished service, and devotion above and beyond the call of duty. During the first attack by Japanese airplanes on the Naval Air Station, Kaneohe Bay, on 7 December 1941, Lt. Finn promptly secured and manned a .50-caliber machinegun mounted on an instruction stand in a completely exposed section of the parking ramp, which was under heavy enemy machinegun strafing fire. Although painfully wounded many times, he continued to man this gun and to return the enemy's fire vigorously and with telling effect throughout the enemy strafing and bombing attacks and with complete disregard for his own personal safety. It was only by specific orders that he was persuaded to leave his post to seek medical attention. Following first aid treatment, although obviously suffering much pain and moving with great difficulty, he returned to the squadron area and actively supervised the rearming of returning planes. His extraordinary heroism and conduct in this action were in keeping with the highest traditions of the U.S. Naval Service.

Lieutenant Finn served in the navy for twenty-one years. He insists on remembering a fellow World War II soldier who is, in his estimation, "the greatest hero of them all": "Henry Erwin was in the Army Air Force, and they were going on a bombing raid over Japan. They used these really bright flares to light up the ground targets for nighttime raids. Well, somehow, the flare ended back up in the plane after it was dropped. Henry picked up the flare. Imagine that! It's like picking up an oxyacetylene torch. He took the flare and walked up to the cockpit, where he chucked it out the window.

It burned off his eyelids, ears, some of his fingers. He was practically burned to death. They thought for sure he was going to die, so they rushed a Medal of Honor to his bedside. It's a miracle he lived. And it's the guttiest thing I ever heard of. Or what about the men who jump on hand grenades, knowing if they go off, they are dead? I don't know how any of them did that. There was nothing heroic about what I did."

NOTES

1. "Medal of Honor Recipients at Pearl Harbor in World War II," Home of Heroes, http://www.homeofheroes.com/pearlharbor/pearl_8moh.html (accessed May 18, 2009).

2. *The Encyclopedia Americana* (Danbury, CT: Grolier, 1998), 21:578.

3. Thomas Parrish, ed., *The Simon and Schuster Encyclopedia of World War II* (New York: Simon and Schuster, 1978), 486.

4. *Dictionary of American History* (New York: Charles Scriber's Sons, 1976), 5:239.

5. Gordon W. Prange, *At Dawn We Slept: The Untold Story of Pearl Harbor* (New York: Penguin, 1981), 460.

6. *Academic American Encyclopedia* (Danbury, CT: Grolier, 1986), 15:126.

7. "Remembering Pearl Harbor, Reading 1," National Register of Historic Places, http://cr.nps.gov/nr/twhp/curriculumkit/lessons/arizona/5facts1.htm (accessed July 3, 2009).

8. Parrish, *The Simon and Schuster Encyclopedia of World War II*, 487.

9. *Dictionary of American History*, 5:240.

ROBERT MYERS
The Final Man from the Committee
That Created Social Security

*"I'm not the child genius who dreamed it up.
I got involved with Social Security only because
I was at the right place at the right time."*

In the recent debate about the privatization of Social Security, Robert Myers argued in an article, "I am completely opposed [to privatization], now and forever. . . . I don't think the program is broken."[1] While this is not an uncommon position, Myers speaks from an unusual perspective: he is one of the last-surviving creators of Social Security.

Social Security was created during the Great Depression, which hit the elderly particularly hard. Many became destitute

Mr. Myers at the time of the interview
photo by Stuart Lutz

because they had savings in banks that closed. Others had pension plans with companies that failed. Often the adult children of the elderly were unable to support both their own children and their parents. Many senior citizens wrote to President Franklin D. Roosevelt, urging him to establish a pension plan for retirees.[2] At the same time, a populist groundswell of support for a national pension plan arose when it became apparent that local and private charities were unable to cope with the prolonged Depression. Roosevelt quickly created a Committee on Economic Security to study various pension proposals.

In January 1935, after reviewing the committee's recommendations, Roosevelt sent to Congress the Economic Security Bill, which was soon renamed the Social Security Act. The proposed plan taxed payroll in order to provide pensions to the elderly. In August 1935 Roosevelt signed the Social Security Act into law, and it went into effect on January 1, 1937. At the bill signing Roosevelt stated, "[W]e are compelled to employ the active interest of the Nation as a whole through government in order to encourage a greater security for each individual who composes it."[3]

Born on October 31, 1912, Robert Myers graduated from Lehigh University in 1933, then received a master's degree in math from the University of Iowa in 1934. His home office has pillars of papers and magazines. The walls hold dozens of actuarial certificates and photographs signed by prominent people. One interesting plaque acknowledges that Mr. Myers holds a Guinness World Record for testifying before Congress 175 times.

Mr. Myers recalls the horrid economic conditions the nation faced when he graduated. "It was the Depression, and many people who thought they had prepared for retirement found their resources gone," he states with a professorial air. "The children couldn't take care of the parents. There was something called the Townsend Plan, suggested by Francis

Robert Myers in Germany in 1931
photo courtesy Jonathan K. Myers

Townsend. He wanted to create a national pension for the elderly. Everyone over the age of sixty would get two hundred dollars a month from the government. Retirees had to spend this every month, and Townsend hoped this would increase spending and end the Depression. He thought that a 2 or 3 percent tax at every stage of the manufacturing process would pay for his pension plan. However, all the best estimates couldn't finance Townsend's idea. After all, the average wage was ninety dollars a month, so it would be hard for a retired couple to get four hundred dollars monthly. And although it didn't make financial sense, the idea swept the country and had many supporters. Also, Louisiana governor Huey Long had a 'share the wealth' plan, but the benefits were not logical. [The famous radio broadcaster, populist, and priest] Father [Charles] Coughlin also had a similar idea. President Roosevelt knew that two hundred dollars a month was impossible. But many conservatives, seeing the support Townsend and the others had, realized they had to do something, so they supported the eventual Social Security idea. FDR got wide backing from the GOP, and 90 percent of all Democrats supported it. Townsend wanted a retirement age of sixty, but that was too low. Roosevelt eventually settled on sixty-five.

"President Roosevelt set up a Committee on Economic Security not long after he got into office. Frances Perkins, who was the first female cabinet member, was on the committee. It had twenty or thirty people, but not all were from the government. The committee borrowed experts from the private field. So there was a man from the AT&T pension plan and one from Traveler's Insurance." Mr. Myers explains how he ended up on the committee: "They needed a junior actuary [an actuary studies the life span of people] to grind out the numbers. One committee member consulted a professor at the University of Iowa, who suggested I be the junior actuary. This was 1934, the middle of the Depression. I guess my main qualification was that I lived near Washington," he laughs. "I took a six-week temporary job with the committee. I was willing to take anything. But the six weeks extended beyond its original intention, and the committee took longer than it planned. I didn't work for the Social Security Administration immediately. There was a slight interlude before I was hired by the Social Security Administration, and they didn't need actuaries to start off. I scraped together money then and worked for a year for the federal relief administration. In 1936 I went with the Social Security Board, who by then got appropriations."

Mr. Myers reviews the accomplishments of President Roosevelt. "He was a very capable, dedicated, well-meaning person. He did a lot for the country and he was instrumental in the Social Security field. He wanted the United States to develop various forms of social insurance, such as medical care and pensions. European countries already had elderly pensions. I had thought that something like Social Security was

**Robert Myers (*back right*) examining
United States government bonds bought by
the Social Security trust fund in 1968**
photo courtesy the Department of the Treasury

eventually going to come to America, but the Depression just made it occur faster.

"Many of the new Social Security Board workers realized that we were on the ground floor of a big thing that would be important for the welfare of the nation," he says, recounting his work at the new agency. "I certainly didn't work for the board on idealistic grounds, for I could have made more in the private sector. But I realized how big it would be in the long run."

As he looks back on the founding of Social Security, Mr. Myers argues that "[s]ome say I created Social Security, but that's not true. I was just there at the birth. I'm not the child genius who dreamed it up. I got involved with Social Security only because I was at the right place at the right time."

Mr. Myers offers both a unique perspective on Social Security and a defense of the program. "Social Security's success is quite evident in looking at poverty figures. For people over sixty-five, the poverty rate is the same as the general population. But the elderly aren't as poor as they used to be since they are not dependent on their children, as used to be the case. So no matter how stupid people are or how bad their luck, people can't fall below the floor Social Security provides. People are better off today and don't realize it. We have so much more than people did fifty or sixty years ago. Things are greatly improved for the average American, though there is still poverty."

He says that Americans should not be surprised that the population is getting older. "Actuarial estimates told about that long ago," he says. "Social Security can be financed with this in mind. If the benefits are too large, then the payroll taxes become a burden. And with the increase in life expectancy, the burden can grow. I feel that the retirement age should increase and we can raise the payroll tax slightly, perhaps a quarter percent on both the employee and employer. It's an unpopular thing to say, but sixty-five does not have to be the fixed age [for retirement]. Problems can be handled by small changes gradually. It's a relative thing, and as people live longer, the retirement age should be raised, perhaps to seventy or seventy-two. For example, if we started Social Security two centuries ago, the retirement age would have been fifty based on life expectancy. There are fewer physically demanding jobs than years ago, and people don't need to retire as early.

"I'm a strong believer [in] Social Security. It's an excellent form of protection, so I'd hate to see it weakened or destroyed. I don't want to see it either privatized or expanded. Social Security was designed as a three-legged stool, combining your savings, a private pension, and Social Security. Social Security provides a guaranteed floor of protection, and it is inflation proof. If we could build private accounts on top of what we already have, that would make the current system as good as possible. But as for funneling part of your Social Security money into private funds, mutual funds don't want that business and they cannot handle it. I've been on the board of two large mutual funds and I know it would be a horrible administrative mess."

In 1947 the young Mr. Myers became Social Security's chief actuarial officer. "I was chief actuary from 1947 to 1970, and it's the best actuarial job in the world. My job was to make estimates for what the program will cost, both long range—up to seventy-five years—and short range. Of course, you can't make these predictions with absolute precision, but these informed estimates give guidance. I left the Social Security Administration for political reasons, since I thought that people at the top were traitorous. A civil servant shouldn't take sides," he says sternly. "I was a professor at Temple University and consulted for the GOP. After Reagan was elected president, I was brought back as the number two person to limit a financial crisis when Social Security was running out of money. I was named executive director of the National Commission on Social Security for a year and a half, and it was quite successful. Our 1983 efforts saved the system.

"I'm still working and I've authored over a thousand articles on Social Security. I get my Social Security check every month and it comes in handy. Of course, a third of it goes off for taxes!" he quips.

NOTES

1. "Lies Clutter the Landscape," North Texas Activists, http://www.labordallas.org/ssa3.htm (accessed July 3, 2009).

2. "Pre–Social Security Period: Traditional Sources of Economic Security," Social Security Online, http://www.ssa.gov/history/briefhistory3.html (accessed July 3, 2009).

3. Franklin D. Roosevelt, "Message to Congress on the Objectives and Accomplishments of the Administration," American Presidency Project, http://www.presidency.ucsb.edu/ws/index.php?pid=14690 (accessed July 3, 2009).

GEORGE PUTNAM JR.
The Last Person Still Alive to
Have Flown with Amelia Earhart

"People are not willing to accept the most logical thing—
[Amelia Earhart] ran out of gas."

Today, we take flying to be a routine—albeit occasionally frustrating—experience. We think nothing of having a soda in a quiet, pressurized cabin at thirty-five thousand feet while city lights twinkle below us. Yet several decades ago, aviation was neither safe nor glamorous.

Amelia Earhart is history's most famous woman flyer. During the Great Depression, her daring flights captivated the country and made her one of the most well-known people on earth. She disappeared over the Pacific Ocean in 1937 while attempting to make the first circumnavigation of the earth by a woman. Earhart's stepson George Putnam Jr., born in 1921, may be the last person alive to have flown with the great aviatrix.

Amelia Earhart was born in 1897 in Atchison, Kansas.[1] An inquisitive child, she enrolled at Columbia University as a pre-med student but never completed her degree.[2] In 1920 her father paid for her first flight, hoping the experience would cure her desire to fly.[3] It did the opposite, and the twenty-three-year-old took lessons from another aviatrix.[4] In 1928 she met George Putnam Sr., a book publisher and a first-rate promoter, and they were wed on February 7, 1931. "Most of the Putnams lived in Rye so they could commute to work," the younger Mr. Putnam explains in his deep and commanding voice. "My father used to be connected to the Putnam publishing firm, but he lost it during the Depression.

"I probably first met Amelia Earhart about 1928 or so. I was very young and I liked her very much. She liked engines and cars. One time she told my father to turn on the car in the morning and let it run for a while to get the oil flowing throughout the engine. Of course, the way cars are now, you don't have to do that. She had a great interest and determination to learn and to perform. She was a great example, but she wouldn't have done it without the encouragement and backing of my father. He always thought that a wife should do what she's best at, and in her case it was flying. She was always nice to me and a good person. She had this ability to deal with anyone. She was awarded a gold medal by President [Herbert] Hoover, and she was just as comfortable accepting that as she was changing oil and fixing cars. One time, my father and Earhart came to Fort Pierce, Florida, where I was raised by my mother. It was a mob scene with them."

In 1928, the year after Charles Lindbergh's famous transatlantic solo flight, Earhart became the first female passenger to cross the ocean when she accompanied two pilots on a flight. This transatlantic voyage made her famous. Not satisfied with merely being a passenger on the plane, in 1932 she became the first woman—and only the second person—to fly alone across the Atlantic.

Mr. Putnam has vivid memories of flying with his world-famous stepmother. "In 1933 I flew with her to the World's Fair in Chicago. I think we left from Newark. In Chicago she was quite a celebrity, and she and my father were busy with all these important people. So they turned me over to a gentleman to keep me occupied. I had a wonderful time, with parades and everything else they had there." He stresses the primitiveness of flight then. "When I was young, it was something to have flown. Back then, no one would fly aboard a plane without a good reason. Today, no one really has any concept of what flying was like back in the 1930s. The planes were very small. There were no facilities of any sort. There was no insulation, and the planes made a complete racket. It was before radar and the global positioning system."

He recounts another flight with Earhart: "She also had an

**Young George Putnam with Amelia Earhart
dressed in her flight suit**
photo courtesy George Putnam Jr.

autogyro, which was a precursor to the helicopter. In order to finance it, my father did an advertisement for the Beech-Nut gum company. The gum came out in these long sheets, about three feet long. She flew this autogyro from town to town. My job was to hand out fistfuls of gum to everyone when we landed."

In 1935 Earhart became the first pilot to fly from Honolulu to the American mainland.[5] Mr. Putnam retrieves from his desk an envelope addressed to him. In the upper left corner, his

The envelope Earhart mailed Mr. Putnam in 1935
photo by Stuart Lutz

stepmother wrote, "Carried by Air Honolulu to Oakland January 11–12 1935," then signed it. "See this envelope?" he asks. "Her flights cost a lot of money, and my father was always thinking of new ways to raise funds. Sure, gas was forty cents a gallon then, but her flights took thousands of gallons. Anyway, a stamp dealer gave my father about two thousand dollars if Earhart would carry two hundred of these envelopes on her famous Honolulu flight. And then the dealer would sell them. This one is addressed to me."

He mentions the difficulty in achieving these early flights. "On her record-breaking trips, she'd have to fly, say, sixteen hours with no break, paying attention all the time. That takes a lot of physical stamina. There was no autopilot in those days. There was no easy way to eat or go to the bathroom. I really admire her much more now."

In 1937 Earhart attempted her most daring exploit, a flight around the world following the equator, the longest possible route.[6] Accompanied by navigator Fred Noonan, her first attempt was launched from Oakland on St. Patrick's Day in 1937. The flight went toward the west, so Earhart flew to Honolulu.[7] When leaving Hawaii, a mishap occurred and the

Lockheed Electra plane was wrecked on takeoff. The plane was returned to California for another attempt, but the next trip headed eastward.

Earhart and Noonan left Miami on June 1, 1937, headed for San Juan, Puerto Rico.[8] "The last time I saw her was the day before she left Miami," he says. "She started her around-the-world flight there. My father was there to see her off. [The years] 1936 and 1937 were extremely busy for her, and I was living in Florida. I didn't get a chance to see her that much. I knew Fred Noonan. He was the best navigator in the country. He received all this bad and false publicity that he was drinking a lot. It's just not true."

By June 29, Earhart landed on Lae, Papua New Guinea, just north of eastern Australia.[9] Her next goal was a speck in the Pacific called Howland Island. According to one biographer, while on Lae Earhart was quite tired from the previous long flights and other commitments.[10] Also, Lae had a short runway, so her plane could not carry as much gasoline as she wanted.[11] Her flight to Howland, which began on July 2, was estimated to be twenty-five hundred miles long and to take eighteen hours; a portion of the flight was to be flown in the dark. At some point during the night, Earhart probably veered slightly northward, off her intended course, without realizing it. Near the end of her flight Earhart radioed that she was running low on fuel and that "we must be on you but cannot see you."[12] In her last radio transmission, she indicated: "We are on the line of position one five seven dash three three seven. . . . We are running north and south."[13] That was the last time anything was heard from the plane. When she failed to arrive as scheduled, search crews were sent out immediately, but no plane wreckage was ever found.

"I was sixteen when she was lost, living in Fort Pierce," Mr. Putnam says. "I probably heard about it on the radio. But I thought at first that she would be found, since she was a

Mr. Putnam at the time of the interview
photo by Stuart Lutz

capable woman. My brother flew out to Los Angeles to be with my father. He was waiting there to greet Earhart when she finished her flight. I saw a newsreel of my brother getting out of the plane in LA. When I was in the navy during World War II, we went on one mission near New Guinea, and we steamed right by Lae.

"Earhart is as famous as ever," he states. "Even more so in the last five or six years. There has always been a mystery about her loss, and that fuels her popularity. People are not willing to accept the most logical thing—she ran out of gas." There have been rumors that she was captured by the Japanese or even executed as a spy. "I know the Japanese are very interested in finding the plane underwater because that gets them off the hook. Several times the Japanese press has been here to interview me about it. And my voice is translated into perfect Japanese! But I still get a lot of calls—many from American World War II veterans who served in the Pacific—who claim she was caught by the Japanese." He shakes his head in dismissal of these rumors.

Recently, Mr. Putnam and his wife were the guests of honor in Earhart's hometown. "Everything in Atchison is Earhart. When we first got to Kansas, I had no idea who to report to. I was driving around Atchison and I saw a sign that pointed to her museum. So I went that way. I found it and knocked on the door. The woman who answered said, 'Are you George Putnam?' even though she had never seen me before. There was an oil painting there of my father and Earhart, and I look enough like him that they figured it was me!" he chuckles. "We went on a twenty-three-minute ride over Kansas in the world's only remaining Lockheed Electra. That's the same type of plane she was flying when she disappeared. It was outfitted exactly the same way Earhart had it, down to the numbers on the wings. The Electra was a ten-passenger plane, and it was the first one designed just for passengers. To outfit it for the around-the-world flight, Earhart took out eight seats. Then they put extra gas tanks in these boxes where the seats once were. To get to the front of the plane from the back area, you had to slide over the tanks, leaving about a foot of room," he explains as he holds his hands about twelve inches apart.

A very rare signed photograph of Amelia Earhart and Fred Noonan, taken just before they left Oakland on their around-the-world flight
photo courtesy Purdue University Libraries' Karnes Archives & Special Collections

"I enjoy being one of the last ones to know Earhart because I like the curiosity other people have about her," he concludes. "And I've met a lot of interesting people in my lifetime because of my association."

NOTES

1. Mary S. Lovell, *The Sound of Wings* (New York: St. Martin's, 1989), 9.

2. Ibid., 29.

3. Ibid., 32.

4. Ibid., 35.

5. *Dictionary of American Biography* (New York: Scribner's, 1958), supp. 2: 164.

6. Lovell, *The Sound of Wings*, 228.

7. Ibid., 246.

8. Ibid., 261.

9. Ibid., 267.

10. Ibid., 269.

11. Ibid., 276.

12. Ibid., 283.

13. Ibid., 285.

BOYCE PRICE
One of the Final Two Officers to Work in
President Franklin D. Roosevelt's
Secret White House Map Room

"Once I worked in the Map Room . . . the military kept me stationed there since I knew too much."

Franklin D. Roosevelt was the only president elected four times. He led the United States through two of its greatest crises: the Great Depression and World War II. The disabled Roosevelt made few trips during the conflict before his death on April 12, 1945, relying instead on a group of select military officers stationed within the White House, in a top-secret place called the Map Room. The Map Room provided the president with up-to-the-minute reports about the course of the war, prepared from information delivered by top army and navy intelligence.

Sixty-five years after Roosevelt's death, Boyce Price of Hanover, New Hampshire, is one of the last two surviving officers posted to the Map Room. Entrusted with the country's greatest military secrets, he had a unique view of the course of World War II. Mr. Price eagerly speaks of his military service while showing his memorabilia, displayed on his coffee table.

Mr. Price was born in Montreal, Quebec, on June 1, 1914. "My mother fell ill just after my birth and died. My father was a successful architect up there. He went back to New York City and worked for several architectural firms. He remarried when I was five to a great woman who quit working as an art director for an advertising agency just to take care of me."

Mr. Price enrolled at Dartmouth "and I intended to major in chemistry. But I switched to English, something I've never regretted. As a junior, I got interested in the theater and designed sets for college shows. After I graduated Dartmouth in 1936, I enrolled for a year and a half of scenic design classes at Yale, but then shifted to industrial design."

Mr. Price at the time of the interview
photo by Stuart Lutz

Mr. Price as a World War II officer
photo courtesy Boyce Price

"Before the war, I worked in New York with designer Russel Wright, then started a small company making clocks. It went well until the war came along. I was drafted into the Army Engineers in March 1941. I was hoping to get into camouflage design and was sent to Fort Belvoir, Virginia. But I was assigned to a heavy pontoon bridge battalion, building and moving pontoon bridges on maneuvers. We would put it up, take it down, and do it again somewhere else." All that changed after Pearl Harbor. "I was supposed to be getting out of the service since I had already done my time. I was engaged and already had my wedding date set for December 20, 1941.

Although at war, I was able to keep it and took a week off before moving with my new wife to Alexandria, Virginia.

"I went to officer candidate school and was commissioned a second lieutenant. I was then made an instructor of military engineering that covered mapping, demolitions, and combat. In 1942 I and another officer, Ogden Kniffen, were assigned to President Roosevelt's secret Map Room. I never knew how we were picked, but I think my experience with industrial design likely helped. Kniffen was picked first, and he probably recommended me. For my new White House duties, I went for special military training, and after a month I was ordered to report to the Map Room. I'm not sure how the government did a background check on me. Occasionally, someone would follow us around when we were in Alexandria. I know they were watching us." He motions with his hand to indicate someone snooping. "After I worked in the Map Room for some time, the military kept me stationed there, since I knew too much. If I were reassigned to the front, I would be too valuable to the enemy.

"I later learned that when the Map Room was getting started, it needed engineering officers to improve the military maps and keep track of movements. It was a top-secret room set up right after Pearl Harbor. It had been a ladies' powder room on the ground floor near the South Portico! Prime Minister [Winston] Churchill had a similar setup in London which allowed him to see the goings-on of the entire war. Roosevelt, at the suggestion of his friend the actor Robert Montgomery, who was in Naval Intelligence, set up the same thing in the White House."

Mr. Price describes the security around the Map Room. "I first had to clear the guard positioned outside the door at all times. After some time working in the White House, I had no problem getting past the White House guards, since they recognized me. No one was allowed inside the Map Room unless they were accompanied by the president or given special

**President Harry Truman posing with the Map Room crew.
Mr. Price is over Truman's right shoulder**
photo courtesy the Library of Congress

authorization. The room was so secure that Secret Service men—the guards who would take a bullet for the president—were not allowed inside. Nor was his valet, Arthur Prettyman. The Secret Service would leave the president at the door, and it was our job to wheel him inside. His wheelchair had a narrow wheelbase and the president was a muscular man from the waist up, making the chair top heavy and unbalanced. We had to wheel him over raised wiring on the floor, and we always feared that we would accidentally dump him!

"The Map Room was about twenty-five feet by thirty feet and brightly lit. There was an island in the middle formed by desks and file cabinets. One wall had a tremendous naval chart of the whole world with movable symbols for our navy and other Allied warships. Right after Pearl Harbor, we didn't have many soldiers on the ground, so it was logical that most of the

An envelope Mr. Price brought back from the Soviet Embassy, addressed to "The President"
photo by Stuart Lutz

maps were naval. Another wall focused on the Soviet front. There were movable panels that slid, which allowed the president to see every major operation, all the way down to regimental combat units. The maps were covered with acetate so officers could show movements with colored pins or paint." Mr. Price remembers which pin was the most important to the president. "Franklin Roosevelt Jr. was serving on a destroyer, so his ship had its own special pin. Whenever the president came in, that pin was the first thing he looked for.

"The Map Room was manned by four navy and four army reserve officers, plus two noncommissioned clerical helpers. This preserved the traditional interservice rivalries. The Map Room was headed by officers who graduated either Annapolis or West Point, and they were selected by the chiefs of the army and navy. Most officers stayed less than a year. One funny thing about the Map Room is that the commanding officers there actually wanted to answer the phones!" he laughs. "After all, it was only the top brass calling, so an officer could pick up the phone and have an important general or admiral— or even the president—on the other end."

The room was staffed at all times. "This way, the president could have an up-to-the-minute account of the war any time he wanted. The secure room also became a way for the president to communicate with other Allied leaders, but it was often in code. For example, there were files there with all the correspondence between the president and [Soviet premier Joseph] Stalin or Churchill. That way, when there were big conferences, such as Yalta, it was an efficient task to prepare for them."

Mr. Price has many memories of the president. "Roosevelt would usually come to the Map Room early in the morning. He was often accompanied by Admiral William Leahy, his adviser Harry Hopkins, or his military aide, General 'Pa' Watson. He would review a one-page brief summarizing the military situation and get a briefing with the maps. One way to tell his mood was from his cigarette holder. If he received good news that morning, his cigarette would be at a high angle. If the news wasn't as good, it would droop a bit.

"I was never formally introduced to the president. I was there as an officer and the president dealt mostly through Leahy. Roosevelt would speak directly with the admiral. He would never raise major issues in the Map Room. Yet the president would ask us questions when reviewing specific operations, and we'd answer. The meetings with Roosevelt rarely lasted more than twenty minutes. When the president wasn't in the Map Room, Harry Hopkins would often sit down and converse with the officers. It would be informal, and he'd ask our opinions on various operations. He was shrewd and had a talent for asking questions that got right to the heart of the matter.

"In the evening, Roosevelt would stop in his doctor's office to have his limbs massaged; it was down the hall from the Map Room. And he'd call one of us in to give him the latest war news. It was really an emotional sight to see this powerful man so helpless. Yet he never complained about his discomfort," he says with admiration.

Mr. Price recounts one unusual task he was charged with. "I had to retrieve top-secret documents from the Soviet Embassy in Washington at night. Because Washington is several hours behind Moscow, Stalin's messages to Roosevelt arrived in the middle of the night. I would get an army car and go to the embassy. There, a beautiful secretary greeted me while I waited to see Ambassador [Andrei Andreyevich] Gromyko. Gromyko was always perfectly dressed, no matter what hour of the night. He would hand me an envelope sealed with red wax addressed to 'The President' on the front. I'd get back to the White House and open it in the Map Room. And we would show it to the president in the morning."

The lonely night watch was fraught with difficult decisions. "I had to decide whether to wake the president with important news. The president's guidelines were, 'If it's important and you don't wake me, you'll be in trouble, and if it's not important and you wake me, you'll be in trouble!'" he chuckles. "The president was rarely wakened, and if I needed more guidance whether to wake him or not, I could confer with his military aide for a decision."

Because of his position, Mr. Price traveled with the president. "I went to Camp David, which was then known as Shangri-La. It was a very informal place in the Maryland mountains with camp-style houses. I was there more often in the summertime. I would deliver materials to him that just couldn't wait to get to him, and if it was late, I would spend the night in the spare bedroom there."

He recalls one of the most terrifying moments of his life:

"In 1944 I was sent to Quebec to prepare a Map Room for the president and Churchill. I had already installed many of the major maps and charts, but I wasn't finished setting everything up. Some new materials had just been delivered to me, and they were still in crates and boxes. I thought I had more time to finish, since I assumed Roosevelt and Churchill would eat lunch together first. All of a sudden, the guard outside announced that the president and Churchill were about to walk in! And there they were, two of the most powerful men on the planet, and I wasn't ready for them. There were still boxes and crates all over the floor. By the grace of God, I had put up the maps they wanted to use. I had to steer the president's wheelchair around the obstacles. He was not happy and I was sweating drops of blood the whole time. But somehow, I was not reprimanded." He winks as he says this.

Mr. Price was privy to D-Day, the massive June 6, 1944, invasion of Normandy, France, by Allied troops. "We knew it was coming ahead of time. It was well planned and well prepared for. I was one of several officers that morning receiving reports on the invasion. But there was one code that I did not know. It was 'Tube Alloys,' [which] I eventually figured out referred to the atomic bomb. This was one of the very few military secrets kept from the Map Room staff. I didn't know about the atomic bombing ahead of time."

He remembers the last time he ever saw Roosevelt. "The officers could see that he was worn out and getting fatigued. At the Yalta conference in February 1945, Stalin reneged on his promise to hold free elections in Poland. I think the deception at Yalta took the remaining life out of the president. The last time I saw him was about a week before he died in Warm Springs, Georgia. That's where he'd go when he wanted to have some time with his girlfriend, Lucy Mercer. She was present when he died. I was on leave in New York City when he passed. I was recalled to duty and served for seventy-two straight hours."

The new president, Harry Truman, "had not been briefed by Roosevelt or his staff, and was not up to speed." He came to the Map Room and "[went] through the maps, theater by theater. At first he didn't get it that he had to make these big military decisions. But he learned very fast. He had a great ability to take over in a positive manner. Yet I could see the start of the Cold War from the messages Truman and Stalin exchanged. The public didn't know about it, but there were some half-joking conversations in the Map Room about using the atomic bomb against the Soviet Union. President Truman awarded the Legion of Merit to the Map Room staff." Mr. Price left the Map Room in 1946 after the war ended.

Mr. Price came in contact with many prominent people during his war years. He has great affection for Eleanor Roosevelt. She "was very pleasant to the Map Room staff. She acted like the White House was her own home. So if you were walking down the hall and she saw you but didn't know you, she'd stop and introduce herself. She'd ask questions about you. She even had the Map Room staff and our wives over for lunch."

He recounts a funny anecdote about Winston Churchill: "He was a night owl, and would occasionally party at the British Embassy before returning to the White House for the night. The Map Room's night duty officer, after erroneously being assured that Churchill was asleep, pulled out the cot and took a nap. He was a stickler, so he took off his uniform pants and hung them from a file drawer to keep the press. About 2:00 in the morning, the Map Room guard announced that Churchill was outside the door. The officer jumped up and accidentally shut the drawer containing his pants, locking them in. He didn't know what to do, so he answered the door wearing his underpants. The prime minister looked at him and said, 'Well, Captain, perhaps it would be better if I visited you in the morning.'

"Also, Churchill liked getting his morning news reports in

his guest bedroom, and he would prop himself up in bed. Other times, he would come into the Map Room for the president's briefing. One Sunday morning, after a hard night at the embassy, he entered the Map Room. He saw a big pile of fat Sunday morning newspapers. He noted, 'The trouble with you Americans is that your newspapers are much too thick and your toilet paper much too thin!'"

Mr. Price concludes with some remarks about Roosevelt, from his unique historical perspective. He recalls that Churchill wanted a series of invasions in the Balkans, but "FDR disagreed, for he wanted a massive invasion of France, which is what he got. When [General George S.] Patton was fighting in North Africa, a lot of people wanted Roosevelt to pull out because of the mounting casualties. But the president stuck with his plan. The Americans established control over North Africa, which created a platform for us to invade Italy.

"Franklin Roosevelt was an amazing man. He engendered respect because he was so able mentally yet so unable physically. His mind was as clear as a bell. He was a real strategist. He knew what he was doing and he made things happen. He was also surprisingly controlled. He was often relaxed and would laugh at things if they were laughable.

"Even before Pearl Harbor, Roosevelt was getting ready for war. He was convinced we would have to come to the aid of France and Great Britain. And when the Japanese attacked, he was mentally ready for it. I'm quite honored that I was able to work with him, and I feel that the recognition of his abilities has increased as the years have passed," Mr. Price says. "As I see it, Roosevelt was a first-rate commander in chief and a great president."

Boyce Price died on November 1, 2007, at the age of ninety-three.

BUDD SCHULBERG
The Last Man to Write with F. Scott Fitzgerald

*"Poor Scott, suffering to his last day on earth.
Such great success in the twenties and bad times in the thirties."*

This Side of Paradise, *The Beautiful and the Damned*, *The Great Gatsby*, *Tender Is the Night*, and the incomplete *The Last Tycoon*—few great American literary reputations are built on so few works as that of F. Scott Fitzgerald. Budd Schulberg, a famous author himself, is the last living person to have written with the legendary Fitzgerald.

Fitzgerald was born in 1896 in St. Paul, Minnesota; entered Princeton University in 1913; and left Princeton to join the army in 1917. Shortly thereafter, he wrote *This Side of Paradise*, and when it was published in 1920 it brought the young Fitzgerald fame and money. In 1925 he released his masterpiece, *The Great Gatsby*. During the 1920s Fitzgerald married a glamorous Southern woman, had a daughter, lived in France, and spent money freely. As the exciting Jazz Age devolved into the Great Depression, the writer faced a number of personal and professional challenges. His wife, Zelda, was admitted to sanatoriums to combat her schizophrenia. Nine years passed before he published his next novel, *Tender Is the Night*, but it was not well received. He battled a vicious case of alcoholism, and he was financially burdened by a sick wife and declining book sales. In the mid-1930s, he was in North Carolina, writing about his famous "crack-up." By the late 1930s it appeared that Fitzgerald's prodigious talents were exhausted. He therefore traveled to the magical place where many struggling writers, including William Faulkner, had headed: Hollywood. In July 1937 Metro-Goldwyn-Mayer agreed to pay him a thousand dollars a week for six months to write screenplays.[1] Whether by luck or design, Fitzgerald met Budd Schulberg, the son of a famous Hollywood mogul.

Budd Schulberg, born in 1914, is the son of B. P. Schulberg, then Paramount's head of production. Raised in Hollywood, Mr. Schulberg met many Hollywood figures throughout the 1920s and 1930s. After graduating from Dartmouth in 1936, Mr. Schulberg remained on the East Coast and wrote his first novel—*What Makes Sammy Run?*—in 1941. It portrays Sammy Glick, an office boy who, through corruption and ambition, rises to head a motion picture studio. Schulberg wrote a second novel, *The Harder They Fall*, about boxing, which was made into a 1956 movie starring Humphrey Bogart. In 1950 he completed *The Disenchanted*, a novel about a famous novelist, Manley Halliday, who was at the nadir of his career. His most famous work is the screenplay for the classic film *On the Waterfront*, which starred a young Marlon Brando. For this masterpiece, Mr. Schulberg won an Oscar for Best Screenplay.

When twenty-four-year-old Budd Schulberg was first told he was going to work with Fitzgerald on the screenplay of the movie *Winter Carnival*, his first reaction was, "I thought he was dead. When [movie producer] Walter Wanger called me in to announce this to me, I hadn't heard about him in a long time, so I just assumed he was gone. I was quite stunned when Walter said he was in the next room and was reading my script for *Winter Carnival*. This was at Walter's office in the old Goldwyn studio. It had to be early 1939, probably January. I was stunned when I first met him, since I knew his work well and read everything of his when I was in college. It was amazing to find myself working with him. After I met him, I thought of him as an old man; he had no color, he was very pale. Everything about him was gray and faded. I didn't know how old he was. I was shocked when I learned how young he was." Fitzgerald was then forty-two.

"At the first lunch we had together, I told him what a big fan I was and that I had read everything. Scott's reaction was,

'I'm amazed anyone of your generation knows who I am. All of my books are out of print. I feel like your generation doesn't have a sense of my work; I feel cut off from them.' I replied, 'I'm sure some people of my age appreciate you.' He asked me to guess his royalties for last year. I assumed, based on the question, that they were low, but I had no idea. I guessed five hundred dollars. He said they were thirteen dollars and change. He challenged me: 'You can't even find a copy of my books in any store, even used books.' And he was right—I tried to order them, but no luck.

"He was a delightful guy to be with; we had many common interests—politics, sports, athletic heroes, and a fascination with Hollywood. We all knew the same circle of people and could gossip about them. We would compare favorite writers. I liked the proletarian writers of the 1930s, such as Steinbeck. We were also both socially conscious, but he was much more so than I anticipated. I was rather left-wing, and I was surprised he was worried about the dangers of Fascism and Hitler. He was also extremely generous. He encouraged young writers and showed a real interest in my work."

Mr. Schulberg found Fitzgerald's attitude toward Hollywood refreshing. "Many famous writers in Hollywood, like Dorothy Parker or John O'Hara, took a cynical, scornful view of the place. I was surprised to find he was so positive about Hollywood. He thought movies were a new creative experience for writers beyond the novel. I learned he had been going to the movies and taking notes. He was interested in being a more proficient screenwriter."

Mr. Schulberg recalls an infamous trip to Hanover, New Hampshire, the location of Dartmouth College, to film *Winter Carnival*. Fitzgerald and Schulberg flew from California to New York, then took a train to New England. Instead of writing the screenplay, they spent most of the trip conversing. Once at Dartmouth, Fitzgerald drank heavily. His interview with the school newspaper was a failure. When Wanger realized that the duo had done much more imbibing than writing, they were both fired on the spot.[2] As Fitzgerald himself later wrote of the trip, "In retrospect, going East under those circumstances seems one of the silliest mistakes I ever made."[3]

Mr. Schulberg recalls the voyage: "The trip to Hanover became a disaster. Poor Scott just unraveled. For three days, it was a terrible ordeal and ended in disaster. Over ten years later, when I wrote about it in *Disenchanted*, it was vivid, like yesterday, since nothing like it had ever happened to me before. On the trip, he got drunker and drunker." Mr. Schulberg has framed in his office Fitzgerald's Social Security card, boasting the author's delicate autograph. He explains how he obtained the card: "We got off the train in Vermont at about two in the morning to get some coffee. Scott was drunk and fell. He was not strong physically. Stuff fell out of his pocket, including his check for working on the film. I helped pick him up, and in the course of it, I guess I got his Social Security card and kept it. Years later, I came across it. He never asked for it or missed it.

"Standing there at the Hanover Inn, Walter fired both of us at midnight. He immediately put us on the first Montrealer [train] and sent us out of town, back to New York City"—Mr. Schulberg raises an index finger to emphasize the point— "without our baggage. The next morning, at some ungodly hour like six, the black porter came to me. Scott and I had adjoining sleeper rooms. The porter told me that he couldn't wake my friend and we only had a couple of minutes before the train departed. So I went in, and Scott was in an unconscious sleep. The porter and I lifted him out of the train, and we got a cab to take us to the Warrick Hotel. This was Monday morning, and we had stayed there just a couple of days earlier, just before we went up to Hanover. They wouldn't let us in. We looked like homeless bums and we were probably

Mr. Schulberg in his study at the time of the interview
photo by Stuart Lutz

wearing the same clothes we had on when we were there a few nights before." Mr. Schulberg chuckles at this old memory. "Well, I have to admit, I had been drinking a bit too on the trip, but I was almost twenty years younger and could carry it better. Anyway, they said the hotel was full, and we didn't know what to do. It was an agonizing few hours until Scott suggested we go to the Doctor's Hospital. He always ended up there after his New York binges."

On February 28, 1939, Fitzgerald wrote to Schulberg of the trip, "I wish you well, and I won't forget the real pleasure of knowing you, and your patience as I got more and more out of hand under the strain."[4]

Two great American books emerged from the bungled trip. "The strangest outcome of the whole fiasco is that we both started writing novels about Hollywood. For me, the trip was the last straw, and my first novel—*What Makes Sammy*

Run?—came out of it. I showed the *Sammy* manuscript to Scott and he was surprised by it. He said it was courageous and excellent since it was critical of Hollywood. He even offered to pen a blurb for the back cover, which he did." Fitzgerald wrote fervent letters about *What Makes Sammy Run?* He told one correspondent, "It's a grand book, utterly fearless and with a great deal of beauty side by side with the most bitter satire."[5]

Fitzgerald's unfinished novel also resulted from the Dartmouth fiasco. Mr. Schulberg continues, "And without knowing it, Scott, who had tried and almost always failed with his screenwriting jobs, began to write *The Last Tycoon*. He told me he was also writing a Hollywood novel and showed me the opening chapters of it. He wrote in bed because of his health. When I read the opening paragraph, I was stunned. I guess it was because it sounded as if I were talking. Having been raised in Hollywood, I always saw it as a factory town, not a glamorous place. It was a hardworking company town. They didn't make tires, but turned out cans of film. Scott made the book's narrator the daughter of a Hollywood big shot. He must have seen the look on my face, since he said, 'I hope you don't mind that I combined you with [his only child, daughter] Scotty.' My feelings were hurt because we got along so well and he seemed fond of me. I thought he liked me a lot, but maybe I was the opportune person for him to meet. I had inside knowledge of the town. Maybe he was using me and he didn't like me as much as I thought. Perhaps he had been thinking of a Hollywood novel and I was the perfect person to meet." Fitzgerald later compared *What Makes Sammy Run?* and *The Last Tycoon*: "Schulberg, a very nice, clever kid out here, is publishing a Hollywood novel with Random House in January. It's not bad, but it doesn't cut into my material at all."[6]

The exchange of novels between Schulberg and Fitzgerald was the last time they ever met, for Fitzgerald died not long afterward. "It was early December 1940, probably the first or second. I then went east to Dartmouth, thinking I'd be back in a few months, and I'd look him up then. I was in Hanover for a weekend, leaning up against the Hanover Inn, the exact scene of our debacle. A professor I had, Dr. West, came up to me and said, 'I know you'll be upset about Scott.' I had no idea what he was talking about. 'He just died.' I was really struck by the loss because I knew he had his comeback novel in mind. When I first met Scott, he was in deep professional and economic trouble. He was in debt and running out of money. People said he was finished. He was hoping to make a comeback with *The Last Tycoon*. Poor Scott was in the middle of the book and he never had a chance to finish the damn thing. I liked him a lot personally and was looking forward to seeing him again. It's a sad thing in life—you never know when the last day is until it's too late to appreciate it."

Mr. Schulberg was offered the opportunity to complete *The Last Tycoon*. "John O'Hara [author of *Appointment in Samarra*, *Pal Joey*, and *Butterfield 8*] and I were approached together—we were good friends. Our feelings were Scott had such a classic style, and no one wrote better than Scott. For us to attempt to do so just wouldn't work. Our tastes were different. It was a no-win situation." Laughing, Mr. Schulberg says, "I could see critics saying they liked the book up to a point—the place where I took over."

Mr. Schulberg knows why Fitzgerald is still so popular. "He was as good as anyone who ever wrote in America. *Gatsby* is really perfect—the style and form came together precisely. I can't say that about *Tender Is the Night*. You can pick that book up anywhere—and I often do—and be captivated by it. The writing is gorgeous, but the structure isn't as good."

Mr. Schulberg has an unusual attitude about being the last coworker of Fitzgerald's. "It's odd. I've attended a number of academic symposiums and conferences on Scott. My main feeling is they stress his achievements, but don't have a sense of what a failure he was in his own eyes. This is a responsibility I inherited by accident, and I feel I need to describe what he was like as a person. I feel the contrast between his poverty—his desperation at paying Zelda's institutional bills and Scotty's schooling, and he borrowed like crazy from his agent until he was cut off—and knowing that today Scott would be a multimillionaire. Poor Scott, suffering to his last day on earth. Such great success in the twenties and bad times in the thirties."

Mr. Schulberg summarizes, "I work every day. And I have a few drinks at night. I go to reunions from my Dartmouth class, and I'm the only one still working. I see my classmates who retire and they begin to fall apart. Senility sets in. I'd be lost without working."

As the interview concludes and twilight intrudes on the room, Mr. Schulberg excuses himself. "I have to check my e-mail now." That is a communication medium that F. Scott Fitzgerald had never used but would have mastered.

Budd Schulberg died on August 5, 2009, at the age of ninety-five.

NOTES

1. Jeffrey Meyers, *F. Scott Fitzgerald* (New York: Harper Collins, 1994), 285.

2. Matthew J. Bruccoli, *Some Sort of Epic Grandeur* (New York: Harcourt Brace Jovanovich, 1981), 455.

3. Andrew Turnbull, ed., *The Letters of F. Scott Fitzgerald* (New York: Scribner's, 1963), 579.

4. Ibid.

5. Ibid., 605.

6. Ibid., 291.

NORMAN VAUGHAN
The Final Explorer to Accompany Admiral Byrd
to the Antarctic in 1929
"Boy was it cold out last night! It was seventy-three below zero!"

The recent interest in polar explorer Ernest Shackleton reminds us of the difficulties in exploring the Arctic and Antarctic. Until a century ago, no human had traveled to either the North or the South Pole, and the polar regions remained two of the greatest exploring challenges. On April 6, 1909, Robert Peary reached the North Pole and on December 14, 1911, Roald Amundsen made it to the South Pole. During Shackleton's 1914 attempt to cross the entire Antarctic continent, his ship *Endurance* was crushed by the ice, stranding his men. Shackleton led a dangerous ocean mission to a nearby island to get help, and all his men were safely rescued.[1]

With the advent of aviation in the early twentieth century, the next great polar challenge was to fly over the poles. Admiral Richard Byrd was ready to try this feat. Born in 1888, Byrd served in the navy for a year and fought in World War I. In 1925 he used an airplane to map more than thirty thousand square miles of frozen Greenland. The same year, he planned a flight over the North Pole and began raising funds for his expedition. On May 9, 1926, he and fellow aviator Floyd Bennett reached the pole and circled it several times. In December 1928 Byrd's expedition to fly over the South Pole arrived in Antarctica and established its base, known as Little America, on the Ross Ice Shelf. On November 28, 1929, Byrd and three other men took off for the South Pole in his plane, the *Floyd Bennett*. Byrd dropped both an American and a British flag over the South Pole; the historic flight took ten hours in all.[2] Colonel Norman Vaughan is the last-surviving participant in Byrd's 1929 Antarctic missions; not surprisingly, he lives in Alaska.

Norman Vaughan, born on December 19, 1905, in Massa-

**Colonel Vaughan in 1928,
training dogs for his Antarctic mission**
photo courtesy Carolyn Vaughan

chusetts, has led a fascinating and unconventional life, seeking out adventure in all forms. As a young man, he became an expert dogsled driver. He left Harvard to help the prominent Canadian doctor Wilfred Grenfell deliver medical supplies in Labrador. Vaughan returned to Harvard but left again to go to Antarctica with Byrd. During World War II he took part in a dangerous mission to recover the top-secret Norden bombsight from some American planes forced to land in Greenland; this prevented the Nazis from discovering how the important bombsight functioned. In 1967 he drove a snowmobile from Alaska to Boston. He represented Alaska in the 1977 Inaugural Parade and has raced in the Iditarod, the world's most famous dogsled race.

His fascination with outdoor sports began when he was young. "As a kid, I camped out in the wintertime in Massachusetts. A friend of mine lived five miles away, and we'd camp outside. This was unheard of by parents there. They thought it was dangerous and we'd freeze to death," he speaks in a strong voice touched by the New England accent from his youth.

Colonel Vaughan first saw Byrd when he was a student at the Milton Academy near Boston. "Byrd gave a talk there one night. I don't remember a single thing he said per se, but it was about the Antarctic. I fell in love with the idea of going with him if I could. I first heard of his Antarctic mission when I was at Harvard. The door opened and I saw the evening paper, the *Boston Transcript*. The headline had five words: 'Byrd to the South Pole.' I read it out loud and I said to my roommate, 'Gee, look at this. I've *got* to go!' Byrd needed dog drivers and that fit me just right."

As much as he wanted to go on Byrd's mission, he needed an introduction to the adventurer. "I knew I had to find a way to talk myself onto the expedition. I went to his house and asked to see him. At the front door was this buxom woman who said I couldn't see Byrd and stated that no one gets past her. She put up her arms like she meant it. So I went and spoke with the newspaper people at the *Boston Transcript*. I spoke to W. A. MacDonald, who broke the 'Byrd to Antarctica' story. He spoke to Byrd for me and told the admiral that I was enthusiastic to go and would do anything. He accepted me and my two friends, Eddie Goodale and Freddie Crockett. We didn't get paid at all.

"Byrd assembled the dogs at Wonalancet, New Hampshire, so we went there first. Dogs were arriving every day. We'd immediately put them in a harness to see if they would work. Those that worked, we trained, and those that didn't, we sent back to the owners. We spent the entire winter of 1927 training them. We worked with over one hundred dogs and found ninety-seven suitable to go. Each dog had his own crate. We traveled with them on the deck of the ship to New Zealand and then onto the ice. We had to do all types of labor on the ship, including shoveling coal into the ship's furnaces and cleaning out the ashes.

"I helped unload the 650 tons of equipment and supplies that needed to be offloaded from the boat. I moved heavy loads between the boat and the camp, Little America, nine miles away. The Antarctic is beautiful. It is snow covered and ice crusted and you walk on top of the crust. The mainland is solid and you can dock your boats easily in the water."

One story illustrates the danger of being in such inhospitable climes. "We were on the poop deck of the boat, which was docked to the Antarctic ice. A sheet of ice fell off and hit the ship's bow. The boat rocked and one man, Benny Roth, was thrown in the water. He started screaming that he didn't know how to swim. He grabbed a piece of ice and started floating by the ship's stern. Byrd started to take off his parka to go in after Roth. We grabbed him and said, 'We don't need two of you in the water.' We held Byrd down. Suddenly, he jerked up and jumped over the ship's railing. We threw a life ring at Byrd. Byrd grabbed it with one hand and Roth with the other. We lowered a lifeboat, picked them up, and returned them to the ship. It was very cold, and their clothing was frozen stiff. We took them to the warm engine room and were able to strip off all their clothing until they were naked. We put shoes on their feet to keep the cinders from their bare feet."

As part of his duties, Colonel Vaughan participated in an experiment with winter clothing. "Admiral Byrd wanted to test furs and a man-made suit. Goodale put on one type and I put on the other. We laid our sleeping bags on the ice and went to sleep. When it's that cold, it keeps you up at night. So I'd be awake and look over at Goodale and see him asleep. I didn't know this then, but he'd be awake and look over at me, thinking I was asleep," he cackles. "Morning came and we were the first ones up. We went in the kitchen and the cook was in there. We were having coffee at the dining room table when the meteorologist came in through the tunnel. There were tunnels connecting everything so you didn't have to go outside so much. He came in and said, 'Boy, was it cold out last night! It was seventy-three below zero!' It was a good thing we didn't know how cold it was before we went outside because I didn't think I could stand that. No wonder we shook and shivered all night. Byrd asked about how our clothing withstood the weather, and I told him that it was so cold that we couldn't tell which one of us was colder.

"I was part of Byrd's flight advance team. We headed toward the pole and went about seven hundred miles from camp. We could travel about thirty or forty miles a day with the dogs, so it took about three weeks. I never actually got to the pole on the trip because you have to climb over some mountains to get on the Antarctic plateau. We helped Byrd complete his flight by using these handheld radios. We created a place for him to land in case he was in trouble. We also made it easy for Byrd to find his way. See, the dogsleds leave a trail in the snow that is easily seen from the air. All he had to do was follow our tracks. We radioed back about the weather ahead of him."

When Byrd finally took off for the South Pole, the headwinds were strong and the plane struggled to gain altitude over some threatening peaks. Byrd and the crew threw 250 pounds of supplies out of the plane to reduce its weight, and it safely cleared the mountains.[3] "About four hours later, we heard the roar of a plane over us. It was awfully low. I was thinking to myself, 'I hope he doesn't land here because it's all snow and ice.' He kept on coming until he got over us. He dropped a box about the size of a shoebox with a homemade parachute. We ran over to get it. There was a note for each one of us on the trail. The day before, he [had] sent a wire to our families at home, and each family sent us a message. Mine sounded just like my mother! She sent her love and was praying for us.

"Byrd's mission helped humanity because we gained a lot of meteorological knowledge. We learned to better forecast how clouds and wind affect the weather. And our Boy Scout, Paul Siple, later developed the wind chill factor. Back in the States, we had a ticker tape parade on Wall Street. Byrd was in the first car with his other officers. I was in the car just behind him. I also got a special medal from Congress. There is a very lovely inscription on the medal about how we were heroes to the country."

Not long after returning to America, "Byrd called me, Goodale, and Crockett to his house. He said that we did a great job and he wanted to pay us, but he was broke. He did something special for us, though. He named an unclimbed Antarctic mountain after each of us. I thanked him and vowed I would climb it one day. He told me that I probably will." In 1994 Colonel Vaughan returned to Antarctica to climb the 10,302-foot Mount Vaughan, the mountain that Admiral Byrd had named for him some sixty-five years earlier; he conquered it three days before his eighty-ninth birthday.

"The last time I saw Admiral Byrd was just before his death [in 1957]. I was traveling through Boston and I stopped at his house. I spent ten or fifteen minutes with him, and he was very happy to see me. I feel great pride in the fact that I am the last one alive from the mission." Seventy-five years later, Colonel Vaughan looks back at what made Byrd a successful leader: "He did the most important thing—he took care of his men. He thought of them as shipmates and thought first of their safety. He did anything to save lives. And if a leader does that, he will do well. We enjoyed his command and respected him. He was still just a commander [in the navy]. He didn't become admiral till after the flight over the Pole. He liked to drink, for he had a cocktail at the end of the day. But I never saw him drunk. He was a well-dressed man and he never wore rags. He was always arranged and pressed."

In his very interesting life, Colonel Vaughan also participated in the 1932 Olympics. "I was stationed up by Lake Placid, New York, and they came to us and asked if we could make a demonstration of dog racing. We harnessed our teams and put on an exhibition. We had races but it didn't count for the standings." Now that he's nearly one hundred, "I'm no longer dogsledding. I had heart trouble in the last year. I did the Iditarod thirteen times, the last one in 1992 at the age of eighty-seven."

Colonel Vaughan still has big plans for his life. "In 2005, for my centennial, I am going back to the top of Mount Vaughan again. Mark it down on your calendar—December 19. I have a specially made dogsled designed for me. The snow is deep and I will try to ride the sled all the way up. We practiced last week. My guides are all chosen, and the lead guide is the one from my 1994 expedition."

Concluding the interview, Colonel Vaughan reflects, "[Y]ou have to eat well, sleep well, and exercise. If you do those three things, you can do whatever you want. If you eat

Norman Vaughan in front of Antarctica's Mount Vaughan in December 1994
photo courtesy Gordon Wiltsie

junk food, you start to weaken, which will affect your exercise. Also, I don't drink or smoke. I'm still going strong and I remain active. With my upcoming trip to Antarctica, I'm proving that centenarians can still do great things. The motto I live by is 'Dream big and dare to fail.'"

Norman Vaughan died on December 23, 2005, just days after his centennial, and his passing made news around the world. Sadly, he was not able to raise the funds to make a return trip to Antarctica for his one hundredth birthday.

NOTES

1. Ralph K. Andrist, *Heroes of Polar Exploration* (New York: American Heritage, 1962), 121–27.

2. Derek Cullen, *Exploring the Poles* (Needham, MA: Schoolhouse, 1988), 41.

3. Andrist, *Heroes of Polar Exploration*, 132–33.

McKINLEY WOODEN
The Last Living Soldier to Serve with Harry S. Truman in Battery D during World War I

"I give [Captain Harry Truman] ninety days at the most."

In 1901 a bright young man from Missouri graduated high school but could not afford college because of his father's recent bankruptcy. Instead, young Harry Truman worked a variety of jobs, including bank clerk, railroad timekeeper, bookkeeper, and mailroom clerk. In 1906, at his father's urging, he returned home to help run the family farm. Nine years later he lost money in a zinc venture, and the following year he lost even more money on a bad oil deal. This thirty-three-year-old man, still unmarried and living with his widowed mother in 1917, might have stayed on the farm forever had it not been for World War I. Truman's military enlistment changed his life—and the course of American history. Truman's presidential legacy includes the Marshall Plan, the Fair Deal, the creation of the Central Intelligence Agency and the Department of Defense, the Japanese surrender ending World War II, the Berlin Airlift, the Truman Doctrine of defending countries threatened by Communism, and the desegregation of the armed forces. Under "Give 'Em Hell" Harry, the United States became the dominant military and economic power in the world.

Young Harry Truman had served in the Missouri National Guard from 1905 to 1911, rejoining it in May 1917. He could have used any number of reasons to excuse himself from military service: He was two years past the draft age, he was a farmer, he was the sole supporter of his mother and sister, and his eyesight was terrible.[1] But Truman wanted the serve his country. Shortly after he enlisted in the army, he was sent to Fort Sill, Oklahoma, for basic training. In March 1918 he sailed to France to attend artillery school, and the next month

An older Mr. Wooden
photograph courtesy
McKinley Wooden

he was promoted to captain of the 129th Field Artillery's Battery D, a group of feisty Irishmen from Kansas City.[2] McKinley Wooden is the last Battery D soldier alive who served under Captain Truman.

Born in 1895, McKinley Wooden was named after the soon-to-be-elected president William McKinley. "I volunteered for the army on June 11, 1917, and I was a corporal. I had tinkered with guns all my life, and I also had taken auto and tractor courses in school that prepared me. I think I own more guns than anybody," he says in his flat Missouri twang.

"I first met Harry in France on July 18, 1918, on Napoleon's old artillery range. That's the exact day Harry took over Battery D. I gotta say Battery D was a pretty rowdy bunch. We were so tough, we already had gone through three captains by the time Harry arrived. On the day he took over, he spoke to the assembled troops, 'I didn't come here to get along with all of you; you are to get along with me.' Right after that, I turned to one of my friends and said, 'I give him ninety days at the most,'" he recounts with a laugh. In private letters to his sweetheart, Bess Wallace, Truman acknowledged that he was very nervous when he first faced Battery D. A few days after first meeting his soldiers, he wrote:

> They gave me a Battery that was always in trouble and is bad. . . . It is the Irish Battery. . . . The men are as fine a bunch as we were ever gotten together but they have been lax in discipline. Can you imagine me being a hard-boiled captain of a tough Irish battery? I started things in a rough-

cookie fashion. The very first man that was up before me for a lack of discipline got everything I was capable of giving.[3]

Eventually Truman managed to get Battery D in order, and he remained with the outfit throughout the conflict. Truman's war experiences gave him the leadership skills to change his life.

Mr. Wooden remembers the first time he ever met Truman face-to-face. "He called me into his office. He promoted me right there to chief mechanic of the battery and I promised him I'd do the best I could. Harry seemed happy with my answer.

"The Battle of the Argonne was the greatest artillery fight the world has ever seen. Just after the battle, a general sent a report to Truman that Battery D's guns were in better condition than any other battery. Truman wrote back to General Peter Traub, giving full credit to McKinley Wooden, an enlisted man. Truman also noted that I was his chief mechanic. I'm proud to say that the original letter is now in the Harry Truman Presidential Library." Truman wrote to Traub, "The Commanding General's letter of October 29th commending this organization on the excellent condition of its Ordnance Materiel is the result of the untiring efforts of Chief Mechanic McKinley Wooden and the enlisted personnel of the Battery to whom all credit belongs."

After the war Truman returned home, married his sweetheart, Bess Wallace, and established a clothing store that soon went bankrupt. He was elected a judge of Jackson County in 1922. In 1934 he won a Senate seat from Missouri and became a strong supporter of President Franklin Roosevelt's New Deal. "After the war ended, I didn't see Truman for about fifteen or so years," Mr. Wooden remembers, "until he ran for the Senate from Missouri in 1934. Times were tough for me then. I went to a Truman rally and he parked two cars away from me. When he first saw me, he ran over to greet me, and

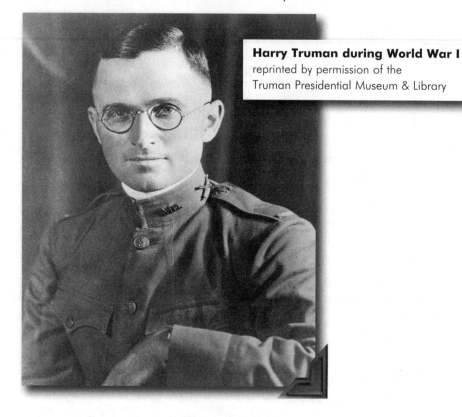

Harry Truman during World War I
reprinted by permission of the
Truman Presidential Museum & Library

he brought with him his wife and daughter. His campaign was taken so lightly that the Democrats didn't even send over a man to introduce him at the rally! There were probably twenty of us in the crowd—really, not a lot of people. I distributed campaign literature for him around the county. Actually, I was the best customer at this gas station near me, and I asked the owner if I could hang a Truman sign there. He said to me, 'Mac, he don't got a chance.' But since I helped him, Harry always put me in the front row at anything."

During World War II Senator Truman saved the taxpayers millions of dollars as the result of his investigation of defense contractors. In 1944 a dying Franklin Roosevelt asked Truman to be his vice president, and he accepted. Truman was in that position for only a few months when Roosevelt died on April

12, 1945, but he was not prepared for the office; for example, as vice president, Truman knew nothing about the atomic bomb program. In 1948 many political pundits believed that Truman would lose his reelection bid to New York governor Thomas Dewey. The president campaigned hard across the country, and he was stunningly reelected in the country's greatest political comeback in history. "I didn't see him while he was president, but I did get some letters from him. When I wrote him letters, I just addressed him as 'Captain Harry S. Truman.'" Years later Truman gave Mr. Wooden a personal guided tour of his presidential library. "I showed my credentials to the guard there, and before I knew it, out came Harry. He spent an hour showing me everything. And then we went back into his private office. He reached into his desk and pulled out a postcard. He said, 'This is something special very few people have.' He inscribed it to me, then signed it. We were friends for fifty-four years, after all."

Truman had a reputation for salty language, a contention Mr. Wooden disputes. "I heard him swear only once. Battery D had two reunions a year. At the fiftieth reunion, I brought a woman along who had never met Harry before. We went to Truman's house and she was in the greeting line in front of me. I just told her, 'State your name when you meet him.' So, as she is doing this, Truman spots me in line. He says loudly to me, 'You don't have a damn bit more hair than you ever had.' That was the only time I ever heard him swear!" he laughs as he remembers this.

Over the years, Battery D had sixty-seven reunion dinners. "When there were only two of us left, we had about fifty-five hundred dollars in the treasury. We didn't know what to do with it, really, so we just gave it to the Truman Library. We figured that would be the most fitting.

"Just a few months ago," he says, "it was the eightieth anniversary of the end of World War I, and a French diplomat gave me a French Legion of Honor for my service. I'm the last Battery D soldier, but it don't make one bit of difference to me."

McKinley Wooden passed away in his sleep on December 7, 1998, at age 103.

NOTES

1. David McCullough, *Truman* (New York: Simon and Schuster, 1992), 102.

2. William A. DeGregorio, *The Complete Book of U.S. Presidents* (New York: Wing Books, 1993), 511.

3. Harry S. Truman, *Dear Bess: The Letters from Harry to Bess Truman, 1910–1959* (New York: Norton, 1983), 266.

Part 2
Survivors

ROSE FREEDMAN
The Final Survivor of the 1911
Triangle Shirtwaist Factory Fire
"I consider it a miracle that I survived the fire."

On March 25, 1911, 146 people, nearly all immigrant women, perished in a fiery fifteen minutes. The Triangle Shirtwaist Factory fire may be the most famous industrial fire in American history, and Rose Freedman is the last miraculous escapee.

The Triangle Shirtwaist Factory, which manufactured lightweight blouses, occupied the top three floors of the ten-story Asch Building, located at the corner of Washington Place and Greene Street in New York City's Greenwich Village. The eighth story, the lowest floor of the factory, was the cutting room where the fabric was trimmed; it was here that the fire began. The ninth floor, where most of the women who died worked, contained the sewing machines, and the top floor had the executive offices. The company had instituted a policy of locking the doors the moment the

The young Mrs. Freedman
photo courtesy Arlene March

The devastated interior of the Triangle Shirtwaist Factory
photo courtesy the UNITE Archives, Kheel Center, Cornell University

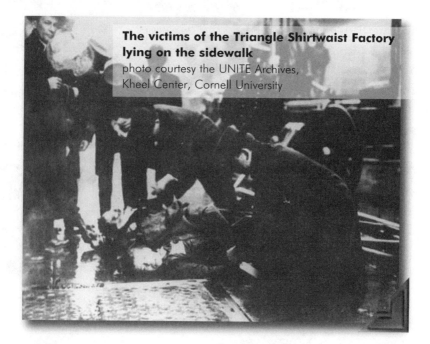

The victims of the Triangle Shirtwaist Factory lying on the sidewalk
photo courtesy the UNITE Archives, Kheel Center, Cornell University

shift started, so that employees who were late for work would lose their daily pay. The doors were bolted so that people could neither enter nor exit the workplace.

The eighth-floor machines sliced through more than one hundred pieces of cloth at once, leaving a fair amount of extra material, which was stored in wooden bins underneath the machines.[1] By the end of a working day, the bins contained thousands of pounds of unused, flammable cloth. New York City Fire Marshal William L. Beers guessed that the fire "started from the careless use of a match from one of the cutters. They were about to leave to go home, and in those factories they [were] anxious to get a smoke just as quick as they [were] through work."[2]

When the fire erupted, the employees could not escape because of the locked doors. Inside the workplace, there were a meager twenty-seven buckets of water to fight the ravenous inferno.[3] The one escape ladder, located at the rear of the building, was inadequate for the number of employees, and it broke when too many people climbed on it at once. The elevator made several desperate trips to the eighth floor to whisk people down, until it could run no longer.

Most of the women died either because they inhaled smoke, slid down the elevator shaft (twenty-five bodies were found at the bottom of the elevator well), or jumped out of the windows to the street, often with their clothes ablaze. Firefighters arrived quickly and tried to catch the women who were jumping, but their nets soon broke, and many more women plunged to their deaths. Yet Mrs. Freedman defeated the odds, walking away from the factory unharmed.

She explains how she started working at the factory. "My sister criticized me, saying that my chores at home were not the same as having 'work' to do. So I decided to get a job. So after the 1909 strike at the Triangle Shirtwaist Factory [over safety conditions], I applied for a job there. They needed

A photograph of the building that once housed the Triangle Shirtwaist Factory
photo by Stuart Lutz

**A wreath laid at the annual
memorial ceremony at the factory**
photo by Stuart Lutz

workers. The factory ordered a machine for me that attached buttons to the shirtwaists. The machine was called the Union Special. They showed me how to use it." For her labors, she earned four dollars a week.

Mrs. Freedman went to work as usual on Saturday, March 25, 1911, two days before her eighteenth birthday; she was stationed on the ninth floor. At approximately 4:45 p.m., as the employees were ending their day and collecting their weekly pay envelopes, a fire started in one of the storage bins on the eighth floor. "We smelled the smoke before we saw the fire," she remembers. "Panic occurred because the doors were locked. Everyone started screaming and running toward the fire escape. I wasn't near the windows. I was further back and stood still in shock."

The flames jumped from one bin to another, spreading quickly. The employees on the eighth floor had the best chance at escape, because the elevator stopped on their floor. The workers on the ninth floor, including Mrs. Freedman, were in a much worse situation, since the elevators made no trips to the higher stories.

Yet Mrs. Freedman was one of the few people from the ninth floor to escape because she had a remarkably clear thought in this desperate time. She asked herself, "What are the executives on the tenth floor doing?" Unlike everyone else, who made the seemingly logical choice of going down to escape, Mrs. Freedman thought about ascending the stairs. "I pulled my skirt over my head and dashed up the interior stairs to the tenth floor." She found the offices empty.

"When I saw the executives were gone, I looked to see how they escaped. I saw stairs on the other side of a broken glass door. I went through the door and up the stairs to the roof. There was one policeman on the roof [of the Asch Building] and another on the roof of the adjacent building [owned by New York University]. One hoisted me up to the other roof. Then I had to walk down by myself ten flights."

At that point, the emotion of the tragedy overcame her. "I stopped going down and cried sitting on the stairs." When she reached the ground floor, she saw her father, who, hearing of the fire, came looking for her. "He fainted when he saw me. He thought I had burned to death."

The owners of the factory escaped the same way that Mrs. Freedman did. When one owner recognized Mrs. Freedman on the street, he tried to bribe her "to testify that I had left through the unlocked doors." Mrs. Freedman, still spunky after all these years, told him, "Nothing doing"—and refused the offer.

The factory's owners, Max Blanck and Isaac Harris, were charged with manslaughter in 1911. More than 150 witnesses were called to the stand, and one of the few survivors testified that she tried to open the door and found it locked.[4] Sadly, the men were found not guilty; although the jury acknowledged the doors were locked, the prosecution was unable to prove that Blanck and Harris knew of these unsafe conditions. In 1914 a judge ordered the owners to pay seventy-five dollars to each of the families of twenty-three victims who sued; this paltry amount equaled about five months' pay.

A new awareness of workplace safety conditions grew out of the flames. New York City created a Bureau of Fire Prevention to enforce stricter safety regulations. Since most of the victims were women, the tragedy ignited a renewed call for universal suffrage. It also strengthened the International Ladies' Garment Workers' Union, whose one hundred thousand members marched in protest of unsafe working conditions. Although Mrs. Freedman was not actively involved in the labor movement immediately after the fire, she comments, "I have always been a Democrat and supported the labor movement."

When she ponders a 1991 fire in a Hamlet, North Carolina, chicken-processing plant that killed twenty-five workers because some of the interior doors were locked, she says, "It brings tears to my eyes to know those conditions still exist. It makes me feel that 146 lives were lost for nothing."

She summarizes her experience this way: "I only recently became the last survivor, and naturally, being 106 years old, I feel blessed. I consider it a miracle that I survived the fire."

On February 15, 2001, Rose Freedman died at age 107, just a month before the ninetieth anniversary of the disaster.

NOTES

1. Testimony of Edward F. Croker, New York City Fire Chief, quoted in "No Way Out: Two New York City Firemen Testify about

the 1911 Triangle Shirtwaist Fire," History Matters, http://history matters.gmu.edu/d/57/ (accessed November 17, 2009).

2. Testimony of William L. Beers, New York City Fire Marshal, quoted in "No Way Out: Two New York City Firemen Testify about the 1911 Triangle Shirtwaist Fire," History Matters, http://history matters.gmu.edu/d/57/ (accessed July 27, 2009).

3. "Leap for Life, Leap of Death," The Triangle Shirtwaist Fire of 1911, http://www.csun.edu/~ghy7463/mw2.html (accessed July 3, 2009).

4. Doug Linder, "The Triangle Shirtwaist Factory Fire Trial," 2000, http://www.law.umkc.edu/faculty/projects/ftrials/triangle/triangleaccount.html (accessed July 3, 2009).

JOHN FULTON
One of the Last-Surviving Ground Crew
from the *Hindenburg* Explosion
*"As soon as the second control line hit the ground,
I felt a change. I felt the sun on the back of my neck."*

The *Hindenburg* was the largest airship ever to fly. Measuring more than eight hundred feet long, it would dwarf today's blimps, airliners, and even the massive rockets that launched astronauts to the moon. The size of the *Hindenburg*, however, is not its claim to fame. In 1937 the airship exploded over New Jersey, killing three dozen people and leaving the ground littered with metal tresses. The disaster also ended the glamorous era of speedy zeppelin travel.

In the 1930s, airship travel, offering the ultimate in transatlantic luxury, was the only commercial aviation across the sea. The *Hindenburg* was specifically built to fly over the Atlantic Ocean, and it could zip from Germany to New York at eighty miles an hour, making the voyage in under three days, twice as fast as an oceanliner.[1] Tickets cost four hundred dollars, and the passengers had their own rooms, complete with beds and sinks.[2] The cuisine, which was first rate, was served on fine china.

During the 1930s both the *Graf Zeppelin* and the *Hindenburg* flew more than 1 million accident-free miles.[3] In 1936 the *Hindenburg* made seven trips from Germany to Rio de Janeiro, Brazil, and ten flights to New York.[4] The New York–bound zeppelins landed at Lakehurst, New Jersey, fifty miles south of the city; the massive airship hangar there covered eight acres.[5] These giant airships had one fatal flaw, however: They were filled with 7 million cubic feet of highly explosive hydrogen gas.[6] At the time, the United States had a monopoly on the much safer and inert helium, which could have been used to lift the airships, but the country refused to

**Mr. Fulton
in the navy**
photo courtesy
Susan Fulton Murphy

sell the gas to Nazi Germany. Additionally, the lighter hydrogen was a better lifting agent than helium.[7]

The ship departed on its fateful voyage from Germany's Rhein-Main Airport at 8:00 p.m. on May 3, 1937, with thirty-six passengers and sixty-one crew aboard. There were usually forty staff members, but the company added twenty trainees who were scheduled to fly aboard the sister ship *Graf Zeppelin II*, then under construction.[8] The voyage was routine, and the airship was originally scheduled to arrive at Lakehurst Naval Air Station at 6:00 a.m. on May 6. Strong headwinds over the Atlantic slowed the crossing, and the landing was postponed until 7:00 that evening. The afternoon weather did not cooperate, however; there was a cold front approaching that brought thunderstorms. The *Hindenburg* cruised south, toward Atlantic City, until the storms passed.[9]

**Mr. Fulton at his
ninetieth birthday party**
photo courtesy
Susan Fulton Murphy

Mr. Fulton in the navy
photo courtesy
Susan Fulton Murphy

John Fulton is one of the last men alive who worked as a member of the ground crew under the *Hindenburg* when it exploded. Born in 1912 in South Carolina, he still has a trace of a Dixie drawl. He explains how he came to be at Lakehurst: "I was already in the navy. I left the destroyer *Conyingham* and was sent to Lakehurst for a five-month concentrated course in weather. Part of our work was helping with the navy blimps that landed at the station. The navy had built landing masts there for its four dirigibles. We would hold the control lines." When the weather was bad, Mr. Fulton recalls, "we'd be dragged over the ground."

Mr. Fulton was excited about the *Hindenburg*'s first Lakehurst docking of 1937. "It had already landed at Lakehurst a number of times in 1936. Every available man at the station was needed for the massive craft, in addition to one hundred civilians brought in specifically for the docking. My class would take positions underneath the dirigible's control car as it neared the ground and catch the short lines attached to the sides of the control car. Other crews would handle the longer, heavier mooring lines that were to be dropped from ports in the bottom of the ship near the bow and stern. Our instructions were [that] once the mooring lines were secured, we would walk the ship over to the mooring mast that secured the nose of the *Hindenburg*. The mast could rotate so that if winds were blowing from a certain direction, the airship would shift with the breeze so as not to damage it.

"We could see the *Hindenburg* approaching the field from the north through the broken clouds that were drifting away eastward." He points to an imaginary spot in the air, as if he has just sighted the airship. "It passed over the field at a height of fifteen hundred feet and made a slow turn to return to a position from which it could make its approach into the wind. I think every man on the field was experiencing some degree of excitement as we moved to take up our positions. We all had our eyes on its great bow as it came toward us, now at a much lower altitude. The ship was two hundred feet up at the time of the explosion.

"As the bow passed over our heads, we could see men standing on the *Hindenburg* just inside the open port in the bottom. Then the first mooring line was dropped. It came tumbling down in a coil about the size of a beer keg. When it hit the ground, the handlers grabbed it. That line was carried off to one side so it could stop the forward drift of the ship. Now, the control car was almost directly over our heads. We had to jog and be ready for the shorter control lines that we could see dangling from the sides of the car. As soon as the second control line hit the ground, I felt a change. I felt the sun on the back of my neck. I was trotting along and I glanced back over my left shoulder and saw a giant flame coming from just ahead of the tail fin." The *Hindenburg*'s passengers, who were hundreds of feet from the initial fire, were unaware at first of what was occurring. They were crowded by the windows, scanning the ground to see their friends and family awaiting their arrival.[10]

"I was terrified at the moment of the explosion," he continues. "I began running for my life, but I couldn't take my eyes off of the ship. As each hydrogen gas bag burst, it blew the ship's skin off, and I could see the metal skeleton showing through the flames. I had run as far as a cameraman who was cranking the handle of a camera mounted on a tripod. I stopped running, thinking I had gone far enough. I could see the tail settle quickly to the ground and the nose was up about forty-five degrees. There, I saw two men jump out of the stern post, which was about forty feet off the ground. The fire had already gone past that area, and I could see their clothes were on fire. As soon as they hit the ground, the ship landed on them and killed them.

"Now the front part of the ship was coming down. I started going back toward the ship to see if I could help at all. Then I saw a crewman jump out of the forward port. It was probably thirty or thirty-five feet down, and he fell over. He tried to get up and fell again and a burned-out section of the bow fell over him. Later, I timed the fall of the ship from the newsreels, and it was only thirty-six seconds." Herb Morrison famously broadcast the docking on live radio. The reporter cried into his microphone, "It's burning, bursting into flames, and it's falling on the mooring mast and all the folks. This is terrible. This is one of the worst catastrophes in the world. . . . Oh, the humanity, and all the passengers."[11]

As soon as it was safe, Mr. Fulton returned to the smoldering wreckage. "I saw several crewmen trapped in the wires and girders, and they looked like they were beyond our help. We lifted three of them out and laid them on the ground. There was nothing more that we could do. I started walking back toward the stern and I was surprised to see people walking out of the passenger section. It was scarcely damaged."

Mr. Fulton comments, "No one could believe that there were any survivors after seeing such destruction." Yet of the ninety-seven people aboard the airship, sixty-two survived.[12] Five people later died at the hospital, and one witness on the ground was also killed. An elderly passenger walked out the normal exit, and a fourteen-year-old cabin boy who was almost unconscious on the ground was awakened when a large water ballast bag burst over him, dousing him.[13]

Mr. Fulton points to his wall; hanging there is a copy of Nazi leader Hermann Göring's letter praising the American crew for helping the *Hindenburg* passengers. Göring wrote, "The unreserved help of the American airmen in coming to the rescue of their German comrades is beautiful proof of the spirit which links the airmen of all nations."[14]

The spectacular explosion attracted curious spectators. "People saw the fire for miles and came over to the base. They were turned away by the Marine sentries. So they climbed over the fences and came in by the hundreds. The station ordered all personnel to guard the wreckage so it could not be taken off as souvenirs. We formed a cordon around the frame, but we were only partially successful at keeping the crowds away from it. People came at us from such numbers in all directions that we could not keep them all away. We stayed on duty for five hours, until midnight, when some Coast Guardsmen from Cape May came to relieve us. I also know that pieces of fabric and framework drifted for miles. People found pieces in their backyards."

At the end of the day Mr. Fulton returned to his barracks, where the communications officer notified him that he had a telegram from his girlfriend. She had heard about the disaster and was concerned about his safety, knowing that he was part of the ground crew. He went to the office to reply that he was safe, then he went to bed. "I have never been before or since as exhausted as I was when I went to bed that night. I was able to go to sleep quickly that night, but I had trouble sleeping after that. I had visions of men on fire."

In the days following the disaster, he says, "I wanted to get it out of my mind, but the investigators made me watch the movies. I had to sit through them because there was no plausible cause for the explosion. After they showed us the movie, we were interviewed individually." Mr. Fulton adds that "all of the people aboard were VIPs, and the cameramen were scattered behind a roped-off area. It was photographed by eight professional photographers and newsreel companies, and they were all taking pictures. But none of them had cameras on the tail section," where the blaze began.

Seven decades after the explosion, there is still no known cause for the fire. Some speculate that it was started by escaped hydrogen gas, other experts believe that it was an electrical discharge, and still others believe it was an act of anti-Nazi sabotage. Still, there is little doubt that the disaster ended the glorious era of zeppelin travel. Two years after the explosion, the first passenger plane flew across the Atlantic.[15]

Mr. Fulton theorizes why the disaster has remained in the American consciousness: "Those newsreels were shown all over the country. It was the most photographed disaster of any magnitude." Today, he says, he is able to watch the films of the *Hindenburg* fire and "it no longer gives me chills down my spine."

John Fulton died on June 6, 2003, at age ninety.

NOTES

Selected parts of the interview came from Mr. Fulton's historical essay "The Hindenburg *Fire."*

1. Shelley Tanaka, *The Disaster of the* Hindenburg (Toronto: Madison Press Books, 1993), 13.

2. Patrick O'Brien, *The* Hindenburg (New York: Henry Holt and Company, 2000).

3. Tanaka, *The Disaster of the* Hindenburg, 13.

4. Len Deighton and Arnold Schwartzman, *Airshipwreck* (New York: Holt, Rinehart and Winston, 1978), 64.

5. Ibid., 4.

6. Tanaka, *The Disaster of the* Hindenburg, 8.

7. Deighton and Schwartzman, *Airshipwreck*, 64.

8. Ibid., 64–66.

9. Ibid., 66.

10. Ibid.

11. "*Hindenburg* Disaster Footage with Audio," http://www.youtube.com/watch?v=xiAT9xvTVKI (accessed May 5, 2009).

12. O'Brien, *The* Hindenburg.

13. Deighton and Schwartzman, *Airshipwreck*, 68.

14. John Clayton, "An Unforgettable Disaster," *Manchester* [NH] *Union Leader*, May 6, 1998, A4.

15. Tanaka, *The Disaster of the* Hindenburg, 60.

FRANK HOLMGREN
The Final Survivor of the USS *Juneau*

"I'm going to die, I'm going to die,
and I'm going down with the ship."

In January 1943, Navy Lieutenant Commander Truman Jones solemnly knocked on the door of the Sullivan family home in Waterloo, Iowa. He told the parents, Alleta and Tom, that a navy cruiser, the USS *Juneau*, was torpedoed by a Japanese submarine. The sinking left all five of their sons—George, Joseph, Albert, Madison, and Francis—officially "missing in action," and they were later confirmed as dead.[1] All that remained of the once large family was a sister, Albert's wife, and Albert's infant son, Jimmie. Although there were over seven hundred sailors aboard the *Juneau*, only ten men were rescued from the water. Frank Holmgren is the last survivor of the tragic cruise memorialized in the movie *The Fighting Sullivans*.

Born in 1922, Frank Holmgren volunteered for the navy as a teenager, just after the attack on Pearl Harbor. "That was my country the Japs were attacking. I enlisted with five friends and I was assigned to the USS *Juneau* with my friend Charlie Hayes. The *Juneau* was an antiaircraft cruiser and I was a deck man. My battle station was at the fantail passing arms to the gun turret."

The ship cruised through the Panama Canal and arrived in the Pacific Ocean. "On the twelfth of November in 1942," Mr. Holmgren recounts in his genial voice, "we were at Guadalcanal, protecting the Marines on the island unloading ammo. We got word that there was a big Jap fleet coming to bombard Guadalcanal and we were sent to intercept them. At 1:00 in the morning of Friday the thirteenth, we ran smack into the middle of them. It was quite a battle, and the *Juneau* was hit by a torpedo in the Number One Fire Room, but it didn't blow up the ship. It knocked out the power, including the guns. So we managed to get out of the battle. The next morning, we were supposed to rendezvous with the remainder of the fleet that survived the battle. At about 11:00 in the morning, we were hit by a sub-launched torpedo. It was intended for the nearby *San Francisco* but missed and hit us instead." He lays one hand flat to represent the *San Francisco* and uses the other hand to show how the torpedo passed under the intended target. "It hit us in the front part of the *Juneau*, and she blew up right in front of my face. It must have hit the ammo section, and the ship went down in a minute or less. It blew up half the ship, I imagine."

Mr. Holmgren tells a desperate tale of survival. "I survived because my battle station was in the tail. When I hit the deck after the explosion, my hand just happened to hit a life jacket, and you better believe I grabbed it! I wrapped it around me. And I held onto the twenty-millimeter gun mount for dear life. Everything was sliding by as the ship turned, and I could hear the roar of the ocean coming. I thought to myself 'I'm going to die, I'm going to die, and I'm going down with the ship.' Well, the next thing I know, I came shooting up out of the water." Mr. Holmgren thrusts upwards with his hands. "If I had died then, I never would have known it 'cause it happened so fast."

Mr. Holmgren found himself in the ocean with other sailors. "There were three rafts in the water, and some large nets that floated because of the cork attached to them. I managed to get on a raft. Now, I estimate there were 75 survivors on the rafts and the nets, but some people guess 100 or even 150. But we weren't interested in counting. Most of the men died of their wounds, and they were dying left and right all around me. As they died, we just pushed them off into the water. And all these men died because we were not picked up right away. The other navy ships left us and didn't come back to check us out."

Mr. Holmgren recounts the quality that enabled him to survive under the tropical sun. "I didn't go out of my head.

Mr. Holmgren as a young sailor
photo courtesy Frank Holmgren

Mr. Holmgren in his USS *Juneau* hat
photo by Stuart Lutz

Some of my shipmates went crazy. They wanted to dive below to the ship and get supplies. But there were sharks all around there and if you jumped off, you were dead. For example, my friend Charlie Hayes survived the explosion. I don't think he was injured in the blast, and he wanted to go down below to the ship. He didn't survive." The naturally jovial man recalls this with some bitterness.

"There was obviously no food. The next day, a plane flew overhead and dropped a rubber raft. One officer and two men hopped in it and made land with it. They were three of the ten *Juneau* survivors. Actually, I could see land some of the time we were in the water. But there was nothing to do but sit there, waiting for a rescue. Finally, someone asked if there were any volunteers who wanted to try to make land in one of the rafts. I volunteered and left Charlie behind. We tried to make land, but never got there because we were rescued first. We were in the water for six days and some hours when we were picked up on November 19. There were only ten survivors of the 725 or 728 people on the ship. Imagine that."

Mr. Holmgren took his first flight that day. "A seaplane just landed on the water to rescue us. I was so damned scared as we zipped along because I thought we were submerging. But I gathered up the courage to look out the window. And while I was scared, it was a lot better than where I had been. My first question to the pilot was if he found the cork nets. He said no, but they had found the other two rafts."

He reiterates, "I just don't understand why the navy didn't come back to rescue us earlier. If they had, a lot more would have been saved. But later on, I learned that Captain [Gilbert] Hoover of the USS *Helena* was the man in charge of the remaining ships because the higher-ranking admirals were killed in the battle. Hoover did not believe that anyone could survive such an explosion and told the other ships to leave due to the threat of the submarines. As a matter of fact, the *Juneau* blast was so big that other ships located quite a distance away were hit by its shrapnel. Soon after, Admiral [William "Bull"] Halsey relieved Hoover of his command for not rescuing us. Hoover claimed he didn't want to break radio silence, but Halsey said that for a rescue, Hoover should have broken it. Hoover didn't do anything for us, and we shouldn't have been out there six days."

Mr. Holmgren notes the greatest irony of his survival: "I could not—and still cannot—swim, so the life jacket saved me," he chuckles. "I cheated on the swimming test during enlistment. I hopped in the pool, got wet, and signed the form attesting that I could swim. A stupid move on my part. During the war, the navy wasn't as finicky about the test. They needed men."

Mr. Holmgren opens Dan Kurzman's book *Left to Die*, a detailed account of the sinking of the *Juneau*. He points to a picture of pilot Robert Gill standing before a plane. "I don't remember seeing any other planes flying overhead, but Gill claimed to have flown over the wreckage and reported not seeing any survivors. I just don't understand," he repeats.

Despite sailing on the *Juneau* for six months, Mr. Holmgren did not know the Sullivan brothers. "I knew they were on the ship, and I'd seen George once or twice. Francis was in my division, but I don't remember talking to him. They were already on the ship when I first came aboard. George is the only one that got off the ship when it sank, but he was so beat up that he didn't last long. I didn't see him when he died, but he was just pushed off when he passed away. There were a couple of guys who claim that *three* of the Sullivans got off, and that's a bunch of hooey. They are wrong, and I think their heads were all screwy then from being stranded. It was just George."

He recalls a less well-known family that also suffered losses from the sinking. "There were four Rogers brothers aboard the *Juneau*. On our last trip out, they decided to break up, and two of them traded places with other people. So only two went down with the ship. I knew them a lot better than the Sullivans. I was also a captain's orderly, as was one of the Rogers, so I knew him pretty well. But here's a sad story. Shortly after the *Juneau*, I was walking down the street in New Zealand and I met up with the two surviving Rogers. They asked about their brothers, and I told them that they didn't make it. They kind of knew, but I just confirmed it for them."

The American public did not learn of the *Juneau* sinking or the Sullivan tragedy for several weeks afterward, but Mr. Holmgren was not sworn to secrecy. "We didn't want the Japs to know which ships they sank," he explains. "My mother and father got my missing-in-action report, and I was taken to a hospital in Fiji. All I got were water sores that turned raw." He pulls up his left pant leg to point them out. "But soon my parents got a letter from me and they knew I was alive. The news of the sinking was released in January or February 1943."

Mr. Holmgren returned to fight on the USS *Oakland*, a similar ship to the *Juneau*. "The captain asked me how I felt about it, and I told him the truth: I was scared to go out again on the same type of ship. I insisted that I be on the top rather than down belowdecks. I'd rather see the action than be helpless below. So I was a gunstriker and ended up a gunner's mate third class. I actually saw more action on that ship than the *Juneau*. I fought at Gilbert Island, the Marshall Islands, and I got off of the ship in June of 1944, after the Saipan battle. I got shipped back to the States and spent six months at Earle [Naval Weapons Station]."

As a tribute to the Sullivan Brothers, the navy dedicated the USS *The Sullivans* during World War II, and the Sullivan parents christened it. "After the dedication of the original USS *The Sullivans*, my friend Lester Zook and I tried to get on that ship, but I couldn't, since I was on the *Oakland*." The destroyer was decommissioned in 1965. Then, during the 1990s, the navy commissioned another USS *The Sullivans*. "I was at the second dedication in Staten Island in, I believe,

1995." He points to a framed picture of himself standing before the new warship. "I was invited with Lester Zook, since we were the only two *Juneau* survivors still alive then. Actually, Lester just died. He was hit by a car in Nevada on Friday, November 13. The anniversary of the sinking. Went through all of that on the ship, only to be killed by a car."

Mr. Holmgren did not tell his family that he had been aboard the doomed *Juneau* until 1987, when he was invited to Juneau, Alaska, to dedicate a monument. "I did what I had to do in the war. There have been a few articles about the *Juneau*, and people started writing to me from all over the country. They tell me that their uncle or father was aboard, and they ask if I knew them. I was in Waterloo, Iowa, for the fiftieth anniversary of the sinking, and they had a lovely parade. I met [Albert's son] Jimmie and his daughter, Kelly."

Mr. Holmgren has a room filled with *Juneau* memorabilia, including a decorative plate with an image of the ship and a large black-and-white portrait of the *Juneau*. He also displays a number of military plaques and local newspaper articles about his service.

The old sailor reflects on his service and concludes with the message, "I think it's good that kids today have to understand that war is no playground out there. It's easy to lose an arm or a shoulder or a leg. It doesn't hurt the kids to have a couple of years in the service to show them what life is really like, and it's not all about partying and drinking."

The film *The Fighting Sullivans*, starring Anne Baxter, was released during the war. "I knew it was out before I got back home, and I was surprised. I only saw it once when it came out, and it was very moving. And pretty sad. I guess the last time I saw it was last year. But the ending, where all the brothers die together on the ship, is all wrong!"

Frank Holmgren died on May 11, 2009, at age eighty-six.

NOTE

1. Dan Kurzman, *Left to Die* (New York: Pocket Books, 1994), 242–44.

CHARLES LINDBERG
The Last Iwo Jima Flag Raiser
*"We tied the flag to the pole, carried it to the highest spot
we could find, and we raised it. . . . We were very proud of it."*

There is a barren volcanic rock sitting alone in the Pacific
Ocean, 650 miles south-southeast of Japan. Five miles long
and eight square miles, the pear-shaped island has a cratered
peak at its southern end. For thirty-six days in 1945, brave
Marines bitterly fought devoted Japanese defenders over this
territory, known as Iwo Jima. It was the bloodiest fight in
Marine Corps history.

Few Americans had ever heard of Iwo Jima before its
bloodbath. The island was strategically important to America
for two reasons. First, its airfields were much closer to Japan,
which would make bombing runs far shorter and safer for
American forces. Second, Iwo Jima lay in the flight path from
the American-held Marianas Islands to Japan, and Iwo Jima
gave Japanese fighter planes a haven from which to harass the
American bombers that flew out of the Marianas.[1]

Admiral Chester Nimitz created a strategy called "island
hopping," in which American forces captured strategic islands
closer and closer to Japan. Planning for the assault on Iwo
Jima lasted for months. Knowing that the island was rocky, the
Marines trained by scaling rocks.[2] The troops packed enough
supplies—including ammunition, food, and medical supplies—to last the entire city of Atlanta for one month.[3] Once
the Marines departed from Hawaii, many of them would not
touch land again until they stormed Iwo Jima's beaches.[4]

The Japanese were similarly preparing the island for an all-
out war. They built defensive tunnels, planted mines, constructed fortified foxholes, and placed guns in strategic positions. And the Japanese soldiers swore to defend the island to
the death.

Photographer Joe Rosenthal, who was on Iwo Jima with the Marines, took what would become the most famous photograph from World War II, showing five Marines and one navy corpsman planting the Stars and Stripes atop Mount Suribachi, the island's highest point. Few people realize that Rosenthal's picture was the second flag raising atop the dormant volcano. The original flag ceremony occurred four hours earlier, when six other Marines hoisted the banner there.

Corporal Charles Lindberg, born on June 26, 1920, in Minnesota, is the last-surviving Marine from the original flag raising atop Mount Suribachi. He speaks in a fast voice in flat midwestern tones. "I enlisted in the Marines on January 8, 1942, one month after Pearl Harbor. I joined because I had no job then. As soon as the war was declared, the factories closed. So I decided I was going to join the Marine Corps."

Prior to Iwo Jima, Corporal Lindberg saw action at the bloody Pacific battles of Guadalcanal and Bougainville. "I was with Carlson's Raiders. They were special troops, and I volunteered for them right out of boot camp. We went to Midway with them, Bougainville and Guadalcanal. Guadalcanal and Bougainville were just jungles. We spent thirty-two days behind the enemy lines in Guadalcanal. Our job was to harass troops and supply lines. We did whatever damage we could. We took a toll of over four hundred Japanese and only lost seventeen men. We thought that was a very good record. The Raiders broke up after Bougainville, and they sent us back to the States with the paratroopers. They put us in the Fifth Marine Division, since they wanted seasoned men in there. So back out we went again and we didn't like that."

Before the Iwo Jima invasion fleet arrived, American naval and air forces strafed the tiny island for seventy-two days to weaken the Japanese.[5] The invasion fleet consisted of eight battleships, sixteen aircraft carriers, fifteen cruisers, and seventy-seven destroyers. For two days before the landing, these

Corporal Lindberg in 1944, the year before Iwo Jima
photo courtesy
Violette M. Lindberg

mighty warships blasted the island from point-blank range.[6] But all this firepower did little to penetrate the island's well-protected subterranean defenses.[7]

Corporal Lindberg remembers being on the amphibious craft that carried the Marines to the island. "Before landing on Iwo Jima, I was tense, for there were shells hitting the water out there, they were throwing mortars every place. But it didn't scare me. That was all part of my 'take it as it comes' philosophy," he chuckles.

At 9:00 on the morning of February 19, 1945, amphibious tractors moved fifty yards inland to create a defensive perimeter; they often bogged down in the soft volcanic ash. Shortly thereafter, the Marines landed on the island's southern

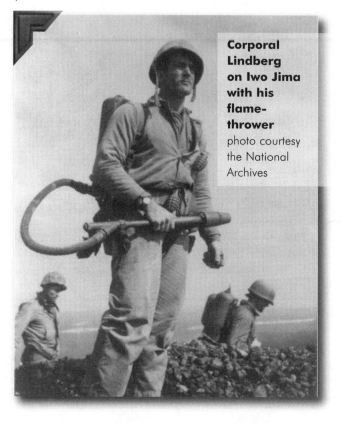

Corporal Lindberg on Iwo Jima with his flame-thrower
photo courtesy the National Archives

beaches. For the first hour, the troops found little opposition.[8] The goal of the Japanese commander was to let the troops land on the beach. "I found out later that the Japanese strategy was to put us on the beach, then annihilate us. I landed at 9:30 in the morning on Green Beach, but we weren't the first wave. The Japanese resistance was very heavy on the sands. They were walking these mortars up and down the beach. Casualties were very high. We finally got off that beach after an hour and we got across the island. We marched to the other side of the island that cut Suribachi off from the rest of the island. [Suribachi was connected to the remainder of the island by a narrow neck.] We did that in the first day, and I think we arrived toward the evening. I can't remember exactly what time it was."

Conventional military wisdom says to seize the high ground, and the 556-foot-high Suribachi, located on the south side of the island and just to the left of the landing beaches, was the first target. "The 28th Regiment was ordered to take Suribachi. The hardest part of taking it was getting to it. It took us from the nineteenth to the evening of the twenty-second just to get to the base of the mountain, and it was only about a block and a half."

Corporal Lindberg operated a flamethrower on February 23, the day of the successful Suribachi ascent. "I went through a lot of tanks of fuel that day. We carried five gallons, and every time we ran out, I went back to get more. It weighed seventy-two pounds. I just heard from a friend of mine who was there. He bet me that I couldn't carry that seventy-two pounds anymore. And I told him that I probably couldn't carry a six-pound rifle at this point!

Corporal Lindberg at the first Iwo Jima flag raising; he is standing above the shoulder of the man holding the rifle
photo courtesy the National Archives

"Sergeant [Harold] Schrier carried the flag up. It was brought over from Honolulu by Lieutenant George Wells in a briefcase. Once up there on the crater, we found a pipe about twenty feet long, for the Japanese must have had a water system up there. We tied the flag to a pole, carried it to the highest spot we could find, and we raised it [at 10:31 a.m.]. That's when the noise started in. The troops down below started to cheer and the ships' whistles went off. Oh, were they noisy!"

Six Marines raised the flag the first time: Corporal Lindberg, Harold Schrier, Louis Charlo, Henry O. Hansen, Ernest Thomas, and James R. Michels.[9] Photographer Lou Lowery captured that historic flag raising. His best image shows several Marines gathered around the makeshift flagpole while the proud banner is rigid in the wind. In the foreground, Jim Michels holds a rifle, and just behind him Corporal Lindberg stands observing the scene. "That day was quite a proud moment," the corporal recalls. "We took their eyes away from them up there. We found telescopes up there in one of the caves that they used for observation."

But at their moment of triumph, the Japanese surprised them. "There was no resistance until we put the flag up. Not too far from us was this cave. The Japanese came out with gunfire and grenades, and James Robeson used his BAR [Browning Automatic Rifle] to chase them back in. We went over there and [found that] the cave had two entrances. One was further down the hill and had caved in, and there was one up above. I put a shot of flame down through there and the guys on the other end were waiting for the enemy to come out, but no one came out. I said, 'That's funny.' So we sealed it, and two days later we opened it again. We found seventy-two dead Japanese in there. We resealed the cave after that because we didn't know what other tunnels led in there."

A week later, Corporal Lindberg's time on Iwo Jima ended. "On March 1 I was shot through the forearm; it went through the bone and shattered it. That put me out of action. I was taken out to one of the hospital ships just off Iwo Jima that had been converted from other ships. They sent me back to Saipan, then to Pearl Harbor, then to San Francisco. I ended up in Charleston, South Carolina, where I guarded the naval brig. The best duty I had in the Marine Corps!" For his service on Iwo Jima, Corporal Lindberg was awarded the Purple Heart and a Silver Star. His citation states:

> Repeatedly exposing himself to hostile grenades and machine-gun fire in order that he might reach and neutralize enemy pill-boxes at the base of Mount Suribachi, Corporal Lindberg courageously approached within ten or fifteen yards of the emplacements before discharging his weapon, thereby assuring the annihilation of the enemy and the successful completion of this platoon's mission. While engaged in an attack on hostile cave positions on March 1, he fearlessly exposed himself to accurate enemy fire and was subsequently wounded and evacuated.

When Corporal Lindberg left Iwo Jima, he knew that Lou Lowery had taken photographs of the flag raising, but he had not seen them. "I first saw Lowery's photograph when I was recuperating in Honolulu. It was in *Yank* magazine. When I returned back from the service, people didn't believe me about what I had done. So Lowery sent me a bunch of photographs. He was a good friend of mine. He took a picture of me alone that I didn't know about. I went to his funeral when he was buried in Quantico."

Four hours after Lindberg's original Suribachi flag planting, the more famous one occurred. "Corporal [Chandler] Johnson was worried about our flag that was up there on Suribachi," he explains. "He didn't want someone to steal it for a souvenir. After all, it was the first American flag to fly over Japanese home territory in World War II, and he wanted

Corporal Lindberg in a more recent photograph
photo courtesy Violette M. Lindberg

to preserve it. So he ordered another flag up. Today, the original Iwo Jima flag that I raised is in the Marine Corps Museum at the Navy Yard in Washington, DC. And that's where Rosenthal got in. He went up with the Marines and took that famous picture. He got the film off the island in a big hurry and sent it off to Guam for development. It then went back to the States and no one ever knew there was another flag raising four hours ahead of the famous one."

Corporal Lindberg was not aware of Joe Rosenthal's photograph for a few weeks. "I saw it when I got to Saipan. I didn't know anything about it being taken. When that photograph took place, I was with my other flamethrower buddy down below loading our tanks." The old Marine remembers his reaction the first time he saw Rosenthal's image. "It made me feel perturbed. We took the mountain, did the fighting, and then they come and changed our flag and put the big flag up. All the recognition went to the second flag."

The government memorialized all Marines by using Rosenthal's photograph as the basis for a massive monument. Sculptor Felix de Weldon created the world's largest bronze statue, rising 110 feet and weighing more than one hundred tons.[10] Corporal Lindberg went to the dedication ceremony in Arlington, Virginia, in 1954. "They put us original flag raisers way at the end of the field, and there we sat. Not a bit of recognition."

Corporal Lindberg saw Rosenthal at Lowery's funeral. He states, "I went over to introduce myself. Rosenthal joked, 'Oh, you were on the real flag raising, weren't you?' and I almost fell over!" After the Battle of Iwo Jima became famous, many people claimed to be at the flag raisings. Corporal Lindberg quickly dismisses the allegations of all the phony flag raisers. "Over the years, I've heard many claims of people who said they were flag raisers. It's still happening today. There was a Marine Corps general who once remarked to me that if everyone who claimed they raised the flag really was on Iwo Jima, the island would have caved in!"

Corporal Lindberg returned to Iwo Jima once, for the fiftieth anniversary of the battle. "The big ceremonies there took up most of our time. You can go there after sunrise and you have to be off before sunset. Also, there were some of the Japanese troops there, and some of their children. I was invited to go for the sixtieth anniversary too, but I have a leg that bothers me and I didn't want to take the chance with it. To mark the sixtieth anniversary of Iwo Jima, I am doing something here in Minnesota with the Metro Marines."

Like any fine warrior, Corporal Lindberg respects the Japanese soldiers. "From Guadalcanal to Bougainville, the soldiers weren't that good. The closer you got to Japan, the better the troops. On Iwo Jima they put up a terrific fight. It was just so hard to take. They had tunnels throughout that entire island. You'd knock out one bunker, then go up ahead and pretty soon, they are coming back out again from the back way. That was really something. If we hadn't taken Japan, we would be living an awful life today. Getting rid of the Japanese government means more to me than anything."

Iwo Jima was the bloodiest battle in Marine Corps history. Of the six original flag raisers in Lowery's photograph, Hansen, Charlo, and Thomas were killed on the island.[11] Lindberg's Third Platoon, the first one that first scaled Suribachi, was originally composed of forty Marines; only four of them left the island without being killed or wounded.[12] From the six flag raisers in Rosenthal's image, three died on Iwo Jima: Harlon Block, Franklin Sousley, and Mike Strank.[13] And William Genaust, who took a color movie of the second flag raising, also died there.[14]

Of the 75,000 Americans who landed on Iwo Jima, one-third of them were casualties, including 6,821 deaths—an average of almost 190 deaths a day over the thirty-six-day fight.[15] During World War II, 353 Americans were given the country's highest military decoration, the Medal of Honor. Twenty-seven Medals of Honor were given for actions on Iwo Jima, and thirteen of them were awarded posthumously (many of them were awarded to men who smothered grenades with their bodies to save their comrades).[16] It is estimated there were 22,000 defenders on the island, and only 1,083 were captured at the battle's conclusion; more than 20,000 Japanese soldiers died on Iwo Jima.[17]

Unlike the troops who stormed the D-Day beaches, the victorious Marines on Iwo Jima were not greeted by adoring Frenchwomen thanking them for their grueling and deadly task. For the survivors of the battle, their reward came six months later, when the Japanese surrendered aboard the USS *Missouri*, thus ending World War II. "It makes me feel good to be the last flag raiser," Corporal Lindberg concludes.

Charles Lindberg died on June 24, 2007, at age eighty-six.

NOTES

1. Bill D. Ross, *Iwo Jima: Legacy of Valor* (New York: Vanguard, 1985), 14.

2. Ibid., 34.

3. Ibid., 26.

4. Ibid., 36.

5. Ibid., 37.

6. Ibid., 48.

7. Ibid., 65.

8. Ibid., 61, 67.

9. Richard F. Newcomb, *Iwo Jima* (New York: Holt, Rinehart and Winston, 1965), 165.

10. James Bradley with Ron Powers, *Flags of Our Fathers* (New York: Bantam Books, 2000), 326.

11. Newcomb, *Iwo Jima*, 224.

12. Ross, *Legacy of Valor*, 103.

13. Bradley and Powers, *Flags of Our Fathers*, 231, 232, 245.

14. Ibid., 235.

15. Newcomb, *Iwo Jima*, xiii.

16. Ibid.

17. Ibid., 296.

CORA LUCHETTI
One of the Final People to Remember
the 1906 San Francisco Earthquake

*"[My father] was killed when a pole fell on him.
The earthquake shook it loose from the ground."*

In 1900 San Francisco was the nation's ninth-largest city, with a population of nearly 350,000.[1] At 5:13 a.m. on April 18, 1906, a massive earthquake shook the city; it originated not far off the Pacific Coast.[2] San Francisco's buildings and structures swayed with the waves, killing many people when they collapsed. Hospitals were wrecked.[3] Roads and tracks were destroyed, making it difficult for emergency crews to travel to where they were needed. The telephone system was down, as was the electric grid. Mayor Eugene E. Schmitz warned the populace: "You may therefore expect the city to remain in darkness for an indefinite time."[4] The water and gas mains were similarly torn up. Fires quickly broke out around the city, fanned by both the gas and San Francisco's perpetual breeze; many victims died in wooden structures that burned. It was nearly impossible for the firemen to fight the blaze, since the water mains were destroyed.[5] The fires raged for four days. The flames consumed almost five square miles, burned twenty-eight thousand buildings, and destroyed entire neighborhoods.[6] The newly completed city hall was almost completely ruined.[7] The earthquake cost a half billion dollars in damages and left more than a quarter million people homeless. The official death total was 478, but this estimate appears to be extremely low based on the size of the fire and the number of collapsed buildings.

Cora Luchetti, born Cora Pinelli in San Francisco on June 11, 1900, is one of the last survivors of the 1906 San Francisco earthquake. "My father owned a fruit store on Fillmore Street near Pine. He sold liquor in barrels in the back. My mother stayed at home. I had a brother, Babe Pinelli, who eventually played professional baseball for the Cincinnati Reds. We lived close to a baseball field and he was always playing at the park. We lived near Fillmore and Bush. There is a little narrow street called Wilmot right off of Webster, and we had a house there. It was across the street from a big grocery store," she recounts in a halting voice.

"Right after the earthquake hit, everybody was out in the street. It only took a minute. Everyone left their house scared, like I was. All were out in the street talking. We had a rail at the top of our steps, and the earthquake broke it up. There was broken glass everywhere. In a way, it was exciting.

"My father went to his store that morning. It wasn't very far away. My mother saw him coming home with his wagon and she was happy, since she had hoped nothing happened to him. As he was walking across the street, he was killed when a pole fell on him. The earthquake shook it loose from the

Crowds milling in the San Francisco streets after the earthquake
photo courtesy the Library of Congress

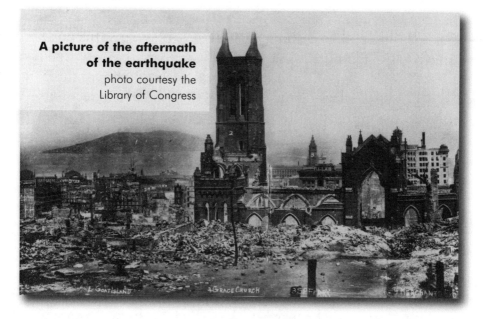

A picture of the aftermath of the earthquake
photo courtesy the Library of Congress

ground," she recites calmly. "We all tried to soothe my mother. She was sitting on the doorstep. People were all so good to her. The Irish had these big dinners. They would put all the leftovers in a bag so we had stuff to eat. Mother then worked for some cleaners washing clothes. She made twenty-five cents an hour."

Mrs. Luchetti discusses her family's evacuation from their home. "The authorities ordered us out of the house for safety reasons. The police were very firm and told us to sleep in the park. The army came and threw us all blankets. We laid on the sloping lawn with blankets covering us. And we watched the city burn. That's my best memory of the earthquake. We walked down to Presidio, where they had set up hundreds of tents. We stayed in the tents about a week or so. Everyone helped everyone else. We didn't get any government assistance. It was a couple of weeks before we were allowed back in the house. The fire missed our home and nothing else happened to it. The fire couldn't cross the wide street near us. We were damn glad to get back. We found the plumbing still worked."

Shortly after the quake, Brigadier General Frederick Funston, stationed in San Francisco, put the city under military control.[8] He ordered some buildings dynamited in order to create a firebreak.[9] Secretary of War William Howard Taft ordered tents and rations be sent to San Francisco to house and feed the survivors. The USS *Chicago* rescued thousands of refugees by sea. The large immigrant population, who had never experienced an earthquake before, had trouble understanding what occurred. Aftershocks worried an already frightened population.[10] To solve the ongoing looting problem, Mayor Schmitz proclaimed on April 18 that "[t]he Federal Troops, the Members of the Regular Police Force and all Special Police Officers have been authorized by me to KILL any and all persons found engaged in looting."[11]

Mrs. Luchetti gathers every year on April 18 with the dwindling number of survivors at San Francisco's Lotta's Fountain to memorialize the disaster. "I've been going for so many years that I can't remember how long it has been," she confesses. "We get there really early and a lot of people come. There were about eight or ten survivors and I was the oldest one of them. This year, they built a nice stage for us. I enjoyed meeting the mayor there. He shook hands with everyone."

A panoramic view of the devastated, flattened San Francisco taken from the airship *Lawrence Captive*
Geo. R. Lawrence Co., 1906. Accessed through Wikimedia. Public domain

Yet even nine decades after the "Big One," Mrs. Luchetti admits, "I get nervous every time the house shakes. I don't have strong memories of the 1989 earthquake. I've been through it and I think, 'I hope it's not another one.' But so far, so good. I just hope there's never another one like the 1906 earthquake."

Cora Luchetti died on December 1, 2000, not long after her one hundredth birthday.

NOTES

1. "Population of the 20 Largest U.S. Cities, 1900–2005," Infoplease, http://www.infoplease.com/ipa/A0922422.html (accessed July 3, 2009).

2. Gordon Thomas and Max Morgan Witts, *The San Francisco Earthquake* (New York: Stein and Day, 1971), 66.

3. Ibid., 98.

4. "Proclamation by the Mayor," April 18, 1906, available at the Virtual Museum of the City of San Francisco, http://www.sf museum.org/1906.2/killproc.html (accessed July 3, 2009).

5. Thomas and Witts, *The San Francisco Earthquake*, 86.

6. Ibid.

7. Doris Muscantine, *Old San Francisco* (New York: G. P. Putnam's Sons, 1975), 430.

8. Thomas and Witts, *The San Francisco Earthquake*, 88.

9. "Timeline of the San Francisco Earthquake, April 18–23, 1906," Virtual Museum of the City of San Francisco, http://www .sfmuseum.org/hist10/06timeline.html (accessed July 3, 2009).

10. Ibid.

11. "Proclamation by the Mayor."

BARBARA ANDERSON McDERMOTT
The Last Passenger of the Sunken *Lusitania*
"All I escaped with was my clothes I was wearing."

When the magnificent *Lusitania* steamship was launched early in the twentieth century, it was one of the largest and fastest vessels of its time. On a springtime Atlantic Ocean crossing, a German submarine captain spied the *Lusitania* off the coast of Ireland. The German sub fired a torpedo at the liner, and it sank beneath the waves in an astonishing eighteen minutes (in comparison, it took the *Titanic* more than two hours to sink). The tragedy killed 1,198 people, including 128 Americans. Of the 1,959 people on the *Lusitania*, only 761 survived.[1] Of the 129 children aboard, 94 perished. Several very wealthy and prominent men died, including a Vanderbilt, a famous theatrical producer, and the founder of the Roycroft Press. Problems releasing the lifeboats meant that many passengers died unnecessarily. In the longer run, the *Lusitania* sinking coalesced anti-German sentiment in the still-neutral United States, paving the way for the nation's entry into World War I.

Although Barbara Anderson McDermott was three when she survived the sinking of the *Lusitania* on May 7, 1915, she remembers the disaster. She has looked for other survivors recently, but concludes, "I can't find any. I think I am the last one."

The *Lusitania* left New York on May 1, 1915, running on partial power to save scarce fuel. It was unarmed but carried five thousand ammunition cartridges; they were entered in the manifest and stored in the lower decks about fifty yards from where the torpedo struck.[2] Mrs. McDermott, born in 1912 in Connecticut, was the child of British parents. She explains how she boarded the ship. "When I was very young, dear, my mother was pregnant and wanted to see her mother, who was still in England. So we took the *Lusitania*." In 1915 the Imperial German Embassy in Washington warned in the press that

The medal memorializing the sinking of the *Lusitania*
photo by Stuart Lutz

Mrs. McDermott holding the *Lusitania* medal
photo by Stuart Lutz

"[t]ravelers intending to embark on the Atlantic voyage are reminded that a state of war exists between Germany and her allies and Great Britain . . . vessels flying the flag of Great Britain . . . are liable to destruction."[3] She doubts her father was aware of this ominous alert, explaining, "Oh, heavens—he never would have let us go if he knew of that."

When the *Lusitania*'s captain, William Turner, approached the war zone off the southern Irish coast on May 7, he was warned of enemy submarine activity in the area and he wanted to be ready for any emergency. He ordered that all lifeboats be prepared for use; the forty-eight boats were more than enough for all passengers and crew. Turner also closed all portholes, dou-

Young Mrs. McDermott's passport
photo by Stuart Lutz

**The *Lusitania* in 1911 steaming by the Old Head of Kinsale
off the Irish coast, near where it was torpedoed four years later**
photo courtesy Peabody Essex Museum

**The *Lusitania*
under construction**
photo courtesy
National Archives of Scotland

bled the number of lookouts, and directed the engine room to keep steam at full pressure in case the boat needed to accelerate.[4]

At 8:00 a.m., Turner reduced the ship's speed from twenty-one to eighteen knots so that it would arrive in Liverpool when the tide was most favorable. When a fog set in later that morning, Turner further slowed to fifteen knots, and when it dissipated, he added three knots. At 12:40 p.m., Turner received an ominous submarine warning and made a hard port turn toward land.[5]

Just forty minutes later, Captain Walther Schweiger of the German submarine *U-20* was floating on the ocean's surface, recharging his ship's batteries. Two days prior, Schweiger's ship stopped the English schooner *Earl of Lathom*, ordered the crew off, and sank it using grenades; U-boats often sank ships with grenades or guns instead of what were then the unreliable torpedoes.[6] On May 7 Schweiger spied a four-funnel steamship in the distance and presumed it was either the *Lusitania* or her sister ship, the *Mauritania*. The German navy believed that both ships were armed merchant vessels and thus legitimate war targets. The *U-20* dived and set an intercept course with the liner. At first Schweiger lost hope of catching the faster liner. He was elated when the *Lusitania*, unaware that the U-boat was shadowing it, changed course and headed directly toward the *U-20*. Schweiger moved his vessel and waited for the *Lusitania* to move into the ideal position. At 2:10 p.m. the *U-20* fired one torpedo.[7]

At 2:00 the *Lusitania* passengers were finishing lunch, unaware that an enemy submarine was only 650 yards away. Ten minutes later, when the ship was ten to fifteen miles from Ireland's Old Head of Kinsale, the second officer reported an incoming torpedo; the torpedo smashed into the starboard side between the third and fourth funnels, immediately sending the vessel toward the cold waves.[8]

Mrs. McDermott recalls that fateful afternoon clearly. "It

Barbara Anderson about age six
photo courtesy Elizabeth DeLucia

was about 2:00 and we were having lunch, dear. We went second class. We were in the upper part of the ship, and by the railing, fortunately, when the torpedo hit. From that spot where we had lunch, we could walk right onto the deck." She pauses. "It was the only reason we were saved, and anyone below[decks] was lost. All I know is that if it had been a different time of day, like night or when I was in the cabin, I would have had no chance. It is just so sad. The boat tilted immediately since the water was rushing in so fast. My mother and I got separated, and she jumped into the water first. She was probably trying to protect her unborn child. And I figure that she must have been close to the water before she jumped. It turns out that she missed the lifeboat but was soon picked up by one."

Many of the *Lusitania*'s lifeboats proved useless. As the ship quickly listed to the starboard side, the lifeboats on the port side rested against the hull, making them impossible to

**Barbara Anderson in the hands of
the *Lusitania* purser who rescued her**
photo courtesy Cliff Barry

lower, and the ones on the starboard side swung out so far from the foundering boat as to make them unreachable.[9] The bow went under so quickly in the shallow sea that it hit the bottom before the *Lusitania* sank completely, leaving the stern exposed.[10] "I can still see myself standing at the railing alone," Mrs. McDermott continues. "Since we were having lunch, I had a spoon in my hand when the ship went down. I still had it when we got to England. I remember my grandmother showing it to people. Gosh, I wish I knew what happened to it. So I saw the ship sinking before me. I was grabbed by a crew member [Assistant Purser W. Harkless] and put into a lifeboat. Lucky for me, it turned out to be the same one as my mother was in." For a short time, this lifeboat was unaccounted for on the open seas, and her father was notified that his wife, daughter, and unborn child were lost. She reads a 1967 Bridgeport, Connecticut, newspaper reprint of the 1915 story about her father collapsing when he erroneously learned that his family was dead.

Mrs. McDermott spreads the blame for the tragedy. "I know the Germans had a lot to do with it. The captain of the U-boat turned around to sink his prize. He didn't listen to all the rules of war. But it also would have been better for us to land in Ireland than to lose the boat. But the *Lusitania* captain had something to do with it too. He got bad warning messages and swerved the wrong way." She uses her hands to illustrate the turning ship.

Mrs. McDermott explains what happened to her in England. "I was stuck in England with my mother and baby brother until the war was over. My mother died just before I was five. It was supposedly TB, but all of my English relatives said her death was caused by the *Lusitania* disaster. I remember the last time I saw her. She was in bed, and when she saw me she gave me a great big hug and kiss. And I did not learn this until many years later, but a baby was born, named

Frank. He lived to be six months old. He is buried in England with my mother. And as hard as I have tried to find her grave, I just can't. My father died in 1974. He remarried, but a step-mother is not like a real mother. Lately I've been thinking about my mother more and more. How I had to grow up without her."

Mrs. McDermott returned to the United States in December 1919. "The funny thing is, I came back on the *Mau-ritania*"—the *Lusitania*'s sister ship. She opens a printed booklet with the *Mauritania* passenger list and points out "Ms. Barbara Anderson" as a traveler. She then unfolds a large blue paper. "This is my passport," she declares. A picture of seven-year-old Barbara Anderson is glued down, and her name is signed twice in a childish script. "Let me tell you, the woman I was sent back with was the nastiest person. And I was pretty seasick too. I really wanted to stay in England, since my school and friends were there. But I hadn't seen my father in four years. When I returned to England in 1974, I met up with many of my English childhood friends there."

She opens a small box, revealing a heavy, drab medal about one and a half inches across. One side has a disturbing image of a skeleton standing behind a Cunard ticket window, dis-tributing tickets to passengers. The case has the following Eng-lish passage printed on it:

> This indicates the true feeling the War Lords endeavour to stimulate, and is proof positive that such crimes are not merely regarded favorably, but are given every encourage-ment in the land of Kultur.

"It's a German medal they printed to commemorate the sinking of the *Lusitania*," she reveals. "See, the Germans minted this *Lusitania* medal after the sinking. The English were so angry with it that they copied it and sold them for propaganda. The money raised went to helping the soldiers wounded in the war. My English cousin Roddy heard about these medals not too long ago when he read an article. So he wrote to the paper, explained that I was a survivor, and asked if anyone could spare one for me. Four people offered medals, and this one came from the family of a man who recently died. The family had no idea why he had it, so they sent it."

Dr. Robert Ballard, the man who located the wreckage of the *Titanic*, has also explored the *Lusitania* wreck. "I'm not opposed to his exploration. All my stuff's down there! All I escaped with was my clothes I was wearing. But I'm not opposed to the dives to learn the truth or to get mementos." Yet she argues, "I don't understand the big deal over the whole *Titanic* thing anyway. The *Lusitania* indirectly caused us to go to war. And unlike the *Titanic*, which was caused because the captain was going too fast in icy waters, the *Lusitania* was sunk because someone gave the order to fire a torpedo," she says incredulously.

Barbara Anderson McDermott died on April 12, 2008, at age ninety-five.

NOTES

1. Charles E. Lauriat Jr., *The* Lusitania's *Last Voyage* (New York: Houghton Mifflin, 1915), 121, 130.

2. Ibid., 132, 136.

3. Vincent Kan, "RMS Lusitania: *The Fateful Voyage*," August 22, 2009, http://www.firstworldwar.com/ features/lusitania .htm (accessed November 17, 2009).

4. Lauriat, *The* Lusitania's *Last Voyage*, 136–37.

5. Diana Preston, Lusitania: *An Epic Tragedy* (New York: Walker, 2002), 184.

6. Colin Simpson, *The* Lusitania (New York: Little, Brown, 1972), 134.

7. Preston, *The* Lusitania, 190–91.
8. Lauriat, *The* Lusitania's *Last Voyage*, 138–39.
9. Ibid., 146.
10. Simpson, *The* Lusitania, 163.

ROBIE MORTIN
The Final Witness to the Infamous
1923 Rosewood Race Riots in Florida

*"I saw so much, awful things. People being shot and hung.
The mob was getting a real joy out of the killing,
and they were drinking."*

The 1923 race riot in Rosewood, on Florida's Gulf Coast, was not the worst incident of racial violence in American history. In 1919 a white mob in Chicago killed many African Americans during a five-day dispute over a segregated beach.[1] A 1921 race riot in Tulsa, Oklahoma, is estimated to have killed hundreds, if not thousands, of people; it wiped out blocks of an affluent area known as the "Black Wall Street."[2] Yet Rosewood is significant in American history because, according to one prominent historian of the South, it was the last of the major race riots in the South.[3] The decade leading up to the Rosewood riot had been one of escalating racial tensions. In 1915 D. W. Griffith's influential film *Birth of a Nation* revived a dormant Ku Klux Klan. In 1920 the Klan began a publicity campaign, and by the mid-1920s it had 4 to 5 million members.[4] At the same time, many African Americans from the South were moving north in search of better wages and living conditions.[5] Their migration drained the South of cheap labor.

Robie Mortin may be the final survivor of the Rosewood Riot; she was born in the town on August 29, 1915. "My mother died when I was eighteen months old," she recounts in the gentle but quick Southern-accented voice of her youth. "I was raised by my maternal grandmother, Polly Cornelius Carter, and I lived with my Uncle Sam Carter and Aunt Katie. My grandparents came from South Carolina after the Civil War—about 1868—and traveled there in a covered wagon. My grandfather was probably a former slave. He raised saplings and owned eighty acres. He split the rails to build the cabin himself. My grandmother was part Cherokee, but you could hardly tell her from the real thing. She could live in the woods as well as she could in a home. She was a tough old lady. My father lived in Rosewood and at the time worked at the mills in Sumner, which was one town over. I know my Aunt Sarah Carrier was born into slavery.

"Rosewood was a beautiful town. It was once owned by mill people, but they cut down all the timber in the area. When my family arrived in Rosewood, it was a second-time-around town. They homesteaded the land and built a house. Every so often, the state would come by to make sure the lots were kept up. If you kept them up, you could always get more property. One family had over one hundred acres. Rosewood had approximately three hundred homes and it did pretty well for itself. And these were no shacks or shanties. You are going to build something nice for yourself, so all the houses were well kept. It was all white paint and picket fences. I was a grown woman before I saw colored paint. It's a shame they burned those beautiful houses down. There was no trouble around that area."

She makes an interesting argument about slavery: "It gave some vocational skills to the people who came from Africa with no knowledge. By the time the people got to Rosewood, everyone had skills to give to the town. The first settlers learned during slavery how to plant sugar cane and how to grind it. We never worried about water since everyone knew how to dig a well. The Goins, one of the town's prominent families, had a thriving turpentine business there. Uncle Sam Carter took care of the businesses in Rosewood."

The Rosewood Riot started on January 1, 1923, when a white woman from nearby Sumner falsely claimed that an African American man from Rosewood attacked her. Mrs. Mortin has firsthand knowledge of the disturbance's spark. "The white people who lived three miles from us in Sumner had shanties. And a lot of people didn't know we were back there in Rosewood. The whole riot was based on envy, since there were black people living way better than the whites. The riot started with a lie. My aunts Sarah and Philomena did housework for Fannie Taylor in Sumner. Now Fannie was a smart girl. She was married, but had a couple of men on the side," Mrs. Mortin says with a wink.

"One man worked for the railroad and he got off the train whenever he came through town. He got off the train on New Year's Day in 1923. This man and Fannie got into an argument. He called her a 'swamptramp.' Aunt Sarah was there, and she heard Fannie yelling at him about other girls he had. Finally, he said, 'So what?' and she went after him. Meanwhile, Fannie's baby started crying and Philomena wanted to go in and help the baby, but Sarah said no. Soon the man came out the door and went back to the train to get to Gainesville. He had beat [Fannie] up bad, head to toe. Philomena ran in there to help her, but Fannie kicked her out. But soon Fannie gave Philomena the baby to look after. Anyway, Fannie's husband would soon come home. She came out of the house hollering like it just happened! She said a nigger came in her house, robbed her, and beat her up. And she looked the part. She never said rape. People in the neighborhood came out. Sarah and Philomena heard her give this wild testimony to the sheriff. The sheriff went to get tracking hounds and tracked the suspect to Rosewood. Let me tell you, the criminal didn't get anywhere close to Rosewood; he went back on the train. She caused all of this," she recounts, shifting in her chair frequently.

Meanwhile, "New Year's Day was a big holiday for us. There was cooking and food and parties. We'd go to church to thank the Lord for giving us another year, then go to dinner afterward." The Sumner mob first came to the home of Sam Carter, believing he was the prime suspect. "During the massacre [Mrs. Mortin pronounces it so it rhymes with 'tea'],

Mrs. Mortin at the time of the interview
photo by Stuart Lutz

Uncle Sam—poor thing—was lynched on New Year's Day during the evening part. He was in our driveway fixing to come up to the house. My grandmother saw them hang him up, but they didn't know she was up there in the house. The mob took him down and dragged him off to the woods and killed him back there. My grandmother lost the last son she had," she says slowly. The mob killed him in the woods with a shotgun blast, then used his body for target practice.[6]

"The lynching of Uncle Sammy was on Monday night. My father went to work on Tuesday at the Sumner mill. He had no idea what happened, but the rumor was that they had hung his brother-in-law. When he found out about it, he had to stay on the job, of course. But then he run right to the house, all three miles. He came in hot and sweaty. He told my sister Sebie to put on heavy clothes and get ready to go. It was so cockeyed cold. He was afraid to take us to the Rosewood train station, so we went to the Sumner one. He put us on a train to Gainesville. He never told us why, and my sister was puzzled he didn't get on. We just did what we was told. We went to Chiefland and didn't arrive until the next morning. Sebie saw the newssheet—we didn't have a real newspaper then—and that's when we found out Uncle Sam was lynched. We didn't worry too much about my father since he was a man and could take care of himself.

"My grandmother grabbed her daughter-in-law Katie, who was Sam's wife and my aunt. She brought Katie up to the house a mile away, threw their stuff in a bag, and put on heavy clothes. They walked at night, though the moon was bright and it was sleeting. They went into a town known as Otter Creek—not near where the mob was—and waited there for a little while. The mailman came by in his mail wagon, rescued my grand-mother, and put her on a train. We never saw Katie no more. My grandmother landed in Chiefland with us. Somehow she got a wagon and horse, and no one knows how she did it. We went back to Rosewood in the wagon. We had to sneak and crawl up there, and we took the back way to our house.

"I saw so much, awful things. People being shot and hung. The mob was getting a real joy out of the killing, and they were drinking. It seems so backward to me, even when I was a child. What was wrong with these people? There was stealing and raiding in that town. Whites were loading up carts with our furniture. Everyone in Rosewood had music in their house, an organ, piano, fiddle, guitar. One white man went into my house and he couldn't figure out how we had a piano. He was very upset about it. I still wish I had my grandmother's bedroom set," she states wistfully. "It wasn't no playground mahogany, but real mahogany."

On January 4, the mob returned and went to the home of Sarah Carrier. The house was defended by her son, Sylvester, who armed himself with guns.[7] "Aunt Sarah told the mob in front of the house that Sylvester was there the entire time [that Fannie Taylor claimed to be attacked] and they all knew it was a white man who attacked her. So they blowed her down, killed dead." In the ensuing gun battle, both Sarah and Sylvester Carrier were killed, but their actions allowed many family members to escape. The mob then torched the Carrier home.[8]

"The Ku Klux Klan misread the intentions of what was going on because they came late. If the mob wanted to burn our houses, they would have done that first. But when the KKK came in, the riot was well on its way. The Klan was the one who burned the houses. That whole town was burned flat to the ground—there was nothing left. The Sumner people wanted our nice houses for themselves. The governor knew what was happening, but he wouldn't send anyone to help the people of Rosewood. After it was all done, the state dug a mass grave and threw everything in there." A month after the riot, a grand jury investigated the entire incident but found insufficient evidence to prosecute anyone.[9] It was also impossible to ascertain an exact number of Rosewood residents who died.[10]

In the aftermath of the riot, Mrs. Mortin says, "My grandmother, my two sisters, and I headed east. We came up on a little place called Osceola. It was a mill town, and we stayed there about a month. My sister got married and her husband had an old Ford. We put fishing poles on the top and when we were hungry, we'd stop to catch something to eat. I learned that God gives us ways to make use of what we know. We had nothing except a car full of junk. We then moved to a town, Argelly. Some guys came by and asked my brother-in-law if he wanted a job, and he got work on the railroad. We stayed in a closed grocery store for about a year, then moved to Riviera Beach. The railroad furnished a house if you worked for them."

Her grandmother, who had money in a Gainesville bank, traveled west to retrieve it. "She wrote to a cousin who lived near there. The cousin came out east by bus and took my grandmother to get her money. While there, she sold a piece of property she owned in Gainesville. She came back loaded! We got to Riviera Beach in 1925 and built a house in 1926. It was beautiful, but not strong, and we didn't know about hurricanes then. The 1926 storm picked it up and took it away." By luck, "I found my father out here on the East Coast a couple of years later. He was working for a mill." She pauses. "He never talked about how he escaped." Once Mrs. Mortin had her own family, "I didn't tell my children one word about Rosewood. I figured they didn't need to know the bad things that happened to my life. My children were growing up beautiful."

About seventy years after the riot, she says, "One of my cousins, Arnett Doctor, was going to bring up the idea of Rosewood reparations to Governor [Lawton] Childs." Mrs. Mortin was in for a number of surprises. "One morning after the Rosewood story broke, my house was surrounded by newspaper reporters. When my children found out about my living in Rosewood, their mouths were wide open. They were dumbfounded." She continues, "Doctor had to hunt up the survivors, and there weren't many. Most were grandchildren and great-grandchildren. They were lucky to find me. When I heard about it, I was working for the Pulitzer family in Palm Beach. I didn't want to be bothered with it anymore; it was already stuck in my heart. I'm a 'let sleeping dogs lie' kind of person. I didn't go looking for reparations, and I stayed out until they drew me into it. If I had my say-so, I never would have said a word about it. One of my friends called to convince me to get involved. He said, 'You are the one who lost family in this.' Also, Levy County took title to our property. I said I wasn't going to Tallahassee, so I sent my lawyer in my place. This was his first case right out of law school! When he returned, he gave me this deposition and I had five days to fill it out. I couldn't get my mind right to do it. Finally my granddaughter, who works for the court, made me answer the questions. I didn't know I was up for reparations and I refused to watch about it on television. I was called down to the state offices in Hollywood to identify the other survivors. Only nine people came up that I knew were in Rosewood on the day of the massacre. The reparations relieved me. I could let it go a little bit, but it didn't take it away completely."

Mrs. Mortin says she is not bitter as a result of the riot. "Hate destroyed Rosewood, so why should I allow it to destroy me? I'm a born-again Christian. Rosewood was the worst thing ever to happen to me, and once you get past the massacre, life has been beautiful to me. I married a good man for forty-three years and had five children." She recalls her one year of high school: "Our books were the trash from the other schools. We had to learn to make do when not too much is given to you. But I have education and books all around me. I love to read and I have three library cards. I want to know. I didn't get a chance to be educated, but I passed it on to my children. We have nurses and schoolteachers in the family. One of my granddaughters wants to be senator. We have come a long way, baby."

In 2003 she returned to Rosewood for the first time since the riot. "I went when Governor Jeb Bush dedicated an historical marker, describing what happened. That put Rosewood on the map. Before that, it had been removed from the map. Which was silly since my mama and grandfather are buried there. I was the only survivor that could be there, and there were thousands of people lined up that day. I just couldn't hold back the tears. I will never forget my home."

If the story of Rosewood is familiar, it may be from the 1997 film *Rosewood*, directed by John Singleton and starring Jon Voight and Ving Rhames. The movie was based on the

1923 riot. Mrs. Mortin strongly dislikes the movie, however. "It is not an enjoyable picture since there is so much badness. None of the movie was accurate. The burning and killing was right, but the rest of it was junk. I think Singleton made it because he is racist. There were no jukes in the town, but there were three churches. It was a clean town. That movie killed the survivor Wilson Hall. Three months after seeing the picture and the way Singleton portrayed Hall's mother, Wilson died."

As Mrs. Mortin lived through segregated America, she was uplifted by the election of President Barack Obama. "I could never have imagined an African American being elected president. I am very, very proud of him. He is young and smart and he campaigned on helping the people. I do wish he was my son. I would enjoy living in the White House."

In her opinion, "race relations have improved, but there is still a lot of envy out there. We still have a ways to go, but I believe it can be done. But I taught my children to live a respectable life and not to hurt anyone else." She pauses, then concludes: "I feel God has truly blessed me. I have to think of the good things that happened to me in Rosewood."

NOTES

1. "The Chicago Race Riot of 1919," Jazz Age Chicago, http://chicago.urban-history.org/scrapbks/raceriot/raceriot.htm (accessed July 3, 2009).

2. Scott Ellsworth, "The Tulsa Race Riot," Tulsa Reparations Coalition, http://www.tulsareparations.org/TulsaRiot.htm (accessed July 3, 2009).

3. George Tindall, *Emergence of the New South, 1913–1945* (Baton Rouge: Louisiana State University Press, 1967), 155.

4. Wayne Andrews, ed., *Concise Dictionary of American History* (New York: Scribner's, 1962), 522.

5. David R. Colburn, "Rosewood and America in the Early

Twentieth Century," *Florida Historical Society Quarterly* 76, no. 2 (Fall 1997): 179.

6. Michael D'Orso, *Like Judgment Day* (New York: G. P. Putnam's Sons, 1996), 4–5.

7. Ibid., 7–10.

8. Ibid., 10–11.

9. "Remembering Rosewood: A Chronology of Events," Displays for Schools, http://www.displaysforschools.com/history.html (accessed July 3, 2009).

10. "Documented History of the Incident Which Occurred at Rosewood, Florida, in January 1923," Displays for Schools, http://www.displaysforschools.com/rosewoodrp.html (accessed July 5, 2009).

ESTHER RAAB
One of the Last Escapees of the
Nazi Death Camp Sobibor
"It's worth it all to survive."

Esther Raab's three-year tale of survival during the Holocaust defies comprehension. A miraculous combination of fortune, finding generous people at the right time, and sheer will enabled her to endure one of the most murderous Nazi death camps. If her survival in the camp were not enough, she rose against her captors, escaped the prison, and hid safely until the end of the war. Out of the million Jews sent to the Nazi's Sobibor death camp in the Polish forest, Mrs. Raab is one of the three hundred who escaped, one of the fifty to live until the German surrender in 1945, and one of the few still alive.

Sobibor was constructed in the first cold months of 1942 with one purpose: to kill as many people as efficiently as possible.[1] This differed from some other Nazi camps, such as Auschwitz, which often utilized slave labor to further the Nazi war efforts (it is believed that 10 to 25 percent of the inmates at Auschwitz worked in factories).[2] Trains brought the victims to Sobibor, where they were almost immediately sent to the gas chambers. The Nazis selected a few fortunate people who were skilled in certain trades, such as goldsmithing, to work as slaves, and these prisoners were the ones who revolted, killed their taskmasters on October 14, 1943, and fled into the dense woods.

Today, Sobibor is not as well known as Auschwitz or Bergen-Belsen. Since Sobibor was the only camp at which there was a successful mass escape, the Nazis immediately closed it, killed the remaining prisoners, tore down all the buildings, and planted pine trees over the site in an attempt to hide their crimes. Unlike other concentration camps, there are no photographs of troops liberating Sobibor. The Nazis also destroyed all but three documents mentioning Sobibor, so if it were not for these brave escapees telling their stories of horror, the world would never know of the brutal and remote death camp and the Nazi atrocities there.

Mrs. Raab speaks perfect English colored by the thick Polish accent of her youth. She was born Esther Terner on June 11, 1922, in Chelm, Poland. "We had a good life in Poland. My father was not a rich man, but we were very comfortable, very middle class. He had a flour mill, but only dealt with Gentiles. We lived in a German neighborhood in Chelm, which was about half Jewish. It was my parents, me, and my brother. After the war began, my father bought goods in case we had to go into hiding." As she speaks, she gazes downward to the couch, where she continually rubs her hand across the smooth leather.

"Soon the Germans came, but left right away. They were replaced by the Russians. After the Russians came, they said we should pack up and go with them, since they thought the Germans would be back. I remember a Russian officer sleeping

Mrs. Raab, standing on the far left, and her family before World War II
photo courtesy Esther Raab

in our house. I was still in school, and my parents didn't believe the Russians. After all, we didn't do anything wrong, and my father wasn't a politician or anything important like that. Then the Nazis returned about December of 1940. The Gestapo rounded up the rich and educated people, about six hundred in all, including my father and brother. They started chasing them out from the city and [they] were shot one by one outside Chelm. When they shot my father and brother, they killed my father but my brother pretended to be dead. He crawled out at night and returned home to warn the others." She recounts this horror in a somber tone with no hint of self-pity, still rubbing her hand across the couch.

"We lived under [Nazi] occupation for about a year. We had to wear a Star of David, but we managed. Toward the end of 1941 the Germans made it into a ghetto overnight. We had twenty minutes to leave home, and we left with my mother. We moved into a room with a woman and her six children. Her husband had been shot too. And I remember there was nothing to eat. Well, my mother couldn't stand that, and we had family close by in an area not controlled by the Germans, so we packed up and a Gentile took us to our relatives. It was quieter there and we had two weeks of peace.

"In that small town, the Nazis made a working camp, and we were ordered to report to it. So my brother and I went to work, and we hid my mother, who was unable to work, behind a false wall. She was really in terrible shape after my father's death. Her sister, who we were staying with, was also taken away." She points to her den wall and shows with her hands how the false partition was constructed parallel to the real one. "So she was all alone. Her husband was dead, her children were gone, her sister was gone. There was only one thing for her to do, since she didn't want to live. She went to the police and asked to be shot. They did it. She was very brave, and she didn't want to kill herself. She didn't commit suicide.

She just didn't want to go to the gas chamber like a dog!" Mrs. Raab chops her hand in the air but shows no emotion.

"The Nazis forced us to dig ditches in a swampy place to drain it and make it productive soil. They marched us off in the morning. We got a loaf of bread for eight people and some fake margarine. Lucky for my brother and me, we still had money and things from home to exchange for food. So we weren't that hungry. And we drained that swamp," she boasts of her forced work.

"That camp lasted until October of 1942, when the work was done. We were told to assemble and we heard they were making that place a Jew-free area. We thought we were going to be killed off. We went to another work camp named Stavnowoshulky in horses and wagons. It was muddy, and we had to drag the wagons out when they were stuck. I remember we walked the whole day until evening. There, they started selecting healthy workers, and someone told us that if we went with the young, we had a chance [to live]. I had on two coats in case they took away our bundles [of possessions]. I was so nervous during the selection. And I was told to go with the older people. But the man who did the selecting had a mistress there whom I had gone to school with. The woman took out her lipstick, rubbed it on my cheeks to make me look healthier, and put me in the back of the line. When I got to the selector again, he thought he had already seen me. But the mistress told him he was wrong, and they put me in the work line." She stops and summarizes: "Luck was with me always."

Esther moved to another labor camp. "Let me tell you, the conditions were unbearable. We got a slice of bread, little water, and bad potatoes. The weather was already very cold, and we dug ditches there too. But I had it better than the rest. Since my father was in the bread business, I knew the man who delivered the bread to the camp. He left extra bread for me and my brother. We ate half and bartered the other half. Then, one

Mrs. Raab just after the war
photo courtesy Esther Raab

**Mrs. Raab at the time
of the interview**
photo by Stuart Lutz

night, we had roll call in the middle of the night. I knew this was bad, because this [camp] was the last stop before the death camps. At the roll call, I couldn't get in touch with my brother. Then I heard shots and someone told me that my brother escaped. I figured they probably shot him."

She recounts her trip to Sobibor. "We went the whole day by wagon. We arrived on the twenty-second day of December 1942. On the way, the Poles shouted, 'You're gonna become soap' and 'Don't give your valuables to the Germans, throw them to us.' They were worse than the Nazis. In some ways, I couldn't wait to get my death over with, but I knew that I wasn't going to die. In fact, when I arrived there, I had a nice pair of boots from my mother. I put them aside right away for my escape attempt.

"We assembled on the platform; there were eight hundred people there. The Nazis came around looking for skilled people. My girlfriend Mira picked out knitters for the Nazis, including me. She picked out eight people and two fathers from the eight hundred. All the rest were soon going to be dead. Me? Isn't that lucky?" She shakes her head in ancient disbelief.

"We were taken to a barracks and told to stay until morning. They brought us coffee and bread, and I thought it was our last meal. It tasted so good. The Jewish commandant, the kapo, brought us blankets. He warned us, 'You work good, you make sure they need you and you behave, you'll avoid the frying pan.' That's what we called cremation." Kapos were the overseers who complied with the Nazis; they supervised and carried out the orders of the camp supervisors. Many of them were nearly as harsh as the Nazis, and a number of them were Jewish; some Jews chose to become kapos to save their lives.

"They made two rooms for us in the barracks and put in a little iron stove where we could burn wood shavings. They brought us a lot of wool, and we had to knit a sack a day per person. Well, we were all good knitters and we did that for two or three weeks. Then the transfers started, so they moved me to a sorting shed—it was freezing in there. I went through the clothes of the dead people and found notes in their pockets. Notes like 'Take revenge' and the number of Jews the Nazis killed. But we couldn't say a word to the prisoners or that was it. We worked sixteen or eighteen hours a day and they gave the eight of us a loaf of bread and soup. On the days there were no transports, we did other work.

"If you missed roll call, you were finished. This was not a

work camp, but a finishing camp. In March they brought in twenty men and no women [to work]. One of them was a cousin of my father's by marriage named Leon Feldhendler. We told him what was going on [with the gassings], but he knew already. He insisted we must escape and we can't wait for them to kill us. He warned us that the plotting must be quiet, but on the day of the escape, everyone would know. After all, we didn't have to pack up our luggage." She smiles for the first time.

"So we started planning and planning. Only a small group, maybe about twenty, knew about the escape plot, but a lot more women [than men] knew, since they could move around the camp better than men. I became the messenger between Leon and the rest of the escape group. There were two Nazi crews maintaining the camp. One was smarter and crueler, and when they were gone, we would escape.

"In April [Heinrich] Himmler came. To show him how well the camp worked, they brought in hundreds of beautiful young girls to kill. Himmler was very impressed with Sobibor, so they closed [the concentration camps] Treblinka and Belzec. So they brought in more boxcars for us. It is reported that 250,000 were killed there [in Sobibor], but I know that was wrong. In August [1943] we were given a day off to celebrate the one millionth Jew killed there."

Mrs. Raab recounts one escape attempt from Sobibor: "In the summer of 1943, there was a successful breakout of two people. There was a crew taken to cut trees. When two of them went to get water, accompanied by an armed guard, of course, they killed the guard with the bucket and escaped into the woods. When the other Nazis went to look for the missing guard, thirteen others also made a dash, but were caught. So the Nazis decided to make them an example to all the workers in the camp. They made the thirteen line up in front of us. Then the Nazis made them choose a companion in death. The Nazis then machine-gunned twenty-six people, punishing people who had nothing to do with the escape. That's when we knew we had to take everyone with us on an escape attempt so there was no one left for the Nazis to kill.

"We made plans the whole summer and knew that we had to leave before it got cold. Eighteen days before the day of our escape, they brought in eighty or one hundred Russian POWs. We didn't think they were Jews at first, but then we realized they were. They had already escaped from four or five camps, and they wanted to join in our attempt."

By the end of the summer of 1943, the Sobibor slaves knew they were running out of time. The Nazi death machine was so efficient that it had trouble finding people to kill. The prisoners understood that once the boxcars ceased, the Nazis would kill them, then close the camp.

"On October 13 we were ready to escape in the late afternoon. We wanted to do it shortly before sunset to make it harder for them to find us. That day an unexpected group of SS came to the camp. We thought for sure that someone gave us away. But they just took some provisions and left that evening. We called off the escape for that day. I was so disappointed. We were afraid word would leak. The rule at Sobibor was you never cried and always pretended to be happy. But the night after we called off the escape, we all cried ourselves to sleep." She pauses and reflects, "It was the only time."

Mrs. Raab moves to the day of the breakout, October 14. "I must tell about the dream I had that night [of October 13–14]. My mother came in the main gate of Sobibor, and she knew of the escape plans. She took me by the hand and showed me a barn in a field. She told me that I would survive there. I recognized the barn; it was owned by a baker that my father knew. They were like family to us, and the children were very friendly with my brother and me. When I got up [on the morning of the 14th], I told the girls in my bunk about the dream, and that if I do get out, I must go to the barn."

The plan to kill the Nazi guards on the day of the escape was tactically brilliant. Playing on the greed of their captors, the slaves invited their overseers to stop at their workshops late on the afternoon of the fourteenth. The workers told the Nazis that they had found, for example, a leather coat, and wanted them to try it on as a gift. Once the Nazis were in the shops, the Jews used axes and knives to kill their captors.[3] By spacing the invitations to the Nazis apart, they were able to clean the shops and hide the bodies before the next Nazi came in.

"We had prepared by making knives, and everyone had to kill his Nazi or Ukrainian watcher," she explains. "We killed off the leaders in the hour before roll call—we did this quietly, of course, by inviting the Nazis to the shops at appointed hours. Roll call was at four. We would get weapons stolen from the Nazis and march to the main gate. It was the only place around the camp with no mines.

"At roll call everything was normal. We had already killed eleven Nazis and a few Ukrainians. We had cut the electricity and the telephone so they couldn't call for help. Also, we were dressed normally. Working in the clothing shed, I could trade my clothes to something better. We had our hair and we didn't have striped clothes. But the big problem just before the escape was we couldn't find the one in charge, [Karl] Frenzel, and I feared that he went out for help. The other rule for the escape was that once we were out, or if anything went wrong, it was everyone for himself."

She recounts her first moment of freedom from the Nazis. "At the roll call, Leon got up and made a speech. He said, 'Our day has come. Most of the Germans are dead. Let's die with honor. Remember, if anyone survives, he must tell the world what has happened here.'[4] As Leon said this, I moved close to the main compound, the one closest to the main gate. There was a big commotion and shooting. I saw someone push a ladder toward the wall—we had hidden them. And I took my chances with the ladder because I didn't know how to use a gun. As I jumped down, I was shot. A bullet grazed my ear, and the blood just gushed." Mrs. Raab points toward her ear. "But my will to live was so great that I just kept running to the woods. I was so lucky." Her gaze turns toward the center of her den wall. She has a framed poster for the movie *Escape from Sobibor*. Starring Alan Arkin, the 1987 film told the tale of the Sobibor uprising.

"I ran into the woods, and we broke into small groups. I was in a group of ten men and one other woman. She was from Czechoslovakia, and was doomed by the language barrier she had with us. The first night out, we finally came to a clearing. It was Sobibor again; we went in circles. But no one knew the directions and we were frozen stiff. We escaped on a Thursday night, and on Sunday morning I threw away my leather coat since it was too much to carry. What a mistake!" She raises her eyebrows and shrugs.

"A few days later we found a hut. I couldn't take being in the woods anymore. I took one of my male friends from the small group, since we couldn't all go in. And another man followed us, making three people. The rest of the group waited in the woods. It was a one-room hut with a stove and two beds. I knocked, and a toothless old man answered. He figured out who we were and said, 'You must be the people from Sobibor. You killed Nazis. You did right. How many are you? What can *I* do for you?' Well, he had to go to church with his sons. Or so he said. I thought he was getting the Gestapo. It was almost dark when he returned with his boys. He brought a meal for a king. I can still taste the borscht, fruit, cheese, warm milk. I showed him my wound. So he boiled a big pot of water and cut off one of my braids. He used unsalted lard as medicine. After I washed up, he asked us, 'What would you like to do?' Well, I wanted to get to that barn my mother showed me in my dream, and I knew how to get there. So I thought. He said he'd help us get there, and if it did not work out, we were free to return to his place. He gave us food for the road, and in the middle of the night one of his sons took us to the woods to show us the way. As for the rest of the group in the woods, they were gone when we came out. None of them survived. I don't know if the Poles killed them, or they were caught by the Nazis, or they froze or starved, or what. But none of them made it."

She describes her journey to the barn her mother had showed her in the dream. "The three of us started walking. From where we were, it was about a day's walk to get to the barn. But we went in circles," she says, twirling her finger over her head. "It took us two weeks to find it. But the farmers along the way treated us well. They knew the war was going to end soon and wanted to make up with the Jews. I think the Poles were more guilty than the Nazis. They could have prevented it all by not being neutral. For example, of all the escapees killed in the woods, it was mostly done by the Poles. The Nazis never went far into the woods around Sobibor because they were afraid. It wasn't their land.

"We hid near the main highway, and then I recognized the village where I picked cherries as a child. My father's friend the baker had what they called a gentleman's farm there. Late at night we found the barn. We climbed the loft and for two days lay in the straw. I knew we'd survive there. We got so hungry that we went to the next village to get something to eat. We'd knock on a door and pretend to have a gun." She makes the outline of a gun with her thumb and index finger. "And they'd give us milk and bread. So, when we returned to the loft, we were climbing up and one of the men dropped the milk bottle. I told him he must find it so there was no evidence of us. I spoke in Yiddish, and someone jumped out of the loft. It was my brother! He had already been hiding there for ten months by himself. We held hands until the sunrise.

"Four days later, the owner of the barn, Mr. Marcynuik, returned. Mr. Marcynuik whistled to my brother to let him know it was safe. And when Mr. Marcynuik saw me, he crossed himself. Well, I only told him that I was there with one other man, I never told him I was there with two other men. I thought that would be too much for him to support. The four of us spent nine months there."

Unbelievably, Mrs. Raab remembers the Nazis holding a trial in the Marcynuik barn to investigate one soldier's shooting another.[5] The runaways feared that as the Nazis gave ground to the advancing Soviets, they would impose a scorched-earth policy and burn the barn; they never did.

She recounts her return to Poland after the war. "Eventually, the Russians crossed the Bug [River], so we all went to Warsaw. Then I returned to Chelm and got an apartment there. A few other Jews returned, but they [the townspeople] did not want us back or [want us] to reclaim our property. The Poles began killing us, so we went with the Russian army for protection. At the time, the Russians were allies of the Jews. And once the Russians left the area, there was no law and order. It was only vigilantes. The Russians crossed Poland and we marched with them until Berlin. I lived there for four or five years. It was a divided city, and we were in the English quarter."

After the war, Mrs. Raab testified at the trials of three of the camp commanders. They were all given life sentences, in part because of her testimony. "It was very difficult to see them, and of course they denied everything. But they didn't deny knowing me. But they used the old excuse of 'We were just following orders.' One of the trials was for [Hubert] Gomerski. We called him 'The Doctor' since he always wore a white lab coat. He would come to the train and take away everyone who was sick. He'd put them on a wagon and shoot them. And with the trial of [Erich] Bauer, I was the one who caught him. I saw him riding on a merry-go-round in a Berlin amusement park. I got the police and had him arrested. But there was also a trial of Kleer, who was in charge of the bakery. When I came to the camp, I had brown leather boots. When they wore out, I told Kleer that I lost my shoes. He sat me down, brought me shoes, and put them on me, like a salesman in a shoe store. He offered me two pairs, but I was afraid to take that many, so I left with only one pair. He always gave us extra loaves of bread. He was never with the transports or mistreated people. So at his trial I told the court he did nothing wrong, and he was cleared.

"In 1950 we emigrated to America. I came to a free country, and I built a family." She shows her gold necklace with several charms on it; each one represents one of her grandchildren. "My children and grandchildren are my biggest revenge on the Nazis. They didn't kill me physically or emotionally. Virtually, I am at Sobibor every night. But in actuality, I have been there ten or twelve times. I was there for the fiftieth anniversary of the escape in 1993. And I returned in 2003 to be filmed for a German television documentary about Sobibor."

Mrs. Raab attributes her improbable survival to one specific trait: "I always had the feeling that I was going to live. I felt I was going to make it. I just couldn't see myself in the gas chambers. And I never gave up my belief in God, as many others did."

Mrs. Raab believes Sobibor is not as well known as the other concentration camps because of the escape. "Sobibor was closed a few days after the escape. There was no liberation of it by the soldiers or press reporters, like Auschwitz. No movies of it. So we were the only witnesses to it. The world didn't want to know about the Holocaust. The world would like to absolve itself by blaming the Nazis, but the Western world didn't do much for the European Jews. They didn't bomb the camps or train lines. Now we find out a lot of countries, like the Swiss, and many companies profited from it all."

As for her feelings on being one of the last Sobibor survivors, she explains, "I feel so sorry for those who didn't make it, and I miss the others. I feel responsible to speak up about Sobibor. I was a survivor and I have an obligation to those who didn't make it. I speak a lot at schools and colleges, and I have received thousands of letters from students. That's my revenge. It's worth it all to survive. Remember, my parents gave their lives so we could survive. I keep in contact with the other living Sobibor survivors. There are maybe seven or eight of us. About six of us are in the United States, one in Australia, and one or two in Israel. We went through hell together and remain close friends."

She rejects the Holocaust deniers, coldly stating, "They should have been there."

Mrs. Raab's extraordinary life has been turned into a play called *Dear Esther*, which has been shown to twenty-five thousand schoolchildren; it is named after the greeting she gets on the letters to her.

She goes into the other room to get some photographs. Many of them have been expanded to poster size, and she points out pictures of herself and her family from the 1920s and 1930s. "After I went back to Chelm, someone had saved these and gave them to me," she explains.

She also shows a hand-drawn diagram of the hayloft she lived in, including the air holes and the underground bunker where four people could sleep. She then presents a photograph of herself and other survivors at Sobibor during the fiftieth anniversary of the escape. Another photograph shows a small hill. "This is the pile of ash from all the bodies. It's about forty feet high," she notes. There is a window cut into the side of the ash hill, and there are bits of bone and a skull showing through the glass. At first the Nazis buried the bodies, but when this proved dangerous for the health of the Nazis working there, the corpses were cremated, further erasing evidence of their crimes.[6]

As Mrs. Raab walks through the kitchen toward the front door, she explains about the dozens of houseplants growing in there. "They are sent to me by schoolchildren from all over the country, and I can't just get rid of them, so I keep them all."

Mrs. Raab tells her sad tale with nary a tear. Perhaps it is that steel that enabled her to survive and escape Sobibor and to have a full life despite being haunted by one of humanity's worst crimes. But, as she herself notes, luck played a great role also in her survival. One of the escape planners, Leon Feldhendler, did not live to see the end of the war.

NOTES

1. Miriam Novitch, *Sobibor: Martyrdom and Revolt* (New York: Holocaust Library, 1980), 24.

2. Ibid., 27.

3. Richard Rashke, *Escape from Sobibor* (Boston: Houghton Mifflin, 1982), 215.

4. Ibid., 299.

5. Ibid., 258–59.

6. Novitch, *Sobibor*, 24.

DAVID STOLIAR
The Only Survivor of the *Struma* Sinking
*"The explosion blew me into the air and I fell in the water. . . .
And the people around me slowly drowned."*

For European Jews in the late 1930s and early 1940s, British-controlled Palestine was a beacon of hope. As the Nazis marched through much of Europe, capturing Jews and sending them to concentration camps, some of the Jews who were still free hoped that passage to Palestine would save their lives. The desperate immigrants crowded on ships and set sail. They rarely received a warm welcome from British officers in Palestine, and they were often either turned away or held in refugee camps. As an example, in November 1940 the British navy stopped two ships taking two thousand Jews to Palestine illegally. The passengers were seized and put aboard the British ship *Patria*. The ship was scheduled to sail to Mauritania. Sadly, some Jews already living in Palestine, in an attempt to disable the *Patria* and prevent the immigrants from leaving, accidentally sank it; 250 people died.[1]

David Stoliar, born in Kishinev, Romania, on October 31, 1922, is the sole survivor of the *Struma*, a rickety ship headed from Romania to the promised land of Palestine. The *Struma* held 769 refugees, including 269 women and seventy children.[2] On the morning of February 24, 1942, a Soviet submarine patrolling the Black Sea torpedoed the *Struma*, killing all but Mr. Stoliar.

David Stoliar was the only child of a father who owned a textile factory in Bucharest; his father owned it until 1940, when the Nazis seized all Jewish possessions in Romania. "In 1939, I visited my mother in Paris," he recounts in the heavily accented voice of his Romanian youth. "When I returned to Romania, things had gotten bad for Jews there. About 1940 there was an order for all Jews between eighteen and thirty to present themselves for duty. Remember that Romania was

Mr. Stoliar as a young man
photo courtesy David Stoliar

BUCAREST
1941.

Mr. Stoliar at the time of the interview
photo courtesy David Stoliar

allied with Germany at the time. I had to go into a forced labor camp. We dug trenches for the German army. The troops were massing to attack the Soviet Union to the east. I was sent to a place outside of Bucharest.

"In 1941 my father purchased my passage on the *Struma*. The price was ridiculous, something like a thousand dollars. The voyage was advertised by a travel agency in Bucharest. Because I had a ticket, I was permitted to leave the labor camp. But there was a period of a few months before I boarded the vessel. First the departure was supposed to be in September, then October, and we didn't leave until December 1941. It was just a few days after Pearl Harbor. I didn't go with my parents, but I went with several schoolmates of mine. Also, I sailed with my girlfriend, Ilse Lothringer, and her parents."

The *Struma* was in very poor condition. "The vessel was originally an old barge for animals on the Danube River. But it had been retrofitted for people. The owners put in these tight bunks, similar to what you saw in concentration camps. The vessel was designed for 150 people"—which means that five times the number of people were crammed aboard. "Everyone was on top of everyone else and we were packed like sardines. When I went to sleep, I couldn't lay on my back, for there wasn't enough room. I had to sleep on my side. They made it so 150 people at a time could go on deck for an hour and get some fresh air. And the food and water were very scarce."

Mr. Stoliar moves to the actual voyage. "The *Struma*'s engine worked for only a couple of days. I later learned that it was a very old motor found at the bottom of the Danube. It had three cylinders, but only two worked. We were then pulled by a tugboat into the Black Sea outside of Romania's territorial waters and we were left just to float there. The captain sent an SOS to the port to pull us back into port. A Romanian tugboat came out and said they were not allowed to bring us back. They made us a deal. If we paid enough, they would try to repair the engine. The problem is that none of us had any money," he sighs. "The Romanian customs officers seized everything of value when we were leaving the country. The only thing we had left were wedding rings. The tugboat people accepted the rings as payment. They worked on the engine and got it running again. The tugboat went alongside us until we reached Turkish territorial waters. It took two days to get there. Once the *Struma* got close to the Bosporus, the tug returned to Romania. And once we reached the Bosporus Straits, the engine quit for good. A Turkish tugboat came and pulled us unto the Istanbul harbor."

Once in Turkey, the passengers were not allowed off the ship. "There was a very strict quarantine. We had no communication with the outside world. Once a week, a supply boat came out to us, furnished by the Red Crescent and the Istanbul Jewish community. Conditions grew worse every day. There was not enough water, and the provisions were extremely meager. Supposedly, the supply boat had problems with an export license. We were there for seventy-one days. On February 23, 1942, the police boarded the *Struma*, cut the anchor, and attached us to a Turkish military tugboat. We turned around and headed into the Black Sea for three or four hours. Once in the Black Sea, they left us there—no engine, no food, no water," he recounts.

"I was sleeping in a bunk just below the deck at the extreme front of the vessel. The explosion blew me into the air and I fell in the water. The torpedo just pulverized the wooden ship. When I surfaced, there was a tremendous amount of debris everywhere and a lot of people floating, trying to survive. We were all trying to hang onto debris. The water was very cold. It was February in the Black Sea. And the people around me slowly drowned. Yet the shore was visible from where I was. I could hear water pumps and engines from land.

"Toward the end of the day I was practically by myself. I found a piece of deck, perhaps six feet by ten, and I stayed on top of it. Soon I found the chief mate floating on a door, and I pulled him onto my deck. He told me an interesting story. He was on the deck that morning, watching the Turkish coast. He saw the torpedo bubbles coming from the shore. He ran to tell the captain about this, and as he open[ed] the captain's door, the vessel exploded! When I found him, the mate was floating on the door he grasped when the torpedo hit!

"All night we shouted for help, and we talked to each other to keep ourselves alive. By morning he stopped talking. He had died. I was rescued shortly thereafter, on the morning of the twenty-fifth. Soon a rowboat came out with six sailors from the Turkish Coast Guard. They picked me up and the body of the mate, and took us to shore. I was half frozen and brought to a fishing village. I couldn't walk and was kept there that night. The next morning I was taken to Istanbul and an ambulance took me to a military hospital. As I rolled in, there were several reporters, and one asked me who I was. I replied and said I was from the *Struma*." What the previously isolated Mr. Stoliar did not realize was that after his rescue, the sinking of the *Struma* had become an international story. There were protests by the Jewish community against restrictive British immigration policies to Palestine.

Mr. Stoliar was in the hospital for seven days while he was treated for his frozen arms and legs. "A policeman guarded my room, and no one was allowed in except for the doctor and nurses. After a week they took me across the Bosphorus to the European side of Istanbul to a police station. I was put at the top of the building in an area that was like a prison. I was locked up for six weeks. Finally, my documents admitting me to Palestine arrived from London at the British Consulate in Istanbul, and I was released from the prison in April 1942. Simon Broad, the president of the Istanbul Jewish community, brought me to his home. The next morning, he took me to the railroad station and gave me a ticket to Allepo, which was the end of the line. I was accompanied by a policeman. When I got off the train, there was a car waiting to take me to Palestine.

"By the end of 1942, when I was in Palestine, I was better and I could walk. I joined the British army in 1943 and was sent to Cairo to serve in the North African campaign. I returned to Palestine in 1946 after the war ended. My father survived the war by remaining in Romania. I learned my mother, who was in Paris, was picked up by the Gestapo in 1942 and killed at Auschwitz."

Mr. Stoliar has done his own research on the *Struma*. "I

know the 'official' reason for the *Struma* sinking," he notes dismissively. "Turkey was neutral but supplying chrome to the Nazi government, which was at war with the Soviet Union. This upset [Joseph] Stalin, so he ordered his Black Sea navy [fleet] to torpedo anything floating there. This is the explanation found in the Soviet navy archives. Yet there are several coincidences that don't make sense to me. I question why we were specifically towed to that area. I don't think it was a matter of being in the wrong place at the wrong time, but I think it was prearranged. The Turkish authorities knew we had no engine, so we couldn't propel ourselves. When they towed us out, they knew we had no provisions. We didn't even have an anchor. We were sitting ducks. I later learned the Turks said they were going to move us on February sixteenth, but postponed this a week. I don't think the sub was there the first date, but it was probably there on the twenty-fourth. If you put it all together—no food or water, no engine, the sudden decision to move us into the Black Sea—it seems that the torpedoing was preordained."

He understands the positions of both Turkey and Britain in 1942. "It was the British policy of the colonial office not to allow immigrants into Palestine. They applied this law until the establishment of Israel in 1948. They didn't want to antagonize the Arab population living there. I cannot blame an entire country because the colonial office made this policy." After the *Struma* incident the British revised their policy, no longer expelling people who entered Palestine illegally. They set free the refugees held in a deportation camp.[3] Mr. Stoliar continues: "Consider the situation in Turkey during 1942. Turkey was neutral, but surrounded by Nazis. Greece, just to the west, was occupied by Germany, and the Germans were just to the north too. I understand that they were very nervous and afraid of the German army. In one document I read, the prime minister of Turkey made a declaration that his country [would] not be used as a refugee area for people not wanted in other countries. They didn't want to be a European Jewish refugee camp. Many people tried to get into Turkey, and I know Simon Broad helped them with money and food. In many ways, Turkey was the only gate open to them.

"A deep-sea diver in England, Greg Buxton, had grandparents who died on the vessel. He got a group of his diving friends to see if they could find anything left from the ship. The dozen divers found other wrecks there, but not the *Struma*. But that doesn't surprise me. The *Struma* was made of wood, and it splintered when the torpedo hit it and was gone. The only thing to find would be the small engine. And the Black Sea has a strong current."

After World War II Mr. Stoliar worked for a Haifa refinery and fought in the Israeli War of Independence. He then lived in Japan for eighteen years. "My first wife, who died in 1961, never knew about the *Struma*," he confesses. "For the first fifty years, I tried to forget about the *Struma*. It took me decades to face reality. Until recently I had survivor guilt. I felt terrible for being the only one to make it. If others had also survived, I would have felt better.

"It is sixty-three years past, and I still see it all very vividly. It changed my life completely. People were very inhumane, especially while I was on the vessel and afterward. The cruelty of people shocked me so much that I couldn't trust anyone for a long time. People are only humane when they have to be."

NOTES

1. I. C. B. Dear, *The Oxford Companion to World War II* (New York: Oxford University Press, 1995), 867.

2. Ibid., 1079.

3. Israel Gutman, ed., *Encyclopedia of the Holocaust* (New York: Macmillan, 1990), 4:1417.

THOMAS TORRESSON JR.
One of the Last Survivors of the *Morro Castle* Passenger Ship, Which Burned in 1934
"The Morro Castle is a deep mystery with no solution."

An unsolved and tragic fire broke out on the Ward Line cruise ship *Morro Castle* in the early morning of September 8, 1934, off the New Jersey shore. In a tale reminiscent of a bad mystery novel, the *Morro Castle* was traveling from Havana to New York when the captain, Robert Wilmott, was found dead in his cabin of a probable heart attack.[1] Several hours later, a fire erupted in the writing room and quickly spread throughout the ship.[2] Chief Officer William Warms, who had been the acting captain for only a few hours, had to contend with horrific winds that helped spread the flames.[3]

The *Morro Castle* was carrying 322 passengers and 240 crew.[4] Some of its lifeboats were launched, but not all were filled. One lifeboat held only Chief Engineer Eban S. Abbott and a few passengers, leading to later charges that the crew had abandoned the passengers. Other lifeboats could not be reached because of the location of the inferno. Additionally, there was a delay in sending out an SOS.[5] Fortunately, some nearby ships saw the fire and steamed over to help with the rescue. The charred hull grounded at Asbury Park, New Jersey. One hundred thirty-four people died, mostly of drowning, representing the worst ocean disaster ever to occur to a United States–flag merchant vessel.[6] Newspaper headlines featured the story of the fire.

Thomas Torresson Jr., one the last living people aboard the *Morro Castle* during the conflagration, was a crewman aboard the ship. He lives in New Jersey, due west of where the ship caught fire. Born in 1916, he comes from a long line of seamen. "My grandfather was a Norwegian sea captain. Things were tight for him over there when ships switched from sail to steam. He came to the United States and began working for the Ward Line; he then sent for his family. Shortly after they arrived, he was lost at sea, leaving behind a wife and five children, with no life insurance. The head of the Ward Line gave my father, who was just fourteen, a job as an office boy. My father stayed with the company for fifty-two years, working his way up to marine superintendent. The Ward Line had a terrific safety record. In its first eighty years, the company never lost a passenger."

Mr. Torresson first saw the *Morro Castle* in 1934 as a high

Mr. Torresson about the time of the *Morro Castle* fire
photo courtesy
Irene Torresson

Mr. Torresson at the time of the interview
photo by Stuart Lutz

school student. "I was preparing for my midterm exams and I developed pneumonia. Our doctor suggested that my mother take me on a trip to Havana to help me recover. The *Morro Castle* was launched in 1930, and it was still brand new and beautiful when I first went aboard. It had a black hull and shiny brass. There was a white superstructure and two swept-back stacks sporting the twin stripes of the Ward Line. We had so much faith in the ship. The *Morro Castle* was constructed for tropical waters. Fresh air was blown throughout via a system of ducts. When the fire broke out, the ducts acted like a chimney flue," he notes.

"Because of my father's position in the company, we had the best room on the ship and I had the run of the *Morro Castle*. I met two young guys who were deck cadets. They learned on the job and were studying for their exam to get their mate's license. I was interested in such work, and I asked my father if I could get a job as a deck cadet. He said there was no chance of me getting a job since the waiting list to be a deck cadet was fifty men long. This was when the idea of cruise ships was still in its infancy."

A few months later, young Mr. Torresson found himself a *Morro Castle* crewman. "One Friday night in early July 1934, I picked up my father at the railroad station and he told me, 'Pack your bag; you are leaving for Havana in the morning.' When I asked how that was possible since there were fifty men on the list for deck cadet, he laughed and said, 'You are not sailing as a deck cadet, but as third assistant purser.' That afternoon, the home office received a radio message that Don Roney, the chief purser, was ill. So each of the staff moved up one notch. This left the third assistant purser open with no one to fill it. My father got me on the one trip to gain experience.

"A purser had three tasks. He had to be able to speak Spanish, type, and dance. Well, I couldn't speak Spanish well, I could hunt and peck on the typewriter, and I was no Fred

Astaire! My father put me in for one trip, and the next morning I went to New York City. I bought two white uniforms with epaulets and a high neck, and white shoes. I got my seaman's passport and reported to the *Morro Castle* just before noon. I met purser Bob Tolman, who gave me a little book outlining my tasks. I had to greet all the Spanish-speaking guests, I had to address all the bon voyage gifts for the passengers, and I needed to buy Cuban stamps in Havana. I had to write all the passport and immigration papers in English and Spanish, and the purser's office was open from 9:00 a.m. to 9:00 p.m., though I didn't leave work until midnight. I stayed on the whole summer and made fifty dollars a month. I also had a fourteen-dollar weekly bar tab that I was supposed to use to buy drinks for the guests. A seven-day cruise to Cuba cost a minimum of sixty-five dollars, but for seventy-five or eighty-five bucks you could get a fine cabin."

Mr. Torresson knew the ship's officers well. "Captain Wilmott was very corpulent and jolly and beloved by the passengers," he remembers. "He ran a tight ship, and made a daily inspection of everything. He stopped by the purser's office every morning about 10:00. The crew liked him. One day he called me into his office. He dictated a letter for me to send to my father, who was his boss. It concerned a canal through the Florida Keys. I took dictation and typed it several times. After having the purser read it, I showed it to the captain. He looked it over and said it was fine, except that 'coral' had only one 'R.' I had to retype it," he laughs. "Chief Officer Warms was the usual tough sea dog type, but it was mostly an act. He was well respected by his men. When I first sailed, I reported to him and told him what a beautiful boat he had. He sternly replied, 'We have twelve boats aboard, and they are all swinging in the davits. The *Morro Castle* is a ship!' There's been a lot of claims written that Wilmott and Warms were not friends. There was no dissention among the deck officers. I had meals with [the *Morro Castle*'s chief radio operator] George Rogers, and there was something weird about him. I also had to be careful with radio operator George Alagna, who was a troublemaker and supposed to be a Communist. Radio operators were not employed by the line, but by RCA."

On the night of the fire, Mr. Torresson says, "we were northbound off Cape Fear and Hatteras in heavy fog. We sounded the foghorn and there was a feeling of gloom in the ship's office. A little after 7:00 the phone rang in the purser's office and we were asked to get Dr. Van Zile, the ship's surgeon, from the dining room. He was needed on the bridge. Twenty minutes later the phone rang again and we learned Captain Wilmott was dead. Warms went to his cabin to check on him and found him with his head in the tub. He probably died of a heart attack. There was a discussion whether to tell the passengers, and the cruise director announced the captain's death and stated there would be no party on the last night of the cruise. I typed thirteen copies of the death certificate for Wilmott, and Warms signed them all. The whole scene was like an MGM set with the fog, the horn, and the death of the captain.

"There was a hurricane south of us, and soon the rain and wind started. There was a fifty-two-knot gale. We were working that night to prepare for our New York docking the next day. My roommate, Les Aronson, and I didn't go to bed until 12:30 or 1:00 that morning. The ship rarely had a full complement of passengers, so the assistant pursers used an unoccupied passenger cabin since it had a private shower."

Mr. Torresson was not asleep for long. "There was a pounding on the door about 2:00 in the morning. Les answered it and there was a crew member from the engine room who said, 'Get up, get dressed, put on a life jacket, and get on the deck. The ship's on fire!' Recognizing us as pursers, he suggested that we help calm the passengers. I put on my uniform and life jacket and even combed my hair.

"We walked up to the purser's office on C deck, and there was no noise or sign of fire. Tolman and the cruise director were there having a discussion about their shoes." Mr. Torresson shrugs in disbelief. "Tolman told me to see the fire for myself. I went up the stairs to the B deck and I saw a massive fire. I realized we had problems. Tolman ordered me to check the passenger cabins. I knocked on the port-side cabin doors, since I didn't have a master key, and found three or four passengers. I told them to move to the stern, which was the only way to the lifeboats. The lifeboats were on the topmost A deck, and were supposed to be lowered to the B deck for boarding." He stacks his hands vertically to demonstrate the ship's layout. "But the fire was on the B deck, so passengers couldn't get in the lifeboats. But the stern of the B deck was open and passengers were standing there.

"I found a priest. He said he already performed mass absolution on the passengers but he gave it to me too. There wasn't a lot of mass panic. People were more stunned than anything. We were ordered to move passengers lower from the B to the C to the D deck. We wanted to get people lower so either the rescue boats could get to them or they would have a shorter jump into the water. The D deck was jammed and I closed the door on C deck to keep the fire from spreading down. I tried to use a fire hose on C deck, but the water pressure was so low with everyone else using them also that the hose was useless."

Mr. Torresson notes that William Warms, the acting captain, was in a quandary. "There was a high gale and he wasn't sure lifeboats could survive such a choppy sea. He told Abbott to get in Lifeboat #1, which was motorized, with a few passengers as a test. I saw that lifeboat when I was on B deck. The lifeboat's engine quit and they drifted to shore."

Mr. Torresson helped a badly injured child off the ship. "Someone gave me a boy named Bobby Gonzalez to look after. He was eleven or twelve. His back was burned and he couldn't put on a life jacket. I told Bobby we [had] to jump into the water and he said he could swim. We climbed over the rail and I jumped alongside him. I forgot to hold my life jacket down and it hit me across the chin. The water wasn't that cold. That kid was gutsy. We were talking for many hours, but I was tired of holding him. There was a woman floating there and I asked her to help with Bobby. She replied, 'Let him go and save yourself.' That was her contribution," he notes bitterly. "Soon Bobby wasn't answering me, and he died of shock or hypothermia. I saw an oar floating by and I tied his body to it."

Mr. Torreson was rescued by a lifeboat from the *City of Savannah*. "I was the last one pulled in, and they wouldn't take Bobby's body. It was so jammed that they couldn't row, so we were just floating out there. A coast guard cutter tossed us a line. The first one broke, and after they sent us a second line, the cutter's engine quit. A small fishing boat towed us to the Manasquan Inlet. I held a woman so she wouldn't roll off the lifeboat. The fishing boat captain kept the towline taut, which kept us from turning over. The New Jersey governor flew overhead in a National Guard plane from Sea Girt the next morning to view everything. We came into the dock and there were ambulances waiting. The people on shore were terrific. I was soaking." He wraps his arms around himself as if chilled. "Someone took off my uniform jacket and he took his son's jacket and put it on me. I went to the Sea Girt First Aid squad and was given a glass of liquid. My throat was raw from the smoke and salt water. It was pure rye! They gave me a pair of Levis and a shirt but no shoes. I never saw my uniform again. I recently received a call from a local doctor who recovered a *Morro Castle* lifeboat bag. He found a home movie—and this was before many people had personal cameras—of me landing on the beach in the lifeboat. You can see me since I'm the only one in uniform," he remarks.

His father soon arrived on the scene. "He asked me if I did

my duty. I said yes. He shook my hand and left. Our family friend Mr. MacDonald took me to the Essex and Sussex Hotel, where my mother was waiting for me. I was in the dining room with bare feet. My mother insisted that I take a bath, after I spent hours in the water! I went to MacDonald's apartment and I passed out. I was injured a little bit. My right eye needed a patch and I had some slight burns to the right side of my face. But I was the neighborhood hero!

"One mistake was that the Ward Line's vice president ordered the crew not to speak to reporters. So the press made up horrible stories instead. One reporter labeled the *Morro Castle* the 'Ship of Shame' since he thought the crew deserted the passengers."

The *Morro Castle* drifted and washed ashore in Asbury Park, New Jersey. "I saw it lying there, but never went on it. It became a tourist attraction, even though it was after Labor Day and all the summer crowds left. It brought thousands to the beach. The number two hold had a cargo of wet hides, and you could smell that miles away. Finally, the hulk was towed to Gravesend Bay near Coney Island, then scrapped in Baltimore. Its sister ship, the *Oriente*, sailed on into the 1950s."

As a crewman, Mr. Torresson was questioned by the authorities. "I was subpoenaed by the Federal Court, Southern District of New York. I was questioned three times by young lawyers who were anxiously seeking something, or anything. One of them accused me of lying about using a fire hose on C deck, claiming that there wasn't one there. When I showed him the hose on the chart of the ship, he didn't bother to apologize. I wasn't allowed to leave the city for a year, so I got a job with a rubber company."

Acting Captain Warms and Chief Engineer Abbott were charged with misconduct, negligence, and inattention to duty; they were convicted.[7] Their guilty verdict still angers Mr. Torresson seven decades later. "If Warms and the others had been tried by a more knowledgeable court, such as an admiralty court, they would not have been convicted. The judge had no idea of the laws of the sea or Warms's quandary. The trial was unfair, and it made me mad. Warms's conviction was overturned the next year. He did everything he could aboard the *Morro Castle*. The conviction ruined him to a degree. Yet during World War II he was a four-stripe navy captain and Abbott served on troop transports. As a result of the *Morro Castle*, there were new laws to increase safety at sea. It tightened the regulations."

No person was ever charged with setting the fire, and no one is certain whether the cause was arson or accidental. Some think the blaze may have been started by radio operator George Alagna, who had caused problems for the Ward Line with labor agitation, and others suspect Chief Radio Operator George Rogers, who died in jail after being convicted of a murder unrelated to the *Morro Castle*. "Rogers later got a job with the Bayonne Police Department at the time when police started using radios. His boss, Lieutenant Vincent Doyle, had a hobby of raising tropical fish. Rogers told Doyle that he built a fishbowl heater and left it on a workbench. Doyle plugged it in, but it was a bomb. It didn't kill Doyle, but Rogers was convicted of attempted murder. He was let out early during World War II because the military needed qualified radio operators. After the war Rogers borrowed money from an elderly couple. When they needed it back, they mysteriously disappeared. Rogers told one of their friends that the old folks moved to Florida. The friend went to the police, who got a warrant and dug the bodies out of their basement. He went to jail for murder and died in the psych ward. He never said a word if he was involved the *Morro Castle* fire."

Mr. Torresson notes, "There's no one today alive who knows what started the *Morro Castle* fire. I don't know if Rogers started it. I don't know if it started in the writing room locker. The investigators couldn't pinpoint the location where it started, or the use of an accelerant."

Recent newspaper stories renewed his interest in the *Morro Castle*. "The local paper, the *Asbury Park Press*, printed stories about the ship that were full of errors, so I wrote letters to the editor. As one of the last people from the ship, I've given talks on the *Morro Castle*, and my intention has been to vindicate Captain Warms and Abbott, because the papers at the time made a circus out of the story. Other history books have jazzed up the story to make sales. In retrospect, the *Morro Castle* is a deep mystery with no solution. That's the bad part."

After the fire Mr. Torresson served in the army air corps during World War II and stayed in the service for more than thirty years, rising to the rank of colonel.[8]

Thomas Torresson Jr. passed away on August 11, 2005, at the age of eighty-eight.

NOTES

1. Thomas Gallagher, *Fire at Sea* (New York: Rinehart, 1959), 26.

2. Ibid., 34.

3. Ibid., 91.

4. Carol MacAllister, "The *Morro Castle*," *Atlantic Highlands Herald*, September 23, 2004, http://www.ahherald.com/news/2004/0923/morro_castle.htm (accessed July 5, 2009).

5. Gallagher, *Fire at Sea*, 125.

6. "Ward Line," House Flags of US Shipping Companies: W, http://fotw.fivestarflags.com/us~hfw.html#ward (accessed July 5, 2009).

7. Gallagher, *Fire at Sea*, 233.

8. "Col. (USAF Retired) Thomas S. Torresson Jr., 88, of Whiting, Manchester" [obituary], *Asbury Park Press*, August 13, 2005.

ADELLA WOTHERSPOON
The Final Survivor of the 1904
General Slocum Fire on the East River

"Anna was found with all her clothes on,
and even her hat was still fastened to her head by the elastic."

Prior to the September 11, 2001, terrorist attacks, the worst fire in New York City history was a 1904 blaze aboard the *General Slocum* excursion ship.[1] The largely forgotten *General Slocum* tragedy killed 1,021 of the approximately 1,300 passengers, mostly women and children. Six of the victims were related to Adella Wotherspoon, the last living survivor of the blaze, as well as the youngest. She was born on November 28, 1903, as Adele Martha Liebenow and was just six months old at the time of the fire; she later adopted the first name Adella.

Unlike the *Titanic*, which sank far from land, the burning *General Slocum* was never more than a few hundred feet from shore, so the disaster was visible to the public. The ship finally ran aground on an island in the East River. Besides taking more than one thousand lives, the fire also destroyed the thriving Little Germany community in the Lower East Side, of which Mrs. Wotherspoon's family was a part.

St. Mark's Lutheran Church, located on East Sixth Street, had arranged the seventeenth annual summer outing for its Sunday school children and their families for Wednesday, June 15, 1904. The plan was to ride the chartered steamboat *General Slocum* to Locust Grove on the Long Island Sound for an afternoon picnic.[2] The vessel, 264 feet long with triple decks, was one of the finest ships to sail through New York Harbor when it was first commissioned in 1891.[3] By 1904, however, it had been surpassed by newer boats. Unbeknownst to the church members, the wooden *General Slocum* was a floating tinderbox. Five weeks before the fire, two inspectors from the United States Steamboat Inspection Service boarded the ship

Young Mrs. Wotherspoon wearing a *General Slocum* mourning ribbon
public domain

The shoes Mrs. Wotherspoon's sister wore when she died
photo by Stuart Lutz

The white dress Mrs. Wotherspoon wore when unveiling the *General Slocum* memorial in 1905
photo by Stuart Lutz

The charred remains of the *General Slocum*
public domain

***General Slocum* victims who washed up on the shore**
public domain

and certified it as safe. They did not notice that a forward compartment, the one where the ship's electricity was generated, was full of flammable items like oily rags and lamp oil.[4] Similarly, the inspectors failed to cite the ship for lacking basic safety equipment: the immovable lifeboats were stuck to the hull with paint, the old life preservers were stuffed with crumbling cork, and the fire hoses were filled with holes.[5]

The old skipper, William Van Schaick, lived aboard the *General Slocum*; he was the only captain the boat ever had.[6] Captain Van Schaick was proud that he had never lost a passenger in fifty years of ferrying travelers.[7] His *General Slocum* crew, however, was inexperienced; the crew had never participated in a fire drill.[8]

On the clear morning of June 15, more than thirteen hundred people boarded the ship at the East Third Street Pier; the *General Slocum* was half filled to capacity.[9] The boat left the pier about 9:45 a.m. and steamed northward up the East River.[10]

Mrs. Wotherspoon explains, "I am the youngest living survivor of the *General Slocum*. I was six months old at the time, so don't expect me to remember it. I'm not certain if my family had been on similar excursions before. Mostly, it was women and children who were on the ship. I'm not sure exactly why my father went with us, but he probably took the day off. He was in the restaurant business somewhere around 13th Street, in Little Germany. So it was my mother, father, and their three children: me; Helen, who was six; and Anna, who was three. Also, my Aunt Martha, for whom I was named, went with her four children. And my Aunt Annie [Weber] and her husband, along with their two children; there was an eleven-year-old boy and an eight-year-old girl. These aunts were my father's two sisters."

At about 10:00, when the *General Slocum* had passed the northern tip of what is today known as Roosevelt Island, a deckhand noticed smoke. A fire of unknown origin had begun in the forward lamp room.[11] Unfortunately for the ship, it was about to pass through the most treacherous part of the river at this time, the perilous waters of Hell Gate. Attempts by the crew to douse the fire were fruitless, for the fire hoses were full of holes and thus useless.[12] Captain Van Schaick, steering the boat from the pilothouse atop the ship, soon learned of the blaze and remained calm until he was greeted by a wall of flames.[13] He rejected the idea of turning the boat hard to the left or right to make a quick landfall, instead charging for North Brother Island, a mile ahead; he hoped to run the dying ship aground there.[14] A flotilla of ships, hoping to rescue the passengers, trailed the *General Slocum*, which was now moving at full speed.[15]

The passengers, seeing the fire, panicked. A number of people tried to grab the life preservers, but they were stored on the ceilings, eight feet above the floor, and secured by wires that often refused to break.[16] Those preservers that were loosed were generally useless, since the cork had dried up over the years. Passengers who tried to lower the six lifeboats were unable to free them because they were stuck to the ship with dried paint.[17] Many of the church members, given the ugly choice of staying aboard a burning boat or jumping into the rushing waters, plunged in and quickly drowned.

Mrs. Wotherspoon is uncertain how she escaped once the fire started. "I assume someone helped me and my mother off the ship. She was very badly burned on her left side—she stayed until her clothes were nearly all burned off. She held the [ship] railing as long as she could, then dropped either onto a boat or in the water. I'm not sure if my father was burned or not. He died when I was seven from TB. My sister Helen was never identified, and we think she was buried in the mass grave at the Lutheran Cemetery [in Queens]. Anna was found with all her clothes on, and even her hat was still fastened to her

**Mrs. Wotherspoon
at the time of the interview**
photo by Stuart Lutz

head by the elastic. She too was buried in the plot. My father got some money for her funeral, but it wasn't like the way people are compensated now."

The beaches of the East River were eventually filled with both corpses and frantic passengers searching for relatives. "My Aunt Martha was one of the identified dead. I know Aunt Annie gave an interview at the scene. She was terribly burned from trying to get the life rafts off the ceiling. She scratched with her fingernails, but the rafts were painted on fast. She died a year later and is buried in the plot in the Lutheran Cemetery." Mrs. Wotherspoon's family suffered six deaths: her two older sisters, her two aunts, and two of her cousins. "My mother said my father walked the streets for weeks and was always at the morgue, looking for Helen."

"There is one story from Aunt Annie," Mrs. Wotherspoon notes. "Survivors from the family got together at the hospital. There was a woman looking for her baby, and thought I was him. She was searching for a boy, and my mother said I was a girl. I don't know if that poor woman ever found her son . . ." her voice trails off.

As word of the disaster spread, there was panic in Little Germany.[18] St. Mark's Church alone lost half its membership.[19] "The Little Germany community broke up as a result, and many moved uptown to the brownstones. There were many classroom seats empty. Families couldn't bear to go back to their old quarters. They used to put a ribbon on the door for each death, and used white for children. Some ribbons went all the way up the door. Our family moved all the way up to 123rd Street as a result. After my father died, my mother had friends in New Jersey, and one of them had a hotel in Plainfield. They convinced my mother that it was easier to raise a child in the country, so she found a place here in Watchung [New Jersey]. I thought the country was wonderful."

The fire and the death of her two daughters scarred Mrs. Wotherspoon's mother for life. "She never talked about the *General Slocum* unless I asked," she observed. "She never dwelled on it. She died at seventy-five, and my parents are buried in Middle Village [New York]. Growing up, I knew I once had a couple of older sisters. My mother told me that they were killed on the *Slocum*. As a child, I remember people discussing the ship with her. Also, we would go to Long Island every year for an annual memorial ceremony. We would take a ferry there, and I distinctly remember her pacing the deck during the ten-minute trip."

One of young Adella's most important roles with the *General Slocum* fire was as a poignant reminder of the fire. On the first anniversary of the disaster, she donned a new white dress. She and her parents went to the Queens cemetery where more than sixty unidentified dead from the fire were buried. Over ten thousand people were there, awaiting the unveiling of a statue commemorating the tragedy. Eighteen-month-old

Adella stepped up and pulled the cord to unveil the monument. Today Mrs. Wotherspoon returns every year on June 15 to the monument for the annual memorial ceremony.

Captain Van Schaick, who showed great personal heroism by not abandoning ship until he had beached it, was badly burned. In 1906 Van Schaick was tried for criminal negligence. The prosecution argued that the captain was derelict for steaming to North Brother Island, while the defense argued that he should be found innocent since the inspectors had certified the ship.[20] Mrs. Wotherspoon played an important role in the captain's trial, reminding the jury of the scope of the tragedy. One New York newspaper wrote of her that "[t]he most remarkable witness at the *Gen'l Slocum* disaster trial . . . is Adele Liebenau [sic], 2 years and 2 months old, the youngest survivor of that awful holocaust. Although too young to go on the stand, the mute testimony of her presence has been sufficient to bring tears to the eyes of nearly everyone who passed through the ordeal of fire and flood on the ill-fated vessel."[21]

Van Schaick was convicted of criminal negligence and sentenced to ten years at the infamous Sing Sing Prison. After remaining free on appeal, he reported to jail in 1908. His supporters gathered more than a quarter million signatures on a petition, and in 1911 a parole board freed him.[22] Mrs. Wotherspoon is sympathetic toward the captain, however. "I guess he could have docked earlier," she sighs. "But my mother told me that the captain claimed the women aboard didn't want to get their shoes muddy. At his trial, he argued that if he docked at another port, he could have spread the fire." She stops her narration. "I just don't know. He kept going, and the longer we were on the river, there was more wind and the fire got worse."

In the collective American mind, the *General Slocum* fire is not as well remembered as a similar maritime accident—the loss of the *Titanic*—or the far less deadly Triangle Shirtwaist

Factory fire. Mrs. Wotherspoon thinks she knows the reason for this: "The *Slocum* people were very poor or middle class. They were often German immigrants. The *Titanic* and other ships had celebrities. It was just a matter of it happening to another group of people. The Triangle Shirtwaist Factory was in reach of people. You can go to where it happened. The *Slocum* was a moving boat."

Mrs. Wotherspoon points to a group of objects lying on a large table in the corner. "I've opened my collection to the public so the fire is not forgotten," she states. "And after I die, the New York Historical Society will get everything." She has two black leather children's shoes tied together. "Those were the ones Anna was wearing aboard the *Slocum*." She points out a small white dress with lace on the bottom. "This is what I wore when I pulled the cord at the monument," she explains. Mrs. Wotherspoon shows a black-and-white photograph of herself in the white dress, wearing a black ribbon memorializing the *General Slocum*. She then displays the original ribbon seen in the nearly century-old image. She also pulls out a newspaper clipping from shortly after the fire; it is entitled "Youngest Survivor At *Slocum* Trial" and it shows her mother, draped in black, clutching a young Adella on her lap. There is also a 1906 deed from the Lutheran Cemetery, made out to Paul Liebenow. It showed that he paid $240.00 for a plot to bury Anna.

Mrs. Wotherspoon points to a thick album on the other end of a long table. She introduces it, stating, "My father made these scrapbooks. It was a form of therapy." Until his death, her father scoured all the New York newspapers for any mention of the *General Slocum* and glued the articles in the scrapbook's pages; many of the articles are in German. The opening page is from a June 16, 1905, paper, and the story is headed "Youngest *Slocum* Survivor, A Baby, Unveils The Monument." The album contains a subpoena dated June 24, 1904, from the

Coroners' Court to her father concerning "the *Gen'l Slocum* disaster." One of the most moving letters in her scrapbook, dated July 19, 1904, is from the Executive Committee of Citizens Relief Committee; it forwarded Mr. Liebenow $91.00 for the burial of Anna. A July 15, 1905, letter from the Organization of the *General Slocum* Survivors thanks young Adele Liebenow for her unveiling of the monument. Another letter from a lawyer offers to represent the Liebenow family in a lawsuit.

The telephone rings and Mrs. Wotherspoon answers it. After greeting the caller, she says, "No, I didn't hear about Mrs. Connelly." She is then silent for a half minute. "Well, I'm very sorry to hear that," she replies. "Mrs. Connelly had a very long life." She chats for a few minutes, then hangs up. "That was the *New York Times*. Mrs. Connelly died last night." Catherine Connelly of Connecticut was eleven when she escaped from the *General Slocum*. She was rescued by a passing tugboat, although she lost her mother, brother, and sister.[23] At her death, Mrs. Connelly was 109 and unable to communicate. Mrs. Wotherspoon pauses. "That makes me the last one," she sighs.

"It's been a long and happy life, in spite of the beginning," she muses. "The *General Slocum* fire never made that much of an impression, I think since it happened when I was so young."

Mrs. Wotherspoon taught high school in New Jersey for decades before retiring. She married James Wotherspoon but had no children. Shortly after her passing, all her family's possessions related to the disaster were exhibited at the New York Historical Society.

Adella Wotherspoon died on January 26, 2004, at age one hundred, five months before the centennial of the disaster.

NOTES

1. James Joyce referred to the *General Slocum* disaster in *Ulysses*, for the tragedy occurred the day prior to Bloomsday. One character utters about the fire, "Terrible, terrible! A thousand casualties. And heart-rending scenes. Men trampling down women and children. Most brutal thing." See "Remembering the *General Slocum*," WNYC, June 15, 2004, http://www.wnyc.org/news/articles/39297 (accessed July 28, 2009).

2. Edward T. O'Donnell, *Ship Ablaze* (New York: Broadway Books, 2003), 37.

3. Ibid., 9.

4. Ibid., 54.

5. Ibid., 51–53.

6. Ibid., 7–8.

7. Ibid., 55.

8. "Adella Wotherspoon, Last Survivor of *General Slocum* Disaster, Is Dead at 100," *New York Times*, February 4, 2004, B8.

9. O'Donnell, *Ship Ablaze*, 84.

10. Ibid.

11. Ibid., 99.

12. Ibid., 105.

13. Ibid., 106–107.

14. Ibid., 126–27.

15. Ibid., 134–35.

16. Ibid., 118.

17. Ibid., 120.

18. Ibid., 191.

19. Ibid., 298.

20. Ibid., 306.

21. This quote came from an unidentified newspaper, dated November 27, 1906, kept in Mrs. Wotherspoon's father's scrapbook. He often did not note which paper he had cut articles from.

22. "Adella Wotherspoon, Last Survivor of *General Slocum* Disaster, Is Dead at 100."

23. "Catherine Connelly, 109; Escaped *Slocum* Fire," *New York Times*, October 19, 2002, A15.

Part 3

Witnesses to Technological Innovation

ARTHUR BURKS
The Last Major Designer of the ENIAC,
the First Electronic General-Purpose Computer

"I was in charge of the high-speed multiplier.
I contributed the plan for the master programmer.
I was the only one to check all the circuits of the ENIAC."

Computers are so ubiquitous and important to modern society that it is difficult to remember that the first electronic programmable machine was created less than seventy years ago. One of the first attempts to create an electronic computer was carried out in the late 1930s by John Atanasoff, an Iowa State College professor, with the help of his student Clifford Berry. The resulting Atanasoff-Berry Computer, or the ABC, was the first electronic computer, and it was powered by vacuum tubes.[1] The ABC was designed to solve sets of twenty-nine simultaneous equations.[2] Its development was abandoned soon after World War II erupted.[3]

During World War II the American military was interested in developing a computer to calculate artillery trajectories. As a result, the Moore School of Electrical Engineering at the University of Pennsylvania created the Electronic Numerical Integrator And Computer, or ENIAC. The ENIAC, powered by thousands of hot vacuum tubes, occupied a very large room and gobbled 140 kilowatts of power. Compared to today's powerful computers, the ENIAC had very little capacity. Its answers were not displayed on a colorful flat-screen monitor but were spit out on IBM punch cards.

John Mauchly and J. Presper Eckert were the two major figures behind the development and construction of the ENIAC. In 1947 Mauchly and Eckert filed a patent for the ENIAC; it was issued in 1964 and eventually passed to the Sperry Rand

Corporation. As with many technological advances, there was a patent lawsuit in the 1970s over the computer's invention. In 1973 Judge Earl R. Larson ruled in *Honeywell v. Sperry Rand* that the ABC was the first electronic computer, not the ENIAC, as Sperry Rand had asserted. While the ABC certainly influenced the later ENIAC, the technical difference between the two was that the ABC was not programmable; it could solve only one type of mathematical problem.

Dr. Arthur Burks is the only computer scientist still living who made major design contributions to the ENIAC. Wearing a professorial gray blazer, he gives a guided tour of the legendary computer, currently located in the University of Michigan's Electrical Engineering and Computer Science building. He walks past students typing away on the latest wireless laptops, oblivious that the grandfather of their machines is strolling by.

"The ENIAC was the first general-purpose programmable electronic computer," he explains in a precise voice as we walk through the halls. "It started a revolution in computers. The ENIAC could not only do addition and subtraction, but it could also multiply, divide, and take square roots. It had a write-read-erase numerical memory and a read-only program memory. An electronic digital computer is a very sophisticated logic machine. This is the link between philosophy and computers. Circuits do 'ors' or 'nots' or 'if/then' commands.

"Ten percent of the ENIAC is here," he explains as he points to the eight feet of ominous-looking computer that has been retired to a sunlit brick atrium. "In the mid-1950s, when the ENIAC [had] outlived its usefulness, it was disassembled and stored in a Quonset hut at the Aberdeen Proving Ground. I was able to get some of it moved up here."

There is a space between the back of the computer and the wall that allows visitors to get a close view of the hundreds of vacuum tubes lining the machine. Dr. Burks points out how the vacuum tubes were cooled and data were entered into the

ENIAC. He motions to the thick wires running from one part of the computer to the other and to the numbered dials.

Dr. Burks asks a young lady walking by to take a photograph. She is wearing a backpack that probably contains a slim computer with thousands of times the power of the massive machine before her. After she snaps the picture, Dr. Burks asks her, "Do you know what this is?" She studies it for a moment, then guesses, "Some type of calculator?" before walking away.

Dr. Burks was born on October 13, 1915, in Duluth, Minnesota, where his father was a high school math teacher. "I was going to be a high school math teacher like my father. When I graduated in 1936, there were no jobs, so I decided to pursue another of my undergraduate interests, philosophy. I received my PhD from the University of Michigan in 1941 in philosophy, concentrating in logic and the philosophy of science."

He describes how he came to work on the ENIAC: "I was standing in line at the Michigan Theater when I ran into a math student named Charles Dolph, who had just graduated. He asked what I was going to do after I got my PhD. I told him I couldn't find a job. He informed me that there was a free government-supported course for math and physics students at the University of Pennsylvania's Moore School. I applied, and soon got a phone call accepting me.

"There were twenty-five students in this summer course. Eckert was in charge of the two labs, the electronics one, where Mauchly was a student, and the machinery one, where I was. At this time, I didn't even know how a vacuum tube worked!" he jokes. "I took over the machinery lab, since Eckert didn't want to do it. In fact, Eckert and Mauchly often talked together in the electronics lab as Mauchly began envisioning what would be the ENIAC. The dean made both Mauchly and me instructors at the end of the course, even though my PhD was in philosophy. I remained as a wartime instructor throughout the conflict. I had an exemption from the army, so I was not drafted. I also had a letter from the Moore School stating that I was doing important war work. For example, I worked with Mauchly on an airplane project and radar antennas. I also roomed with him for a year."

Dr. Burks remembers the two men who brought the ENIAC to life. "Eckert was an electronics wizard and brought his genius to the ENIAC. He was just getting his master's degree and was a rising electronics star at Moore. Mauchly was inquisitive and persistent. He knew a lot and was widely read, but was more of a visionary than an inventor. He was outstanding at absorbing new ideas, reflecting on them, and discussing them. Mauchly also knew how to frame important questions. For example, he got the ENIAC project off the ground when he asked Eckert if an electronic counter could work at one hundred thousand pulses a second. The two of them made a terrific team. I was a good supplement, for I had other knowledge that they didn't. It was harmonious."

Dr. Burks explains that Mauchly had visited Atanasoff in 1941. "Mauchly was inspired to build the Moore School a general-purpose computer that was programmable. Atanasoff's machine only solved one kind of problem. Irven Travis had the idea of using a computer to solve multiple problems. Then we got the ENIAC contract in May 1943. Eckert and Mauchly drew up a proposal as requested by Lieutenant Herman Goldstine, the army's liaison man with the Moore School. Goldstine was a mathematician who understood what we were trying to accomplish for the military. He presented the Eckert-Mauchly proposal in April 1943 to a committee headed by the mathematician Oswald Veblen. Veblen heard this idea while leaning back in his chair. He brought the chair down hard and said to the army colonel there, 'Simon, give Goldstine the money.' It was a civilian who made this decision. The original cost estimate was one hundred thousand dollars, but

Dr. Burks in front of a portion of the ENIAC housed at the University of Michigan
photo by Stuart Lutz

it kept increasing until it was finally five hundred thousand dollars.

"The computer research was done by Mauchly, Eckert, myself, and seven other engineers the school brought in. I

A young Dr. Burks in front of the massive ENIAC
photo courtesy Alice R. Burks

Dr. Burks in 1946
photo courtesy Alice R. Burks

began lab work on May 31, 1943, with Mauchly and Eckert. I had to get a security clearance and was told the ENIAC project was classified. We were ordered not to talk to anyone other than the Moore School design team about the ENIAC. No regular member of the faculty contributed to it technically. A Moore School professor, Carl Chambers, argued that it wouldn't be finished before the end of the war."

Dr. Burks recounts his important duties. "I worked with Eckert on the design of the electronic counting circuit, which is the basis of the accumulators. The twenty accumulators each held ten decimal digits and a sign, and they constituted the only write-read-erase memory. That was half of the machine. The ENIAC also had programming circuits all over its face. I diagrammed the program for these circuits to calculate an artillery shell trajectory, the first computer program ever to be executed. I was in charge of the high-speed multiplier. I contributed the plan for the master programmer. I was the only one to check all the circuits of the ENIAC. There were eighteen thousand vacuum tubes in it, and it was a big job. My undergraduate work in statistics was important when working with the ENIAC, for I had to estimate the failure rate for the computer. After Eckert and Mauchly, I was the next most important person there, you could say," he notes quietly.

The professor next identifies the others who helped create the ENIAC. "Harry Huskey was the one who designed the ENIAC's electronic equipment for input and output. He figured out how to connect the ENIAC's units to IBM's punch card reader and punch card printer. Another person who worked on the machine was Chuan Chu. He designed the divider and square-rooter under my help. You have to understand that earlier computers were used for arithmetic. The IBM machines, for example, were primarily used for payroll, so there was no need for division. Chu called me about 10:30 one night. He was having trouble with the ENIAC's divider.

He said it kept running and running and wouldn't stop. I asked what number he was trying to divide by. Finally, he answered sheepishly, 'Zero.' Now, you can't divide anything by zero. That was one contingency we hadn't planned for. Chu made very important contributions, as did T. Kite Sharpless and Robert Shaw."

There was a tremendous excitement among the designers as the ENIAC neared completion. "It was wartime, the computer was classified, and there was this pioneering spirit. And there were doubters, of course, who thought it wouldn't function. But none of us working on the ENIAC had any doubts it was going to work. The first thing we did was design the accumulators, and this was accomplished in about a year. In early August of 1944 the famous mathematician John von Neumann came to visit. He saw how the machine could solve sine, cosine, and exponential function problems. He was very impressed."

The goal of the ENIAC was to calculate artillery trajectories for battlefield use. "Every time the army designed a new gun and shell," Dr. Burks reveals, "it would fire the projectile through two coils in the basement of a building at Maryland's Aberdeen Proving Ground. These coils were made of copper and were located a hundred feet apart. The loops fed into an electronic circuit, and the results were used as a parameter for calculating projectile trajectories. They would calculate three thousand trajectories and this would be transformed by IBM punch cards into a firing table. That way, an artillery officer would know just how to aim the gun."

Dr. Burks was charged with introducing the machine to the public. "On February 1, 1946, I showed the ENIAC to reporters. They were impressed that it could add two numbers together five hundred times a second. The reporters were looking down when I did the first test and they missed it! So I did it again. The ENIAC's development made the *New York*

Times. Two weeks later, I demonstrated it for high-ranking army people. The army thought it had spent its money well. There was a banquet in a university dining hall. At the head table was a big button that Dean Pender pushed to symbolize the startup of the computer. I wasn't at this dinner, since I was getting ready to run the computer for the attendees.

"After the war, two fellows came from Los Alamos to use the ENIAC for an arithmetic calculation. It was classified work. The ENIAC was punching out cards all the time. They took a suitcase full of cards and shipped it back to Los Alamos with a cover letter stating, 'Gentlemen, here is your answer.'

"Not long after the dedication of the ENIAC on February 15, 1946, von Neumann offered me a job at the Institute for Advanced Study in Princeton to work on the institute's stored program computer. It was there that I coauthored with von Neumann and Goldstine the paper that provided the paradigm for nearly all computers to come.[4] I came back to the University of Michigan in the fall of 1946 as a professor of philosophy and then also of computer science. I have been here ever since. I started the first graduate program in computers. I did not imagine computers the way they are today. No one at the time could have.

"The ENIAC deserves credit for helping to foster the information age and the Internet. Of course, there is a downside. I found 217 spam messages in my inbox one day last week!" he chuckles.

Arthur Burks passed away on May 14, 2008, at age ninety-two.

NOTES

1. Alice R. Burks and Arthur W. Burks, introduction to *The First Electronic Computer: The Atanasoff Story* (Ann Arbor: University of Michigan Press, 1988), n.p.

2. *Dictionary of American History* (New York: Scribner's, 2002), 2:154.

3. Burks and Burks, *The First Electronic Computer*, 8.

4. Arthur W. Burks, Herman H. Goldstine, and John von Neumann, *Preliminary Discussion of the Logical Design of an Electronic Computing Instrument* (Princeton, NJ: Institute for Advanced Study, 1946).

PEM FARNSWORTH
The Final Witness to the First
Electronic Television Broadcast in 1927
"Eventually, the world would beat a path to our lab door."

Most people recall that the Wright brothers invented the airplane, Alexander Graham Bell created the telephone, and Thomas Edison perfected the lightbulb. The prime inventor of one of the twentieth century's most widely used electronic items—the television—should be a household name, but sadly, Philo Taylor Farnsworth is nearly forgotten. In 1957 Farnsworth appeared on the television quiz show *I've Got a Secret*, but none of the contestants could identify him. Fortunately, the host downplayed this ignominy when he quipped, "We'd all be out of work if it weren't for you."[1] In 1927 Farnsworth made the first successful electronic television broadcast. His wife, who also served as his laboratory assistant, Elma "Pem" Farnsworth, is the final witness to that technological revolution. Mrs. Farnsworth, who was born in 1908 and was married to Philo on May 27, 1926, lives in a modest green house on a quiet street in Fort Wayne, Indiana. She has a small television satellite dish attached to the roof of her home, near the chimney. Her living room is cluttered with some old television sets at one end and a few portraits of her husband on the walls.

Philo Farnsworth was not the first person to attempt to show moving pictures on a small screen. Shortly before Farnsworth's development, the Englishman John Logie Baird and the American Charles Francis Jenkins succeeded in showing images on a small screen.[2] Their techniques, however, used intricate mechanical spinning discs, and the resulting image was of low quality. Farnsworth was the first one to perfect the all-electronic television, which is far clearer and much less complicated than the mechanical version. For nearly the entire twentieth century, people watched electronic televisions derived from Farnsworth's invention.

Philo T. Farnsworth, who was called Phil, was born in a log cabin near Beaver, Utah, on August 19, 1906.[3] He moved several times when he was young and eventually settled on a ranch nearby Rigby, Idaho.[4] His family first saw his mechanical ability when, as a young boy, he repaired the family's electric generator.[5] He was fascinated with the photoelectric cell and electricity. Soon thereafter, he won a national contest with an invention to prevent cars from being stolen.[6] One of his farm jobs was plowing the fields. He would guide the horses up one row, then neatly steer them down the next. Using the plowing of the rows as his inspiration, he thought he could transmit pictures through the air the same way; he would use an electron gun to "shoot" the picture at a screen, one horizontal row at a time. His proposal was certainly a simpler idea than the mechanical disc invention, and it required no moving parts. He was only fourteen at the time of his inspiration.[7]

The next year, in 1921, young Farnsworth explained his idea to his flabbergasted high school science teacher. He even drew a sketch of the camera, known as the Image Dissector, and gave it to the teacher. Making this drawing proved to be a fortuitous move many years later.[8] He enrolled at Utah's Brigham Young University but never graduated college.

In 1926 Farnsworth explained his radical television idea to a group of wealthy men who agreed to finance his dream. In the autumn of that year he established his laboratory at 202 Green Street in San Francisco.[9] Mrs. Farnsworth recounts in a slightly hoarse voice, "We had that bare loft on Green Street in San Francisco. Phil asked the bankers for twenty-five thousand dollars for one year. The crew was my brother and I, and we put our whole lives into it. We wanted to have a studio but didn't have enough money to do it. At one point, Phil's friend Skee Turner went to Europe and returned with some money,

The young Mrs. Farnsworth on television in 1931
photo courtesy Kent M. Farnsworth
and the Farnsworth Archives

**Mrs. Farnsworth at the
time of the interview**
photo by Stuart Lutz

and they thought that would be enough to create a better studio, but the president of their company said that money was better used for next year's budget."

Without the benefit of a local electronics store, Farnsworth learned to blow the unusually shaped glasses needed for his cameras and cathode ray tubes.[10] On September 7, 1927, twenty-one-year-old Farnsworth was ready for a television demonstration. His assistant, Cliff Gardner, the brother of his wife, was in the next room. On Farnsworth's instruction, Gardner put a slide with a line etched on it before the camera. In the next room, the line appeared clearly on the screen. Gardner then turned the slide ninety degrees, and the televised image similarly turned. In one of the understatements in history, Farnsworth announced, "That's it folks! There you have it. Electronic television."[11] Shortly thereafter, when showing his invention to some backers, Farnsworth asked Gardner to blow cigarette smoke near the camera; the result was the first electronic television transmission of a moving picture.[12] On September 1, 1928, Farnsworth demonstrated his device at a press conference, and shortly thereafter his backers created a company named Television, Inc.[13] "I knew that his television would succeed," she remembers. "We knew that eventually the world would beat a path to our lab door. I was away from my family for several years while the television was being perfected. My younger sister saw a newsreel about the television in a theater. She jumped up and shouted, 'There's my sister!'

"When I married Phil, I knew I was also marrying television. We decided to have a family after three years of marriage. I told Phil, 'I'm not going to have a family and live in an apartment. When we have a child, we will buy a home.' Our family was among television's first advertisers. To show how simple the television was to operate, we had a living room set up with a TV in it and a newsreel filmed us. Our first son, Philo, who was about six, asked, 'Mother, can we watch TV?' I said he could turn it on, and he did it to show people how easy it was to operate."

Dr. Vladimir Zworkin, working at the same time as Farnsworth, also attempted to develop electronic television while working for Westinghouse. He applied for a patent in 1923, which was finally granted in 1938. In 1929 he presented a paper on his work; the conference was attended by David Sarnoff, president of the Radio Corporation of America (RCA). The next year Zworkin paid Farnsworth a visit at his San Francisco laboratory. Sarnoff gave Zworkin his own laboratory and Zworkin continued to improve the television.[14] By the early 1930s, people understood there was great money to be made in television—and the financial battle was on. In 1934 Farnsworth filed a patent infringement suit against Zworkin, contending that Farnsworth was the inventor. Farnsworth's strong claims were upheld that year, and again in 1936 by an appeals court.[15] Farnsworth's high school teacher, who still had the old drawing the teenage inventor made of television, provided key testimony upholding Farnsworth's patent applications. In 1939 an unhappy Sarnoff signed a nonexclusive licensing arrangement with Farnsworth, and that same year many people were first introduced to television at the World's Fair in New York. During World War II the government suspended the manufacture of televisions, which was a deathblow to Farnsworth's company. He was unable to compete with the much larger RCA after the war.

"We had our adversary in David Sarnoff and RCA," Mrs. Farnsworth notes without bitterness. "They went to any length to erase Phil from the history books. We relocated near Philadelphia in 1931. In 1934 we were down at the Franklin Institute in Philadelphia and we made a television demonstration. We later went back to Philadelphia and they had no record of our being there. RCA, who also made a demonstration, somehow managed to erase any record of our being there." Mrs. Farnsworth does not receive any royalties for her husband's revolutionary invention. "The patent rights are good for seventeen years [the Farnsworth patents terminated about 1944]. Phil knew it would be a long war with RCA, and by the time it was over his patent rights would have expired."

The Farnsworth family celebrated the seventy-fifth anniversary of the first television broadcast. "We were planning to go to San Francisco to see the lab. The people who occupied the building were going to let us in. We put up some money for it, but at the last moment, they said no. In 2002 I was invited to the Emmys to spotlight both me and the Sarnoffs on the seventy-fifth anniversary of television. I didn't want to go! I haven't forgiven Sarnoff. I was prompted that I had to go or else it would look like I was wearing a big chip on my shoulder. So I went, so no one thought I was holding any grudges. There, Thomas Sarnoff, the son of David, shook my hand. After the program, we all went to dinner, and he brought his wife to meet me. We all had our photo taken together. I've been on TV a few times in the last few years. There was one show where the preamble was shocking—there were more four-letter words in it! I told them I would not go in person to receive the award, but I'd be happy to do so when they cleaned up their act.

"I was recently made a lifetime member of the Academy of Television Arts and Sciences." She searches a table and finds her prestigious membership card. "There are very few of these around."

According to his wife, Mr. Farnsworth's "favorite television moment was the moon landing. It was the best event we ever watched on television. The camera for that followed Phil's plan. It was a receiving and sending unit about the size of cigar. Every early space shot had one of these, and we could see what the astronauts could see. When Armstrong was on the moon, Phil said to me that seeing it made it all worthwhile. He was again right. Phil always said television would make us a global community, since we could see things happening around the world."

She jokes with an easy laugh about the number of sets she has in her house. "I have about seven televisions, but none of them seem to work right now. I have one of the Farnsworth French Provincial sets! The tube broke and someone shipped a replacement one to me, but I don't have anyone to put it in."

Farnsworth continued to invent throughout his life. "No longer are inventions done solo, but people are brought in to help the inventor. But they always boil down to one person first. Phil never patented anything to do with the livelihood of people. He always put it this way, 'I am a conduit through which things were given to people.' We lost our second son to strep throat. So Phil invented an isolette, or incubator. He told ITT [International Telephone & Telegraph] that he would work on fusion if they agreed to give it to the starving countries. He trained engineers from those countries. But he concluded that the world was not advanced enough to handle fusion for everyone, and Hitler was an example of that. When he knew he only had a few years of life left, he wanted to solve the problem of human waste before we were covered up by it." During World War II, Japanese snipers were climbing trees and shooting American troops as they went by. "Phil invented a sniper scope with IR [infrared] to see in the dark. He put it on a soldier's gun." Yet after the war he had another reversal when "he had a nervous breakdown and went to Maine. We had three thousand acres of woodlands there. In 1947 our house burned in a forest fire.

"His whole life Phil said he wanted to go into space, and he never gave up that dream until the last six months of his life. He predicted that in space, there would be as much to learn on the microscopic level as the macroscopic. There will be a time when we discover units so small that we cannot see them, but only know of their presence by our reaction to them."

Today Mrs. Farnsworth works hard to make her husband's name known. "Everything I do is to ensure Phil's name recognition. My family recently formed the Philo T. Farnsworth Foundation. Also, there is a group getting together of people who lived a century, and they are filming a video. Now, I haven't had that century achievement yet, but I wanted to be in it because it would publicize his achievements. I wrote my husband's biography, entitled *Distant Vision*. *Distant Vision* didn't just mean television. It meant seeing the future. The world is finally catching up to the things he told me. He said there would be a picture on your wall, which now we have with these very large televisions. My biggest aim is to let children know who they are and why they are here. I can't do it anymore because of my age, but I used to go into schools a lot and challenge the students to visualize the future they want to have. If they can see it badly enough, they can do it, though they will have to work for it. One day, they will be the bosses, and it's never too early to get them thinking about the future."

After losing control of his beloved television invention, Farnsworth fell into a depression, eventually sold his interests to ITT, and later worked on nuclear fusion research. He died in 1971 in Utah. "My husband is buried in Provo, Utah, with a double headstone. All that is needed for me is the date. He wrote his own epitaph: 'He loved his fellow man.'"

In 1999 *Time* magazine reviewed the greatest scientists and thinkers of the past century; the prestigious list included Albert Einstein, the Wright brothers, Jonas Salk, and Sigmund Freud. The magazine told Phil Farnsworth's forgotten tale and tried to resuscitate his name, noting that "we ought not to let the century expire without attempting to make amends."

Pem Farnsworth died on April 27, 2006, at age ninety-eight.

NOTES

1. Russell Roberts, *Philo T. Farnsworth: The Life of Television's Forgotten Inventor* (Bear, DE: Mitchell Lane, 2003), 43.

2. *Dictionary of American History* (New York: Scribner's, 1976), 7:21.

3. Elma G. Farnsworth, *Distant Vision: Romance and Discovery on an Invisible Frontier* (Salt Lake City, UT: PemberlyKent, 1989), 23.

4. John A. Garraty and Mark C. Carnes, eds., *American National Biography* (New York: Oxford University Press, 1999), 7: 726.

5. Farnsworth, *Distant Vision*, 33.

6. Ibid., 36.

7. Ibid., 37.

8. Ibid., 39.

9. Ibid., 68.

10. Ibid., 73–74.

11. Ibid., 90.

12. Ibid., 97.

13. Ibid., 108.

14. Garraty and Carnes, *American National Biography*, 24: 270–71.

15. Ibid., 7:727.

ROBERT HALGRIM
The Last Man Alive to Work with Thomas Edison

"[Edison] told me 'You've had more education than me, and I've done all right.' So while I didn't get a degree, I sure got an education!"

In 1999 *Life* magazine ranked the most influential people of the previous millennium. History's greatest inventor, Thomas Alva Edison, was rated first, besting luminaries like Christopher Columbus, Albert Einstein, George Washington, and Johannes Gutenberg. Edison patented more than one thousand items, such as the phonograph and the lightbulb, and it is easy to take for granted how much he helped create modern life. Seventy years after the inventor's death in 1931, Robert Halgrim of Fort Myers, Florida, is Edison's last-surviving employee.

Edison, born in 1847 in Milan, Ohio, later moved to Port Huron, Michigan. His formal schooling totaled three months, supplemented by his mother's tutoring. He was a prolific reader, with an unending curiosity and an unmatched work ethic. At age fifteen he lost most of his hearing. Also at this time he became manager of a telegraph office, and this work provided him with the inspiration for his first invention, a transmitter and receiver for an automatic telegraph. By twenty-one, he had produced his first major commercial invention, a stock ticker. He sold it for forty thousand dollars, and with the proceeds he established a laboratory in Newark, New Jersey, which he soon relocated to Menlo Park. In 1877 he created a phonograph, using wax cylinders to capture sounds.

The following year he focused on creating an electrical light and spent months trying hundreds of different filaments. On October 21, 1879, his lamp glowed for forty straight hours. Since there was no electrical system in the United States at that time, his light was not commercially feasible. In 1882 he opened the first central power station; it was located in Lower Man-

**Mr. Halgrim
at the time of the interview**
photo by Stuart Lutz

hattan and could illuminate more than seven thousand lights. While experimenting with bulbs, he discovered what would come to be known as the Edison effect, in which electricity flows from a hot filament across a vacuum to a wire. This was the basis of much of the twentieth century's electronics.

History would remember Edison if he invented just the electric light and the phonograph, but he continued by designing the movie projector and establishing the first film studio. He also experimented with microphones, concrete houses, trees that produce rubber, and storage batteries.[1] Thomas Edison died on October 18, 1931.

Mr. Halgrim's modest Florida ranch house is a private shrine to history's greatest inventor. A pristine phonograph player with a huge flowered bell guards the front door. "That phonograph is over one hundred years old. I bought it in Canada," Mr. Halgrim explains as he lays in a blue recliner. "It plays as good as ever." There is also a small statue of Edison and a larger bust of the inventor. Ironically, Mr. Halgrim shuns using lightbulbs, giving his residence a gloomy mood.

P E T I T I O N
- - - - o - - - -

TO THE COMMISSIONER OF PATENTS, OTTAWA:

The petition of Thomas Alva Edison, of Llewellyn
Park, in the County of Essex and State of New Jersey, Inventor, showeth:

That he has invented new and useful Improvements in
Process of Duplicating Phonograms, not known or used by others
before his invention thereof, and not being in public use
or on sale, for more than one year previous to his application, in Canada, with his consent or allowance as such inventor.

Your petitioner therefore prays that a patent may be
granted to him for the said invention, as set forth in the
specification in duplicate sent herewith, and for the purpo-
ses of the Patent Act of 1872, your petitioner elects his
domicile in the City of Ottawa, Province of Ontario.

Signed at Orange, Essex County, State of New Jersey,
this ~~~ day of August 1888.

Thomas Alva Edison

**Thomas Edison's signed application to obtain a Canadian patent
on his improvements in duplicating phonograph records**
photo courtesy Stuart Lutz

Robert Halgrim was born in Humbolt, Iowa, on September 9, 1905. Geographic luck played a role in his meeting Edison, who wintered in Fort Myers. "Around 1920 my father, Colonel Halgrim, ran a silent movie theater in Fort Myers." He speaks slowly yet deliberately. "Whenever a new movie was showing, Mr. Edison wanted to be notified. He would set a date and bring in guests for a private viewing. I was the one who would show the guests to their seats, and on many occasions I was also the one who showed the film. Here's the interesting thing. Mr. Edison was deaf, so he was only able to hear the music by the vibrations from the piano player, this being before 'talkie' movies."

Mr. Edison brought his grandchildren to Fort Myers for the 1924 Christmas vacation. "He had asked the local Boy Scout leader who would be a good teacher and nanny for them. I was nineteen and in the Scout troop, so I was recommended and hired. I took care of the children, and many times I went up to New Jersey to care for them there. I really felt I was a personal friend of the family, and Mrs. Edison told me she wanted me to be a part of the family. I lived in his home in New Jersey, there in Llywellyn Park. Once they took me to Edison's box at Carnegie Hall and I watched a play with him. He also gave me a party on Broadway."

Edison furthered Mr. Halgrim's formal education. "After I tutored the grandchildren, the Edisons decided that I should go to college. He paid for me to attend Cornell. In exchange for helping me through college, I would stay with them and look after the grandchildren. I went to Cornell for three years, but he took me out of school. He decided that if I hadn't learned all that I could in three years, he'd teach me whatever else I needed to know. He told me, 'You've had more education than me, and I've done all right.' So while I didn't get a degree, I sure got an education! My one disappointment is I never graduated from college."

"I went to work as his personal assistant and did that until his death. I was part of the 'Insomnia Squad.' I got to work at seven in the morning, and there were always people around to see him. One of my most important duties was to insist Mr. Edison eat the special diet he was given, since he was a diabetic. So every two hours I had to go in and make sure he ate. There were times he didn't want to. So I was given instructions to leave him alone for five minutes, then come back. If he hadn't eaten, I was to sit down and wait until he finished, which he normally did at that time. His diet consisted of strained spinach, herring, and a solution of a milky substance that came from seaweed. Back then, I guess it seemed to work since he lived to a ripe old age." He cackles at the thought of the unappetizing meal.

Soon Edison gave Mr. Halgrim scientific work. "Edison correctly predicted after World War I that we were going to have another war," he continues, "and rubber is the only thing that we don't produce in the United States. And we needed rubber for cars. So I worked in his nursery, which consisted of growing twenty-by-forty-foot beds of goldenrod. It was hoped to grow a plant that could be harvested in a year to use for rubber. Mr. Edison even set up factories for the tire manufacturer Harvey Firestone, knowing that the need for rubber and tires was going to be enormous.

"Mr. Edison was terrific to work for. He had a great sense of humor. If he saw someone was having trouble at work or getting irritated with a problem, Mr. Edison would go over to him, involve him in a joke, thus relaxing him, and then the worker could turn around and do what he had to do. But he also taught me a great life lesson. Once he caught me standing around just a few minutes before work was over for the day. He approached and asked me what I was doing. I replied that I had done everything for the day. So Mr. Edison told me to go and get a large glass cube and a hacksaw. Mr. Edison told me to cut the glass into one-inch cubes. I was irritated, since there were electric-powered saws in the lab and he wanted me to use an old saw. It took me roughly two and a half hours to do it. I thought the task was stupid. Finally I told Mr. Edison that I was done. He asked me if I did the best I could do, and I said yes. He replied, 'That's all I ever ask of you. I wanted to see if you would do what I asked you to do, and you did it well, even though you were upset with me.'" Mr. Halgrim stops, then proclaims, "I've based a lot of my life on that lesson.

Mr. Halgrim (*standing behind the statue*) at the unveiling of a bust of Thomas Edison in the 1960s
reprinted by permission of the Edison and Ford Winter Estates

"Mr. Edison was a very disciplined and dedicated person. He expected the best from everyone around him, but didn't expect more than he could do. He'd always say, 'You can't succeed if you don't work' or 'Work is the key to success' or 'If a man can conceive of an idea, then he can find a solution for it.' He was seldom ever satisfied. It was work, work, work, and more work. Let me give you an example. Once, Mr. Edison and his wife, Mina, were having a party. He wanted to leave, so he would go out to the dock and pretend to be fishing. Since he couldn't hear the people anyway, people would leave him alone. They would assume he was busy fishing. He was just thinking of what he can do next. I learned he could hear more than he admitted. He used that as a crutch. If he wanted to hear you, he would.

"He was incredibly capable. He had twenty businesses going at once and ran them all," he recalls, shaking his head in amazement at Edison's abilities. "But he refused to delegate authority. Unfortunately, he didn't show others how to do things, and his businesses died with him. Did you know that you can't buy a single Edison product today?"

Mr. Halgrim believes that the phonograph was Edison's proudest achievement. "He felt that music elevated the spirit of man, and it is something that everyone understand and enjoys. It can soothe your moods and relax you—it makes people have fun together. The strongest point that sticks in my mind is that he couldn't hear it, but yet he could see the look on people's faces and see their feet tapping and their hands clapping. He knew this feeling was something that he created."

Despite his incredible and prolific success, Edison cared little for money. "He truly wanted to improve things for mankind. He wanted money only to get materials for more inventions. I was with him when Henry Ford and Firestone gave him $92,000 each to form the Edison Botanical Research Corporation. And do you know that Mr. Ford made three autos and named them after Edison? The Model T was for

'Thomas,' the Model A was for 'Alva,' and the Edsel was for 'Edison.' I think he named his son Edsel after Edison, but I can't say for sure. But I now wonder if Ford would have created the car if he knew what it was going to do to the world as far as wiping out our lands and putting roads down and having people driving away from each other. But here's a difference between Ford, who I didn't like, and Mr. Edison. If I asked Ford a question, he'd say, 'I'll tell you tomorrow,' and then would consult with others before answering. He didn't trust himself. If I asked Edison a question, he would answer it right away."

Yet Edison was not above playing pranks on people. Mr. Halgrim giggles when he remembers that "Henry Ford, the famous naturalist John Burroughs, and Edison took some women to the mountains to spend a weekend. Burroughs never slept outdoors, but always inside. It was so cold that Edison vowed to invent a fur-lined condom. Another time, at the shop, he turned a lathe slowly, and it had a roll of ball bearings on it. He then poured four inches of latex on it and kept turning the lathe. He shouted to the poor operator that his balls don't hang even. I think the smartest thing he ever said to me was that he didn't understand women and he didn't think anyone else did either."

Not long after Edison died, Mrs. Edison asked Mr. Halgrim if he wanted to be the curator for their winter home, which was being turned into a museum. "I said that I would enjoy it. She told the city of Fort Myers that she would donate the home only if I was the curator. I made many trips to New Jersey and brought much of the furniture down to Florida. I ran it until 1963, when I retired and passed it on to my son. I enjoyed the job tremendously. When I married, my wife, Mary, and I would go on trips and find things to put in the museum. When Ford sold his home to his city, the combination of the houses was overwhelming. The Ford and Edison Winter

**Mr. Halgrim driving Thomas Edison's 1914 Model T
in the annual Edison Pageant of Light parade in
Fort Myers on February 18, 1967**
reprinted by permission of the Edison and Ford Winter Estates

Estates is one of the biggest attractions in the Fort Myers area. We have a monthlong activity celebration with picnics and block parties. The last night of the celebration, we have the Pageant of Light, which was started by my brother. Now it is the biggest one in the world, and participants from all over America come to it. We are very proud of it here."

As the last living employee of the greatest inventor, Mr. Halgrim reflects on the advancements he has witnessed in his long life. "I think the automobile and airplane come to mind as the greatest changes because they brought the world closer together, for pleasure and business. The changes over the years have been so impressive that I don't even know what to think. How many people would ever have thought that we could fly to the moon or see images from the other side of the world in your living room? I still get surprised every now and then." Yet technology has not been completely beneficial to humanity, in his opinion. "I'm sorry to say the world is a sadder place because people are afraid to relate to each other anymore. Computers—they may be helpful—but I think they are the damnation of the future. They don't allow people to think for themselves and learn on their own. It's taken people from a family circle and forced them into individualism. People need each other, and the computer forces one person to be in front of it at any one time. Evenings are tied up with the computer instead of the family. We are definitely losing the family unity, which, in many ways, has caused a lot of the problems that we see today. I don't think we are ever going to get it back. Sometimes I wonder if all these inventions have done us any good in the long run," he sighs.

"I just feel lucky to have been in the right place at the right time. It's just too bad that more people didn't know Edison, since he left such a lasting impression on our lives as we see it today. I don't think of his inventions as much as I think of the way my life changed because of him.

"Look around you!" he chides. "Edison is present in many things we see today, from cement sidewalks to tubes for television images. You have to remember, he invented 1,087 different things in one way or another. There wasn't a thing he wasn't interested in! Many young people have no idea who he was or how he influenced daily activities, such as the radio, the CDs, the computer, the VCR, air-conditioning, and having cold milk for breakfast. It's all due to electricity, and children take it for granted, as I'm sure we all do. It's really hard to picture that one man could do all this. Think about it. Just the lightbulb brought about so many things.

"The thing that is so sad is that he kept all his knowledge to himself, so no one could carry on his thoughts and produce any of the things he made. When he died, it all went with him. It's a shame, but I cannot imagine anyone who has done more for the world as we see it today."

Robert Halgrim died at age ninety-nine on May 2, 2005.

NOTE

1. *The Academic American Encyclopedia*, 7:58.

HARRY MILLS
The Final Person to Hear the
First Commercial Radio Broadcast
"I let out a yip of some kind."

Today's ubiquitous commercial radio programming was not around ninety years ago. Early radio often consisted of two amateurs with homemade transmitters and receivers, communicating to each other using slow Morse code. It was one-on-one communication, too slow and clumsy to be profitable.

The story of commercial radio broadcasting begins with a Pittsburgh area scientist, Dr. Frank Conrad, who worked for the Westinghouse Electric Company. Every day, the Naval Observatory near Washington, DC, broadcast the exact time over the radio. In 1915 Conrad bet a friend that his watch was accurate and he could prove his point by comparing his watch's time to the Naval Observatory's time. Conrad built a radio receiver to listen to the observatory's transmission of the time.[1] On August 1, 1916, Conrad was granted a broadcast license by the Department of Commerce and assigned the call letters 8XK. He transmitted Morse code out of his garage in Wilkinsburg, Pennsylvania. His station lasted nine months until it was shut down because of World War I, but when the war ended in 1919 he resumed his programs.[2] In 1919 Conrad decided to transmit music instead of Morse code. Listeners from around the area wrote to him, requesting he play their favorite songs. He broadcast in two-hour blocks every Wednesday and Saturday night. An enterprising merchant offered to loan Conrad the records for the shows if he would, in exchange, mention the name of the store on the air. This was the first radio advertisement. Then, in September 1920, a Pittsburgh department store advertised that it was selling radio receivers, then known as crystal sets. People wanting to hear Conrad's popular broadcast could purchase them there.[3]

Mr. Mills sitting in front of his ham radio station at the time of the interview
photo by Stuart Lutz

Mr. Mills's license issued by Herbert Hoover
photo by Stuart Lutz

Harry Mills of Hendersonville, North Carolina, is perhaps the last man to hear Conrad's first commercial radio broadcasts.

Harry P. Davis, a Westinghouse vice president, saw the store's advertisement boasting that these receivers would let people "tune into the Westinghouse station."[4] Davis realized the moneymaking potential of Conrad's broadcasts; thousands of customers could be reached cheaply and simultaneously. On October 16, 1920, Westinghouse applied for a radio license, which was granted on October 27. The station was assigned the name KDKA. In another brilliant marketing move, KDKA decided to make its first commercial broadcast on the night of November 2, 1920. That was the evening of Election Day, and listeners were anxious to hear the results of the presidential contest between Warren Harding and James Cox.[5] The first KDKA "studio" was a shack on the roof of one of Westinghouse's buildings in East Pittsburgh.[6] As the election results came into the *Pittsburgh Post*, they were broadcast over KDKA.[7] As a result, voters did not have to wait to read the next morning's paper to hear that Harding would be the next president. Conrad was promoted to assistant chief engineer of Westinghouse; he died in 1941.[8] Sadly, the originator of commercial radio is almost completely forgotten today. His house was recently demolished, although his historic garage was dismantled for future assembly as a museum.

Mr. Mills's house has a gigantic radio antenna sprouting out of the side wall. He wears a professorial tweed jacket with a row of different colored pens neatly inserted in his shirt's breast pocket. He was born on September 19, 1907, in Beaver, Pennsylvania, about twenty-five miles from Pittsburgh. "When I was twelve, I joined the Boy Scouts and my folks, for Christmas, gave me the Scout handbook. The last chapter was how to build a wireless station. So I built a receiver and listened to it through earphones. It was quite crude, since there were no Radio Shacks back then. I built my own parts. The

Some of Mr. Mills's vacuum tubes
photo by Stuart Lutz

The spark transmitter
photo by Stuart Lutz

coil was an oatmeal box wrapped with wires. I used old telephone parts for earphones, but I couldn't hear out of them very well. And I can't remember for the life of me where I got the crystal from. I stretched out a wire for the antenna. And I've been into electronics ever since.

"Back then, there were also no radio stations per se, but just a bunch of amateurs talking to each other. When I [say] 'talking to each other,' it is not through voice, as we have today. Instead it was using Morse code's dots and dashes. 8XK was Frank Conrad's call. He had it all set up in his garage, and his wireless was set up with a spark signal. Well, this required equipment other than vacuum tubes, and he got his equipment through Westinghouse. One night I was listening to him in my room, and Conrad set up his phonograph next to his microphone. He said, 'Now, I'm going to send some music.' His voice startled me! I let out a yip of some kind. Dad got out of the bath and asked me if I was all right. We then shared headphones to listen to him. I had no idea where Conrad was broadcasting at the time." Mr. Mills never traveled to Conrad's garage and never met him.

Using the new radios, Mr. Mills helped the local newspaper, the *Beaver Times*, get the results of the 1920 election. "With this receiver, we tuned in to KDKA and got the presidential election results that went on for several hours during the evening. We posted the returns on the front window of the news office, and people outside could read them as they came in. To the best of my knowledge, this is the first time that election results were broadcast on the radio. KDKA was a pioneer in that field.

"After a few months, Conrad moved his station to the Westinghouse roof, and KDKA got its license in 1920. It didn't take advantage of its marketing and advertising potential for several years. It was merely a Westinghouse company promotion. Westinghouse would build receivers and sell them in

Mr. Mills and his family, circa 1963
photo courtesy J. Richard Mills

Pittsburgh department stores. I have one of those old original receivers. KDKA had no programming, and it was very chaotic. Someone would play piano or a company employee who could sing would go on the air, or someone else would play phonograph records. In fact, the record stores would loan the station disks to advertise the stores."

Mr. Mills received his first radio license in 1922 and his first commercial license in 1927. He explains, "There was no Federal Communications Commission then, so it was granted by the Federal Department of Commerce. Mine was issued by Herbert Hoover, the secretary of commerce. I had my own amateur station and I talked to people. I was the first one in my high school with a station. Of course, I had to do it at school since my mother wouldn't let me do it at home! Once I had my license, I went to sea for a year on a tanker. I was an omnivorous reader. I would fill up on books before leaving for sea. I wanted to try my hand at broadcasting, so about 1930 I went to Florida as the chief engineer of WMBR in Tampa. I spent a year there as the station's operator, and I then returned to Beaver. I built their police department's first radio.

"I have a degree in radio engineering. Back then, the only schools that taught this were Harvard, Michigan, and Cal Tech. None of them suited me or were affordable to me. I went to a local college, but I gave up since I wasn't getting what I wanted. Finally, Tri State College in Indiana gave wireless courses, and I took 1938 off to get a degree in radio engineering. Just before World War II, I trained pilots to get their radio license for flying. In exchange, they taught me to fly. I never got my pilot's license and haven't piloted since. I joined RCA during World War II and I installed the first radar for submarines. I spent the next thirty years with RCA, retiring in 1971."

He jauntily walks into a room filled with ancient machinery; it is reminiscent of a museum, with shelves of wizened vacuum tubes filtering the sunlight. "Let me show you some of the old radio equipment I still have in use." In the middle of the room is a formidable piece of equipment containing two circular coils and an ominous "High Voltage" sign on the front. There are two metal prongs facing each other with a small gap between them. Mr. Mills powers up the equipment, then presses a key to make a spark jump the narrow chasm between the prongs. "It's a spark transmitter," he clarifies. "In order to send Morse code over wireless, you need this device. You press the key in the 'dots' and 'dashes' to spell out words." He taps in the familiar SOS code of dot-dot-dot, dash-dash-dash, dot-dot-dot, and the sparks flutter in response. "I may very well have the only spark transmitter in the country. Finally vacuum tubes came along, and I didn't have to make all my radio parts by myself. The transistor has been an amazing development. Before it, everything used to be bulky and power hungry. There was no such thing as a portable device. It has revolutionized the electronics business. In fact, I have one of the earliest vacuum tubes in existence," he claims, pointing to it on the shelf.

Mr. Mills walks outside his home and opens the work shed behind his house. Inside are thousands of vacuum tubes of various sizes and types in storage boxes along the walls. In one corner, there are unopened boxes containing vintage radios from all over the country. "People are still sending me their old radios to fix," he says with a shrug. "Everyone's headaches end up on my bench. I also provide museums with examples of old radios."

Looking back on the development of radio, he comments, "The advent of broadcasting has been very great. We no longer need to rely on newspapers or magazines, since radio has brought information to people all over the world. It is a useful mode of communication, but can also be used for propaganda. For example, back in the 1930s the only source of information for ships near the North Pole was what they could get on radio. Even today, at the South Pole, the only way to talk to people is by ham radio. It's great for people in isolated places, and I know many missionaries use it. But radio means more than what you listen to in your car. Now there are satellite signals and the cell phone. The growth is amazing."

Mr. Mills is still true to radio's roots of two people speaking to each other one on one. "I still operate my ham radio every night," he admits, "and I speak to friends I've spoken to for fifty years now."

Harry Mills died on August 9, 2008, at the age of one hundred.

NOTES

1. Stanley Leinwoll, *From Spark to Satellite* (New York: Scribner's, 1979), 83–84.

2. Ibid., 84.

3. Ibid., 84–85.

4. Leonard Maltin, *The Great American Broadcast* (New York: New American Library, 1997), 3.

5. Leinwoll, *From Spark to Satellite*, 85–86.

6. Sam J. Slate and Joe Cook, *It Sounds Impossible* (New York: Macmillan, 1963), 15.

7. Leinwoll, *From Spark to Satellite*, 85.

8. "Dr. Frank Conrad, Radio Pioneer, Dies," *New York Times*, December 12, 1941.

JERRY MINTER
One of the Last People to Have Known
Edwin Armstrong, the Creator of FM Radio

*"[Armstrong] called me again to see if my plane was still available.
. . . The next day, he killed himself."*

The September 11, 2001, terrorist attacks on the World Trade
Center towers knocked out nearly all of the area's television
transmitters. The local stations scrambled to find an alterna-
tive antenna and settled on a seventy-year-old one just north-
west of New York City, in Alpine, New Jersey. This tower is
more than four hundred feet tall and sits on land five hundred
feet above sea level. The tower is significant because it was
built by Edwin H. Armstrong, the forgotten genius who created FM radio and the inventor of many of the devices that
enable modern radio.

Armstrong was born in 1890 in New York and raised in
Yonkers. He studied electrical engineering at Columbia University.[1] While still an undergraduate, he discovered the prin-
ciple of regeneration, which allows signals to be amplified
many times. He also designed the triode feedback circuit to
strengthen and amplify incoming radio signals.[2] Eventually
Armstrong was involved in a patent lawsuit over the regener-
ative circuit with fellow radio inventor Lee De Forest, which
Armstrong lost before the United States Supreme Court.[3]

During World War I, Armstrong served in France, where he
developed his second great invention, the superheterodyne
receiver. It revolutionized radio by combining two frequencies,
the incoming signal and a locally generated signal, to produce
a third signal that could be easily amplified. Today nearly all
radio and television tuners are based on this invention, though
it was not widely adopted until the end of the 1920s.[4] In 1920
Armstrong sold his feedback and superheterodyne patents to
Westinghouse for $335,000.[5] Armstrong's third great radio

invention came in 1921: superregeneration, which allowed very weak radio signals to be amplified to audible levels without having to use a tremendous amount of power to do so. The Radio Corporation of America purchased this patent.[6]

Armstrong's most famous development was frequency modulation (FM) radio. It is superior to amplitude modulation (AM) radio because it is subject to far less interference from static, such as the crackles produced by electrical storms.[7] Armstrong demonstrated it to RCA in 1934 and he set up an FM station in 1940.[8] After World War II the Federal Communications Commission changed the frequencies allotted to FM, instantly rendering a half million radio receivers obsolete.[9] In 1948 the lone inventor sued the giant RCA, whose president was David Sarnoff, over FM patent infringements.[10] Tired from years of legal fighting, Armstrong jumped from his New York City apartment window on the night of January 31, 1954. At the time of Armstrong's suicide, FM was dwindling, though it increased in popularity shortly after his death due to its superior quality over AM.[11] As one historian of science summarized Armstrong, "No inventor contributed more profoundly to the art of electronic communication."[12]

Jerry Minter lives in northern New Jersey, a half hour's drive from Armstrong's famous FM tower. He is one of the last people alive to have known Edwin Armstrong. Mr. Minter was born in Fort Worth, Texas, on October 31, 1913, and graduated from MIT. "I came up from Texas in 1935 and got a job with Boonton radio. I made test equipment for the United States Navy. Early radio was quite primitive. To select a station, you moved a loop antenna. AM doesn't have as good performance characteristics as FM. FM had more truthful fidelity. You can broadcast AM from here to California if you have enough power. You can send AM over the horizon. But even with high power, using AM you get static interference, such as when there is an electrical storm. There was a station

Mr. Minter at the time of the interview
photo by Stuart Lutz

in Cincinnati that used five hundred thousand watts of broadcast power. It was so much that farmers in the area couldn't turn off their lights. In Juarez [Mexico], there was a five-hundred-thousand-watt station that could broadcast anywhere in the United States."

Mr. Minter recounts the first time he ever met Armstrong. "The Radio Club of America was founded in 1909 and I went into New York City for their meetings. Armstrong was also in the club and he published papers in its journal. The first time I ever saw him was at a Radio Club meeting. I heard him give his original lecture on FM. It was very impressive. Another time, one club member gave a presentation on AM radio. He was deliberately spoofing Armstrong, and Armstrong was there. He got up and they had the biggest argument you ever saw! Armstrong was the type of guy who would get up and confront you," he remembers in his light Texas accent laid over a slightly hoarse voice.

Mr. Minter recounts being at Armstrong's apartment shortly before his suicide. "We were dinner guests at Armstrong's house. There were three servants there that night to serve us our meals. Mrs. Armstrong took us into a room with a large table piled with documents. She was upset and had papers all over the place. His apartment was neat, but the room with the papers was a total mess. A few months after the dinner, he called us on the phone, about Christmastime. First he spoke to my wife, then he spoke to me. He knew that I flew airplanes. He asked if I could fly him around to make measurements. He wouldn't say what it was, so I thought it was a classified military project. Someone told me it was for a low-frequency transmitter, about fifty kilocycles. Armstrong wanted to know how far I could go and if I could reach Pittsburgh.

"About a month later, he called me again to see if my plane was still available. I bought a converter for the plane with 150 watts of power, since the plane was wired for DC. The next day, he killed himself. What I later learned was that he had a disagreement with his wife, so Marion left him for Christmas to go to her sister's house. Armstrong had licensed some patents to RCA in 1922 and he was in court over this at the time. He was already very upset, and he got suicidal when she left him. I later learned that Armstrong called other people in those last days too."

Armstrong's death made the headlines, according to Mr. Minter. "There were some Radio Club members who were investigating his patents and his suicide. Armstrong was dealing with a lot of people, and they wanted to make certain it was a suicide and not a murder. I went to his funeral. The Radio Club arranged the funeral and there were many members there, of course. David Sarnoff was an honorary member of the Radio Club, but never went to any regular meetings. He went to the funeral and may have been very upset. He shook hands with everyone there, including myself, even though I had never met him before. In a sense, he was responsible for Armstrong's suicide. He probably felt guilty and was trying to make amends. He probably gave up much of the fight right there. After the funeral was over, we all walked off. Sarnoff was still standing there, looking off into space. His big limo was there in front of the door.

"More people should know that Armstrong was the founder of FM," Mr. Minter states. "But he wasn't much of a showman or very articulate. His station was one of the first FM stations, but he probably didn't speak on it. And he generally only spoke to technical people, so his circle of friends was small. There has been a big conflict over who invented what, but he created the superheterodyne, the superregeneration, and FM. He spent a lot of his life in court. Edison did everything the hard way since he had no formal education, unlike Armstrong."

In 1923 Armstrong married Marion MacInnis, who had been Sarnoff's secretary. After Armstrong's 1954 death, she pursued the patent cases against her former employer; she won twenty-one cases and $10 million in damages.[13] She also asked Mr. Minter to sign off Armstrong's FM station, W2XMN, for good a few weeks after his death. "Mrs. Armstrong, who was a very sweet woman and gave a lot to charity, wanted certain musical numbers for the sign-off, so we accommodated her. For the W2XMN sign-off, we put everything on a tape, including some music and words from various Radio Club of America members and the club's president. I still have the tape somewhere in my basement. I was always interested in recording and made thousands of tapes. We got a shock, though, when we went to broadcast that last time. No one had been allowed in Armstrong's room at the base of the tower. We went in there and set the tape recorder equipment on the floor. His station used open-wire antenna leads that were a foot apart. We plugged in and got feedback and oscillation like crazy. Some of the signal was radiated inside the station. We grounded out the equipment directly and that solved the problem. Armstrong used direct feeds from CBS. No wonder! He couldn't use a tape machine in there! But I haven't been up to his Alpine transmitter since then. There's a man in Philadelphia who still uses the tower for transmissions and has invited me up to see it. I have been informed recently that Armstrong's station W2XMN will be put back in operation in the near future."

Mr. Minter discusses the importance of Armstrong's broadcast tower after the September 11 attacks. "It is pretty high, over four hundred feet tall. It can easily get signals out, so several stations were run out of there after the September 11 attacks. In fact, one of the past presidents of the Radio Club was scheduled to be on the top of the World Trade Center on that fateful morning, but had to be home because the telephone company was coming to install a phone line. But I know that two radio engineers were up there on the World Trade Center roof and couldn't get down. The heat draft at the top of the building was so strong that rescue helicopters couldn't land."

He recounts his own life working with technology. "I have twenty-six patents, all used in my own work or for the company I used to work for. I have six patents on an aviation electronic collision warning system. It feeds a stated signal to the pilot's ear to tell him what direction another plane is coming from. I started my graduate thesis at MIT on a filter for FM. As a matter of fact, Armstrong's first FM transmitter had one of my filters on it, but I never tried to license it. It's sad that I'm one of the last ones who knew Armstrong. But I am very proud that I did know him."

Jerry Minter died on May 19, 2009, at age ninety-five.

NOTES

1. Charles Coulston Gillespie, ed., *Dictionary of Scientific Biography* (New York: Scribner's, 1970), 1:287.

2. Stanley Leinwoll, *From Spark to Satellite* (New York: Scribner's, 1979), 64.

3. Ibid., 65.

4. Ibid., 74–75.

5. *American National Biography* (New York: Oxford University Press, 1999), 1:610.

6. Gillespie, *Dictionary of Scientific Biography*, 1:287.

7. Leinwoll, *From Spark to Satellite*, 163.

8. Ibid., 163–64.

9. Gillespie, *Dictionary of Scientific Biography*, 1:287.

10. *American National Biography*, 1:610.

11. Leinwoll, *From Spark to Satellite*, 164.

12. Gillespie, *Dictionary of Scientific Biography*, 1:288.

13. *American National Biography*, 1:610.

ALBERT WATTENBERG
One of the Final Physicists Present
at the First Controlled Nuclear Reaction
"We knew it was critical when the neutrons grew exponentially."

In August 1939 President Franklin Roosevelt received an ominous warning letter from Albert Einstein. It noted that "[s]ome recent work by E. Fermi and L. Szilard . . . leads me to expect that the element uranium may be turned into a new and important source of energy. . . . [I]t may become possible to set up a nuclear chain reaction in a large mass of uranium, by which vast amounts of power and large quantities of new radium-like elements would be generated. . . . This new phenomenon would also lead to the construction of bombs."[1] Einstein cautioned Roosevelt of the possibility of nuclear weapons, and this famous correspondence set forth the experiments that led to both nuclear power and the atomic bomb. The great physicist Dr. Enrico Fermi was the man chosen to

**Dr. Wattenberg
at the time
of the interview**
photo by Stuart Lutz

put into practice what Einstein warned about. At 2:20 p.m. on December 2, 1942, Fermi's team created the first controlled nuclear chain reaction. Dr. Albert Wattenberg, who is now nearly blind, is one of the last scientists present at that historic experiment.

Fermi was born in Italy in 1901 and educated in Europe. In 1938 he was awarded the Nobel Prize in Physics in Sweden. Instead of returning to Fascist Italy after the awards ceremony, however, he emigrated to America and began teaching at Columbia University, then went to the University of Chicago in 1942.[2] At the same time he received his Nobel Prize, two German scientists—Otto Hahn and Fritz Strassman—announced that they had split an atomic nucleus.[3] In January 1939 Fermi reproduced the Hahn and Strassman experiment in the United States and became a candidate to lead the American effort to create a sustained nuclear reaction. In a chain reaction, neutrons split a few uranium nuclei, which then send off more neutrons to split other nuclei, which then send off more neutrons to split yet more nuclei; this creates a self-sustained chain reaction.[4] By using graphite rods to absorb neutrons, Fermi was able to control the chain reaction and keep it from getting out of hand and exploding.

Albert Wattenberg born in 1917 in New York City. He was educated at City College and Columbia, and received his PhD in physics from the University of Chicago. He was a student in Fermi's first physics courses after he joined the graduate faculty at Columbia. "Dr. Fermi was a very friendly man and great to work with. He also had a good sense of humor. Our relationship developed in such a way that I went from being his student to being one of his assistants." He answers in precise sentences, showing that his analytical mind is very active. "I helped him with a variety of experiments and scientific research projects. But I also socialized with him. He liked to have lunch with his students and we'd talk after class all the time. He was forever giving me scientific problems and challenging me to solve them."

He recounts one funny story about the great scientist: "Dr. Fermi wasn't a very good driver. And he was impatient too. One day he was driving with me as a passenger in the car and we came to a railroad crossing. He was anxious to cross even

Scientists involved in the first controlled nuclear chain reaction. Dr. Wattenberg is front center and Dr. Fermi is in the front row, far left
photo courtesy the Argonne National Laboratory

though there is a train passing. As soon as the first train passes, he starts to move, but there is another train right behind it! We lived through it and he remarked, 'That's why it is terribly important for me to drive with you—my time may be up, but yours isn't.'"

Fermi specifically recruited Dr. Wattenberg to the University of Chicago to work on nuclear fission. "We even traveled to Chicago on the same train. See, the Manhattan Project as we knew it truly started in Chicago. I had to get a security clearance, but it was a lax process. I was a known radical working on the project, but that did not interfere with my clearance." He hesitates, then states, "Of course, there were others who were not cleared."

As for Dr. Wattenberg's duties, "I assembled and tested equipment in preparation for the nuclear experiment. First we'd built a small graphite structure over the course of a few days, and if that worked, we'd build it larger and kept modifying it. We were always doing experiments and trying new materials. I worked on the order of eighty or ninety hours a week. In order to house the first nuclear reaction, we required a much larger structure. It was constructed under the grandstands at the university's Stagg Field. We needed space, and the abandoned stands had it. In fact, the University of Chicago's president did not know about the testing. Dr. Fermi decided that the school shouldn't have to take responsibility for the experiment, so he didn't discuss it with the president. Dr. Fermi also knew that the school president wouldn't be sticking his nose inside the dirty stands.

"The big graphite structure took a number of weeks to construct. It was high-purity graphite, but it leaves a black residue everywhere. We looked like coal miners! The dust was all over me and in my lungs. When we built the structure, we wore these black overalls. But we couldn't go outside like that because it would give away the secret that we were doing war work. So we would change clothes to look like ordinary graduate students dressed to do research!" he laughs.

He discusses December 2, 1942, the day of the fission experiment. "I wasn't nervous about it working. It was just the opposite. We had done the theoretical work and had complete confidence. Dr. Fermi gave us a lecture on how it should work and the equations. We were very quantitative and had a precise set of measurements. Everything was well established and calculated. In fact, we were irritated with professors who wanted us to take unnecessary precautions. We felt they didn't understand the experiments and calculations. Which they didn't. We were very careful, and there were radiation monitors on all of us, which were checked every day. We thought of every contingency, including the possibility of an earthquake. We were not far from a fault line that runs through Illinois. So in case there was a quake during the experiment, there were buckets of cadmium sulfate that we could throw on the pile."

The experiment hadn't started by noon, so Fermi did something unusual. "It got to be lunchtime, and most people didn't think Dr. Fermi would stop for lunch. But those that knew him well were not surprised at all when he called a lunch break. It was a crazy break. We were in our blackened clothes. We had to change completely, then go to lunch. Then change back again. After lunch we did a series of measurements, removing the control rod six inches at a time. We watched our instruments when the experiment was still subcritical. As we removed the control rods, the neutron level would rise, then level off. Dr. Fermi said to Arthur Compton, 'Now I'm going to move the control rod out another six inches and the neutron intensity, instead of remaining constant, will rise exponentially.' That was the announcement that we were moving from subcritical to supercritical. The new measurement kept rising and Dr. Fermi allowed it to keep going. He didn't interfere with it. There was a dramatic break as we were watching the instruments. We knew it was critical when the neutrons grew exponentially. The experiment did not stop until we put the control rod back in.

"When we saw it was successful, we broke into smiles. There was no cheering. Eugene Wigner brought a bottle of Chianti wine to celebrate, and we all had a little bit. With forty-five of us in the room, there wasn't much chance of us getting drunk. We raised our glasses to Fermi. I had the actual bottle in my basement and it was known as 'Al's Chianti bottle.' There was a lot of interest in it, and I was asked to send it to Fermi when he opened a new lab. So it moved from one lab to another as he moved."

On July 16, 1945, the United States tested the first atomic bomb in New Mexico. Surprisingly, Dr. Wattenberg admits, "I did not know of the Trinity Test. We knew they were going to do a test down there, but the details of when and where were secret to those of us still in Chicago." Dr. Wattenberg later became a professor at the University of Chicago, then worked at the Argonne National Laboratory.

Despite his work on fission, he had mixed emotions about the product of his work. "I felt that the atomic bomb should not be used on humans," he states strongly. "There was a big argument about giving a convincing demonstration, and I was in favor of that. We should have shown the Japanese that the bomb was feasible. I signed a petition to that effect and sent it by messenger to Truman. My brother was in the army, and he felt that the atomic bombings saved his life and the lives of the other soldiers waiting off the coast of Japan for the invasion. His military status wasn't a conflict to me, but he was a consideration in my mind."

Dr. Wattenberg is still concerned about nuclear weapons today. "I had hoped there would be better treaties so other countries wouldn't develop their own nuclear weapons. It should have been done as a United Nations–type thing. Now there are too many rogue nations capable of creating disastrous consequences. I'm thinking specifically of the Pakistan and India situation. I think nuclear weapons are more likely to be used in Kashmir, and that is the situation likely to break the rule of not using nuclear weapons. I think this is the worst development I've witnessed in my lifetime. Yet I feel that atomic power has been beneficial for humanity, and that is the best development I've seen. We demonstrated that we can get power from atoms and we don't have to blow up the world to do it."

Albert Wattenberg died on June 27, 2007, at age ninety.

NOTES

1. Emilio Segre, *Enrico Fermi, Physicist* (Chicago: University of Chicago Press, 1970), 111.

2. *American National Biography* (New York: Oxford University Press, 1999), 7:842–43.

3. Segre, *Enrico Fermi*, 99.

4. *American National Biography*, 843.

Part 4

Athletes and Entertainers

SLIM BRYANT
The Final Musician to Play with
Country Music Star Jimmie Rodgers

"I can play with anyone. . . . I listened to [Jimmie Rodgers's] records and I knew what to expect."

"The Singing Brakeman." "The Mississippi Blue Yodeler." "The Father of Country Music." These are nicknames for Jimmie Rodgers, one of the most popular and legendary American musicians of the first half of the twentieth century. Like many other famous entertainers, Rodgers died young, in 1933 at the age of only thirty-five. Seventy-five years after Rodgers's early death, there is only one musician still alive who played with him, the longtime country picker Thomas Hoyt "Slim" Bryant.

James Charles Rodgers was born on September 8, 1897, near Meridian, Mississippi. His aunt, who had a degree in music, mentored him. He started performing in barbershops before he was a teenager and later won a local amateur talent contest. He created his own traveling tent production, then ran away with a medicine show. His father found him, and young Jimmie began working on the railroads, earning the moniker "The Singing Brakeman." His goal, however, was always a singing career. In 1924 he was diagnosed with tuberculosis, the same disease that had killed his mother when Rodgers was just a boy. His illness ended a decade of laborious railroad work.

Rodgers relocated first to Tennessee and then to North Carolina. He performed on a radio program, although he was soon dropped. By chance he met Ralph Peer, an employee of the Victor Talking Machine Company, who sought to record local acts. Rodgers recorded two solo songs for Peer, which were released to minor success. He traveled to New York and recorded more works, including "Blue Yodel (T for Texas)," which sold a million copies. He followed up with "In the Jailhouse Now," "Dear Old Sunny South by the Sea," "Treasures Untold," "T.B. Blues," and a string of other "Blue Yodels." He even performed with jazz trumpeter Louis Armstrong on "Blue Yodel #9." But as his success grew, his health worsened.

In February 1932 Rodgers made a dozen recordings in Dallas, and in August he traveled to Camden, New Jersey, to cut more songs. There he played with Slim Bryant. Rodgers continued to record in 1933, but he knew his time was short. On the way back from a New York recording studio, he fell into a coma. He died on May 26, 1933, at age thirty-five as a result of complications of tuberculosis. His body was returned to Meridian by train, and he lay in state before he was buried.

Rodgers's shooting-star career lasted six years. As one music writer summarized, "his influence on subsequent American artists is incalculable. Many of the top [country] stars, including Gene Autry, Jimmie Davis, Hank Snow and Ernest Tubb started their careers almost as Rodgers' impersonators."[1] He was the first musician elected to the Country Music Hall of Fame. His plaque summarizes his accomplishments: "Jimmie Rodgers' name stands foremost in the country music field as the man who started it all."[2]

Slim Bryant was born in Atlanta in 1908. "But I left when I was twenty-one or twenty-two," he notes in a slight Georgia accent. He comes from a musical family, and his living room contains a few guitars, amplifiers, a tuning machine, and some CDs with his name on them. "My mother was a piano and guitar player and my father played the mandolin and fiddle. I always wanted to play the piano, and I regret that I never took it up. My brother Raymond played bass in my band, and my other brother, Pete, also played guitar."

For such an accomplished guitarist, Mr. Bryant started the instrument quite late. "I learned it after I graduated from high

Mr. Bryant as a young musician
photo courtesy Thomas Hoyt "Slim" Bryant

Mr. Bryant at the time of the interview
photo by Stuart Lutz

school. It was handy, and I took it up and played it by ear. I liked it very much. Anyway, I heard this fellow on Columbia Records named Perry Bechtel, and I learned that he taught in Atlanta. He was a fine guitar and banjo player. I studied under him for sixteen months, and he taught me a lot, including how to play solos. I was introduced to [musician] Clayton McMichen by his cousin, and I played with him on WSB in Atlanta with the Georgia Wildcats. We then did personal appearances in Kentucky and Tennessee."

Despite his burgeoning career, Mr. Bryant temporarily left the music scene to pursue his true passion. "I loved baseball more than music," he admits. "I went back to Atlanta to pitch [in the church leagues], and my brother played for the Boston Braves. But there was just no living in baseball."

He resumed music, playing in Cincinnati, Cleveland, Richmond, Pittsburgh, and New York City. "We played in theaters, high schools, dance halls, gyms, wherever. We just moved onto new radio stations, for that's where the money was." As his musical skills expanded, his band was later billed as "The Georgia Wildcats with Slim Bryant."

Mr. Bryant recalls the time he saw Jimmie Rodgers perform live. "I saw him at the Capitol Theatre in Atlanta. We had six boys in our house and my parents had trouble feeding all of us, so we couldn't afford a record player. My neighbor, however, had one, and I listened to Rodgers there. That's why I went to see him in Atlanta."

He met Rodgers through McMichen, who knew the musical superstar. "He [Rodgers] was making personal appearances and wanted a band to back him in Camden [New Jersey, in August 1932]. Jimmie had never heard of me, but said, 'If he wants to come along, I'll pay his expenses.' So I went, and I traveled with Jimmie from Washington with Ralph Peer to Camden. I told Peer that I had this song, 'Mother, the Queen of My Heart,' and Peer insisted I be there the next morning at eight. He told me that Rodgers couldn't record too many songs because of his health, and he didn't want to over-work Rodgers. It took three or four days, but we recorded 'No Hard Times' and 'Mother, the Queen of My Heart' and a number of others [including 'Whippin' That Old T.B.,' 'Rock All Our Babies to Sleep,' 'I've Only Loved Three Women,' and 'Miss the Mississippi and You'].[3] We soon moved to New York, and Peer asked if I could play with the New York musicians. I told him, 'I can play with anyone.' We did there four songs with a clarinet and fiddles—it had a more modern sound. Jimmie was hoping to make a trip to England, but a doctor warned him that it might shorten his life. Rodgers went back to Texas, and McMichen and I played some vaudeville dates, then went to Louisville to do radio. I was one of the first guitar players to play a solo on the radio. It was the last time I ever saw Rodgers. But he sent me a postcard after hearing me on the Louisville radio, and I sent him one back. He was a nice guy, a fine fellow."

Mr. Bryant opines on what made Rodgers different from the other country music stars of the day: "It was his magic voice and his yodel—it was a good, clean-pitched yodel. If you heard it, you knew it was him. It has often been copied, by singers like Gene Autry, but he never got it. Rodgers was unique to work with, and you had to be on your toes. He'd stick in an extra measure. But I listened to his records and I knew what to expect. Also, you should know that Rodgers couldn't read music."

Mr. Bryant wrote "Mother, the Queen of My Heart," one of Rodgers's biggest hits and still a well-known song today. He recounts how he was inspired to pen the song. "I was in a restaurant right across the street from a fire station in Atlanta. Two men sat by me talking. One said that he had been out all night gambling, and he swore he was quitting after he lost everything. This fellow said that he had promised his mother he wouldn't drink or play cards, but he was hooked on it. So he tells this story that he was playing cards, and all he needed was a queen. And that's what he drew. And he saw his mother's picture on the card, yelling at him, 'You broke your promise!' I thought it would make a good song, and I struggled with it for a few days. But Mr. Peer said yes to it, and Rodgers recorded it. I have three or four CDs with 'Mother' on it, and it came out twice last year," he says as he motions towards a stack of compact disks. "It is on at least fifteen albums, and it's been recorded by Merle Haggard and Pete Seeger. And four times a year, I still get royalty checks for it."

Mr. Bryant owns an unusual musical first: He was the first person to broadcast live music from a plane. "We flew over the World's Fair in Chicago because it was a good promotion for us. It was a few of us Wildcats in there and then we got a cue from the engineer. I played a guitar solo on 'A Little Bit of This and That' and a few other country tunes."

He toured across the country throughout his early days. During World War II, when there was a gas shortage, touring was hampered by gas rationing, so he turned to radio programs. "After the war, I bought a home here [in Pittsburgh]. Television was just starting, and I was on TV for ten years in the early days. Our first broadcast was from a mosque, and the next day an agency called. They offered to put us on the air five nights a week for fifteen minutes. Let me tell you, the first studio was size of a kitchen, so we eventually moved to a larger studio. We did a variety program, and Burl Ives was one of our first guests. It was sponsored by Duquesne Beer at one point, then Iron City Beer. That show expired about 1960."

At this point Mr. Bryant pushes away from his small table and reaches for a syrup-colored hollow-body guitar. He briefly tunes the instrument. "I hurt my arm recently and can't play the way I used to," he mutters. He strums, adding the melody of "Sophisticated Lady" to a country song. Proving that he is capable of playing music from many decades, he then performs the Beatles' "Yesterday." He plays for ten minutes before putting the guitar back in its holder, adding, "If you learn to play guitar, you can play anything."

Mr. Bryant declines to give his opinion on current country music. As for being the last musician to play with the legendary Rodgers, he laughs, "I hate to admit it." He quickly adds, with a touch of deserved pride, "It was just my seventieth anniversary of being in the musicians' union."

Mr. Bryant is indeed a fortunate man to have created timeless music that will be heard many generations from now.

NOTES

1. Colin Larkin, ed., *The Guinness Encyclopedia of Popular Music* (Enfield, UK: Guinness Publishing, 1995), 3540–45.

2. Vladimir Bogdanov, Chris Woodstra, and Stephen Thomas Erlewine, eds., *All Music Guide to Country: The Definitive Guide to Country Music* (San Francisco: Backbeat Books, 2003), 652.

3. Jimmie Rodgers, *No Hard Times 1932* (Rounder Records, 1991). This information was taken from the CD liner notes.

GEORGE R. GIBSON
The Final Player on an NFL Team
That Folded during the Great Depression

"In addition to Sundays, we would play on Wednesdays. . . . Boy, was I sore!"

Today professional football is one of the nation's most popular sports. The Super Bowl charges millions of dollars for a thirty-second television advertisement, players make millions per season, and franchises sell for hundreds of millions. Yet the National Football League was not always so wealthy or popular. During the Great Depression, some teams went bankrupt. Dr. George R. Gibson, the oldest former NFL player, recounts a league where paychecks were week-to-week, games were played frequently, and not all franchises survived.

The history of organized football begins in November 1869 in New Brunswick, New Jersey, when Rutgers University and Princeton University played the first intercollegiate football game.[1] In 1897 the Latrobe Athletic Association created the first all-professional football team. Football was a very dangerous sport, so a few years later the forward pass was introduced in an attempt to reduce the brutal violence of an all-running game. In 1913 Jim Thorpe, the winner of the decathlon and pentathlon at the 1912 Olympics, played with an Indiana team.[2] By 1920 football was in crisis, as professional players quickly moved from one team to another and college players infiltrated the professional ranks. A meeting was held to create a unified league, and the result was the American Professional Football Association; some of the long-forgotten teams included the Canton Bulldogs, the Dayton Triangles, and the Rock Island Independents. In 1922 the league's name was changed to the now-familiar National Football League—the NFL—and some recognizable franchises, such as the Green Bay Packers and Chicago Bears, emerged. The

Dr. Gibson in his football days
photo courtesy Richard Gibson

**Dr. Gibson in front of
his football memorabilia**
photo courtesy Richard Gibson

**A Green Bay Packer contract for Dr. Gibson,
and a signed letter from Curly Lambeau addressed to Dr. Gibson**
photos courtesy Richard Gibson

league's leading team in those days was the Bears, led by
owner George Halas and running back Red Grange. In 1925
the Bears played eight games in just twelve days, attracting
more than seventy thousand fans in New York City.[3] Despite
this success, the Great Depression had a chilling effect on the
NFL, and the league shrank from eighteen teams in 1924 to
just ten by 1931.

George Gibson was born in Canandaigua, New York, on
October 2, 1905; when he was five, his family moved to Med-
ford, Oklahoma, where he graduated high school in 1923.

"For three years, I followed the harvest fields, chopping wheat up to the Canadian line. I had saved enough money by 1925 to enroll at the University of Minnesota with my brother. He saw the freshman football practice. He said that the players didn't look tough and suggested we try out for football. We both made the squad. I was made captain in 1928 and I was an All-American guard that same year. I was a teammate of [the legendary player] Bronko Nagurski. Back then players had to play both offense and defense. There was a rule that if you came out during a quarter, you couldn't go back in during that same quarter. The professionals continued that platoon system until World War II," he notes.

Dr. Gibson says he had no plans for a career playing professional football. "I graduated in 1930 and started graduate work in geology. I also got a job as the assistant line coach. I got married in 1929, then the Depression hit. I couldn't get a job anyplace. There were some long times between paychecks. I moonlighted by coaching the Minneapolis Red Jackets in 1929. Our camp was in northern Minnesota and the squad was twenty-two men. The owners asked if I wanted to play and coach, so I did. But I still graded papers at school!"

He discusses the beginnings of his football career. "In 1930 we played teams like the Portsmouth, Ohio Spartans that were the forerunner of the Detroit Lions. We tied the Chicago Cardinals featuring Ernie Nevers, a great triple threat. We played Green Bay in Minneapolis. We also took on the Chicago Bears when George Halas ran and owned the club. They featured both Nagurski and Red Grange. Grange was over the hill by then, and they never let him run through the line of scrimmage. But he was spectacular in the open field! In addition to Sundays, we would play on Wednesdays. We played a Wednesday night game in Des Moines. Boy, was I sore! In some places, we had to play on Saturdays because of the blue laws."

The Depression continued to affect the professional game. "My team, and much of the league, was strapped financially. After the games, the owners paid us off from the gate receipts. The gate was the only source of income. Unfortunately for the Red Jacket owners, it rained two Sundays in a row, so they didn't get any money for tickets. I knew they were struggling financially, but they told me, 'We're broke. The Frankford [Pennsylvania] Yellow Jackets want you, and they said bring four or five players.' If it weren't for the rainy Sundays, we probably would have survived. We got on a train on Tuesday to go to Philly to meet up with the Yellow Jackets. They told me that they fired their coach and they wanted me to coach them. So I did. Saturday we beat [the] Providence Steam Rollers. We were badly beaten by the Giants at the Polo Grounds. We played the Bears three times that season. We also took on the Newark team and the Staten Island Stapletons. The Yellow Jackets were really a traveling squad, sometimes playing two or three games a week.

"The last game of the season in December, we played the Giants. It was a close game, but we were beat by one touchdown. They held the train for a half hour so we could get into our suits without showering. We had to be in Portsmouth, Ohio, for a game the next day. We played on back-to-back days. But Frankford went broke too. It was tough for the working man," he laments. "Tickets were a dollar and programs were a dime.

"Although the Red Jackets and Yellow Jackets have disappeared, some of the teams did make it. Green Bay was run by the town, so they gave the players jobs. Their halfback was a county attorney! In Chicago, Halas kept the team together. The NFL started in 1920, but Halas had a team before that."

Dr. Gibson compares his NFL to today's league and feels the greatest difference is television. "The early Bears broadcast on radio," he notes, "but television was a much greater change. Money came in from advertising. And there have been a few rule changes. It used to be that the ball had to pass one yard from the center to the passer. When that was changed, it was decided to hand it directly from the center to the passer. Also, a passer couldn't throw a ball unless he was five yards behind the line of scrimmage. The next big offensive change was that blockers were allowed to use their hands. This was the start of the three-hundred-pounders. I was six foot and two hundred pounds, but I was fast. Speed was needed to protect the passer, since we couldn't use our hands to block. Also, the NFL went to an offensive platoon system with unlimited substitution. It's a very brutal game now and bad bodies are the result." Dr. Gibson admits that he's "never been to the Super Bowl, but the league wants me to be at a Hall of Fame game this upcoming July." As a result of his college days, he always roots for the Minnesota Vikings, but now that he lives in Texas, he also cheers for the Dallas Cowboys.

He bemoans the low pay of the early players. "Linemen got fifty to one hundred dollars a week. Coaches were paid twenty-four hundred dollars for a season. Grange was the highest-paid player, and he made five thousand dollars for the season, and Nagurksi got four thousand. I made thirty-nine hundred for both coaching and playing. I was offered a Green Bay Packers contract for the 1932 season with [Packers coach] Curly Lambeau, but I didn't take it. Eventually I was both an assistant professor of geology and a football head coach at Carlton College in Minnesota, but I quit coaching in 1938." He earned a PhD in geology from Minnesota and worked for decades in Texas doing oil exploration.

George Gibson died on August 19, 2004, at age ninety-eight, two years after the NFL Hall of Fame recognized him as the oldest-living former player. The University of Minnesota's football complex is named the Gibson-Nagurski Football

Complex in honor of the All-American teammates from the 1920s.[4]

NOTES

1. Dave Anderson, *The Story of Football* (New York: William Morrow, 1997), 10.

2. "NFL History by Decade: 1911–1920," NFL.com, http://www.nfl.com/history/chronology/1911-1920 (accessed July 3, 2009).

3. "NFL History by Decade: 1921–1930," NFL.com, http://www.nfl.com/history/chronology/1921-1930 (accessed July 3, 2009).

4. "Photo Gallery: Gibson-Nagurski Football Complex," GopherSports.com, http://www.gophersports.com/PhotoAlbum.dbml?DB_OEM_ID=8400&PALBID=15990 (accessed July 3, 2009).

KITTY CARLISLE HART
The Last Starring Actress from a Marx Brothers Movie
"When you hear that high C [in A Night at the Opera*], it's mine!"*

Kitty Carlisle Hart is in her eighth decade of performing. She began her career in the 1930s, when she acted in the Marx Brothers' masterpiece *A Night at the Opera*. In that classic film, she starred as Rosa Castaldi, the Italian opera singer who performs the song "Always." She is the last-surviving cast member of a Marx Brothers movie, and she is also the last person alive to have performed with George Gershwin.

In 1946 she married the Pulitzer Prize–winning dramatist Moss Hart; he is best remembered for his comedies *You Can't Take It with You* and *The Man Who Came to Dinner*. Their marriage lasted until he died of a heart attack in 1961. In 1956 Mrs. Hart starred on the television show *To Tell the Truth* and also continued her singing career. She became vice chairwoman of the New York Council on the Arts in 1971 and was later appointed chairwoman by Governor Hugh Carey; she held that position for two decades.

Mrs. Hart lives in a beautiful prewar building on the Upper East Side, overlooking Madison Avenue. Her apartment is the throne room of an era of theater and music that is quickly fading from the American memory. There is a wall of books and music, and one shelf features a large reproduction of the Moss Hart stamp issued by the United States Postal Service. A shiny black grand piano sits alone in one corner, buried under sheet music. She still tours regularly and practices her singing while the sounds of car horns and sirens rise from the active avenue just below.

The immaculately dressed Mrs. Hart was born Catherine Conn on September 3, 1910, in New Orleans; she has no trace of a Southern accent, however, since she spent her adolescence in European finishing schools.

She was an unknown performer when she first met the Marx Brothers on the set of *A Night at the Opera* in 1935. "MGM put me in the film in an unsuccessful attempt to get rid of me. They sent me home and paid me off. I thought it was the end of the world. I cried big tears on the upper berth of the train. But my voice got me the part. The music had a high C in it, and I could manage that. But the studio wanted to dub my voice for the film. I was on the set for the first day. There were a hundred extras there and I was supposed to sing [the opera] *Pagliacci*. It was the big scene at the Metropolitan Opera. I started off . . . [Mrs. Hart sings several bars in her still-formidable voice] . . . and I stop. The movie's director, Sam Wood, was on a boom and yelled down to me to start again. So I sing again and then I stop. He gets off the boom

Mrs. Hart at the time of the interview
photo by Stuart Lutz

and tells me that I should just go ahead and sing and he'll explain everything later." She shrugs. "I walked off the set. It was the bravest thing I ever did. My agent told me to be ready in my makeup at eight and to stay in my dressing room until he comes to get me. He took me to see [legendary director] Irving Thalberg. I cried in his wastepaper basket, on his head, on his desk. But I got the job! When you hear that high C, it's mine!" she boasts and punches the air.

Surprisingly, the always-joking Marx Brothers treated her well. "They were all very nice to me; they didn't play any tricks on me. I don't know why. Groucho would come up to me and recite a line from the movie. First he would say it in a way that wasn't funny, then he'd repeat it in a way that was funny. Chico was always in his room with either a drink or a girl. One of my favorite memories is Harpo playing the harp. He didn't read music, but he was wonderful; he was so good at it."

She first met her husband on the movie set. "George Kaufman was writing the dialogue, and he introduced me to Moss. They invited me that night to come up to the room to sing for them. So I did it. I didn't get the job, but I got the man nine years later. I had my eye on him all that time. And I was getting a little long in the tooth."

Mrs. Hart reveals one anecdote about Harpo: "Moss bought a farm in Bucks County, Pennsylvania, and kept adding to it until it was a showplace. He invited Harpo for a weekend. Moss learned that the local minister was going to pay a call, and he didn't have anything to discuss with the minister. He instructed Harpo to interrupt them after ten minutes. So ten minutes go by, and Harpo walks out onto the balcony overlooking the room. He's wearing nothing but a towel and is holding a big shaving brush. He yells down to Moss, 'Time to shave the cat!' The minister fled," she recounts with a chuckle.

She first met George Gershwin on the set of a radio show.

A Ronald Reagan photograph inscribed to Mrs. Hart
public domain

To Kitty Carlisle Hart
    With warm regards, & Warmest Friendship &
Affection. Ronald Reagan

"He said to me, 'Let's go over the song,' and I was terrified. If he didn't like it, I had no other way to do it, for that's the way I had always performed it. I was trembling beside the piano, but he liked my performance. That night we went to a party hosted by [the famous gossip columnist] Elsa Maxwell. In those days, artists and society mingled, but that tradition has long since stopped. George and I did a song together at the piano. Other times, we'd go out together to dance at El Morocco. We had this little bet going, to see whose song would be played first that evening. My favorite Gershwin song is 'The Man I Love.' I also remember going with [the American entertainer] Oscar Levant to see George rehearse, and we'd later walk home together. I once went to the theater with him to see *Porgy and Bess*. I thought it was wonderful," she adds with emphasis. "Women just loved George, and he returned the compliment. He had this little trick he used on the ladies. He had created this little waltz, and if he met a woman he liked, he would take her to the piano. Anyway, he had this little spot in the lyrics where he could fill in her name. So he'd play the tune, then add in 'Betsy' or whatever her name was. You could call it his mating call." Before she met Hart, Gershwin proposed to her. "He asked me to marry him, but I declined. He didn't really love me, but he thought he should be married and I was eminently suitable. I had just started my career, and if I married him I'd have to be Mrs. George Gershwin." Gershwin died six months later, at age thirty-eight.

Mrs. Hart is still an active performer. "I gave a concert on my ninety-fourth birthday, and am already booked for my ninety-fifth. I'm going to [pianist Michael] Feinstein's, where I started a renaissance." She pronounces "renaissance" with the French accent learned in her youth. "Now I'm in great demand and I've been singing all over the country recently. I'm still a good singer, and there are not a lot of us around at ninety-four. It's one of my claims to fame. Five years ago I performed a concert in Palm Springs. To my astonishment, the piano accompanist was Harpo's son, who trained at Julliard. I've had a wonderful career and I'm still singing and earning money. Soon I go to Palm Beach for a two-week engagement. They are paying me a fortune. And I use that money to travel with my family."

Mrs. Hart is not only the last person to work with the

Marx Brothers and George Gershwin, but she is the final representative of an entire New York City scene. For decades, there was a sophisticated world of literary and musical theater, created by George S. Kaufman, Oscar Levant, Irving Berlin, Moss Hart, Cole Porter, Rodgers and Hammerstein, and Jerome Kern. Mrs. Hart, who is still out on the performance circuit, is keeping that fading flame alive.

Kitty Carlisle Hart died on April 17, 2007, at age ninety-six.

PAUL HOPKINS
The Last Living Pitcher to Give Up a Home Run
to Babe Ruth in His Historic 1927 Season
"I thought I could outsmart Ruth, so I decided to throw him another curve. . . . Grand slam."

In 1884 slugger Ned Williamson of the Chicago White Stockings established a major league mark when he socked twenty-seven home runs in a season. This record remained for thirty-four years, until 1919, when a brash young outfielder named Babe Ruth clobbered twenty-nine. The next season Ruth hit an unimaginable fifty-four home round-trippers, followed by fifty-nine in the 1921 season. Ruth hit home runs at an astounding pace throughout the 1920s, culminating in his greatest season—1927—when he smashed sixty. This record would last for thirty-four seasons, until Roger Maris hit sixty-one in 1961, in an extended season. Today the single-season home run record is held by Barry Bonds, who smacked seventy-three in 2001. For every home run that Ruth hit in 1927, there was a poor pitcher humiliated by the Sultan of Swat. Former Washington Senator Paul Hopkins is the last living hurler to surrender a home run to Ruth in 1927.

Mr. Hopkins, of Deep River, Connecticut, is a tall, lanky man with the ideal build for a pitcher. He dropped out of New York's Colgate College to pursue his professional baseball dream. "I was signed secretly by [Hall of Famer] George Weiss in my junior year for four thousand dollars. He owned the New Haven minor league team. I came back home and surprised the bank teller by giving him one of the largest checks he ever saw." Mr. Hopkins throws back his head and laughs at the memory. "I was assigned to the New Haven team of the Eastern League, named the Profs. I didn't know it at the time I was pitching, but [Hall of Fame pitcher] Walter Johnson had been sent up all the way from Washington to scout me.

Imagine that—to scout me! After the game he came up to me and told me he enjoyed watching me play. He went back by train—not having planes in those days—to Washington to speak to the owner of the Senators, Clark Griffith. And that's how I was signed by the team. They bought my contract from the Profs, but I didn't think they offered me enough money. I held out for more, but when the team threatened to suspend me I hopped on a train quick. I didn't want to miss my chance." He chuckles heartily.

Toward the end of the 1927 season, Ruth had already hit fifty-seven home runs and was threatening to break his own 1921 record. The Senators played the Yankees in New York on September 29. Mr. Hopkins recounts, "I didn't start the game. Actually, I never had been in a major league game before. So Ruth hits a home run in the first inning [pitched by teammate Horace Lisenbee]. Then, in the fifth, the bases are loaded with two outs. Manager [Bucky] Harris summoned me to pitch and I had no idea at the time who I was facing. I walked up to the mound and saw Ruth at the plate. Well, I had a pretty good fastball, but an even better curve that I could control more. Anyway, I got Ruth to a full count by throwing him three straight curves. I thought I could outsmart Ruth, so I decided to throw him another curve, figuring he really wouldn't be expecting it. He started to swing too early, and for a flash, I thought I had him. But the son-of-a-gun held up for an instant and hit the ball into the right field seats. Grand slam." Mr. Hopkins makes a swinging motion with both of his arms and demonstrates the minute pause in Ruth's swing that allowed him to hit the home run.

The *New York Times* the next day described the shot: "Then the fifty-ninth! That countrymen, was a wallop. . . . The ball landed half way up the right field bleacher." The home run pitched by Hopkins tied Ruth's single-season record of fifty-nine. It was also Ruth's second grand slam in three days, the other one coming off one of the greatest pitchers in history, Lefty Grove. The next day Ruth hit number sixty off Hopkins's teammate Tom Zachary, setting a major league record that stood until Roger Maris's efforts—and Zachary became the answer to a great baseball trivia question.

After the Ruth home run, Mr. Hopkins remained in the game. "I think I pitched five innings in all. Ruth got another hit off of me, a bloop double that he hit off the end of the bat. [According to the box score, the rotund Ruth hit a triple.] The outfielders were playing really deep, and it just went over the shortstop. When he was standing on second, Ruth yelled over to me something about throwing me a better pitch next time." The Senators lost 15–4 as Mr. Hopkins surrendered eight hits and four runs, with all four runs coming on Ruth's slam.

Even as a rookie pitcher, Mr. Hopkins understood Ruth's legend and obtained a piece of memorabilia for himself. "After the game I wanted to get Ruth to sign a ball for me. I found one in the Senator clubhouse, so I took it to the Yankee clubhouse. I was stopped by the attendant, who said no one was allowed in. He said he'd get Ruth to sign it for me, and he did. I eventually gave the ball to a young kid who pestered me for it. He was the son of the Senators' club doctor."

A look of sadness drapes him as he describes the end of his pitching career. "The next year I signed with the Montreal team of the International League. I pitched quite a lot for them, and also played in Baltimore and Jersey City. I was quite friendly with the manager. And in 1929 I returned to the majors. I played for the Senators and the old St. Louis Browns. I was pitching in spring training and felt something pop in my pitching arm. I spent all of my money to take care of my arm. Then there were no real team doctors, and I was on my own. So I went to this small town in Ohio where there was a doctor named 'Bone Setter' Reese. Claimed he could fix any ballplayer . . . except for me!" He laughs aloud. In his career,

**Mr. Hopkins at the time
of the interview**
photo by Stuart Lutz

Mr. Hopkins as a young pitcher and an old man
photo courtesy Henry E. Josten

A baseball signed by Mr. Hopkins
photo by Stuart Lutz

Mr. Hopkins pitched in eleven games and compiled a 1–1 record, with a very respectable 2.96 earned run average.

He is also the last-surviving teammate of the great Walter Johnson. Nicknamed "The Big Train," Johnson was perhaps the greatest pitcher ever, compiling a record of 417–279 despite playing for a basement ballclub; he threw an amazing 110 shutouts. At age thirty-nine, after two decades in the majors, Johnson retired after the 1927 season. "Walter was the player I enjoyed the most. He was revered in the clubhouse. Just absolutely revered. He would have made a great minister," Mr. Hopkins recalls.

After his brief baseball career ended, Mr. Hopkins remained in obscurity until 1998, when two events returned him to the spotlight. One occurrence was the well-publicized home run chase between Mark McGwire and Sammy Sosa, when McGwire broke Roger Maris's record by finishing with seventy. Waving his right arm in the air, Mr. Hopkins says, "There was much more publicity in 1998 than before that. My wife died just a few months ago, but she used to keep all the letters I got. During the home run chase, the mail became staggering." He points to a large box on a bookshelf overflowing with pleading correspondence and prepaid return envelopes. "After McGwire hit number sixty-two, sportswriters really started getting into it, and it became an unusual situation for me."

That same year, the United States Postal Service honored Ruth on the fiftieth anniversary of his death by issuing a new stamp and invited Mr. Hopkins to The House That Ruth Built to take part in the ceremonies. Mr. Hopkins leans back in his chair, looks upward, and speaks in a deliberate manner, "There is something unique about Yankee Stadium. It thrills and amazes you. [Yankee owner George] Steinbrenner would be crazy to leave that place. Anyway, I could only throw the ball halfway to the catcher." He pops out of his chair and demonstrates his limber pitching motion. The ninety-four-year-old pitcher is six feet tall and gangly, but he moves like a man a few decades younger. "Of course, I can't wind up as much now as I did when I was younger."

Mr. Hopkins retrieves an ancient photograph of the fans milling by the gate to the Washington Senators' Griffith Stadium. "I've seen the audience for baseball change over the years. Back then, all the men were dressed in suits and hats," he points out. "And no ladies.

"I figure this. If I had done my job and struck out Ruth, nobody would have ever heard of me. But any fame I have is a direct result of Ruth. If I had become famous because of what I did on my own, that would be a much better story." Baseball, more than any other pastime, is built on its history, and Mr. Hopkins, who appeared in only eleven major league contests, perpetuates the game's most valuable asset.

On January 2, 2004, Paul Hopkins died at age ninety-nine. At the time of his passing, he was the oldest-living major league player.

ROBERT LOCKWOOD JR.
The Final Musician to Play with
Blues Legend Robert Johnson

"Robert [Johnson] didn't want to teach nobody. . . . I was learning so fast, I blew his mind. . . . He never had to show me but twice."

In an African American neighborhood in Cleveland, a group of teenagers, just released from high school for the day, walk down the street. One of them carries a radio wailing rap music. The adolescent is unaware that one of the forefathers of his music, Robert Lockwood Jr., lives in the finest house on that decaying block. Mr. Lockwood is the last musician alive to have played with the legendary bluesman Robert Johnson. Johnson, though only four years older than Mr. Lockwood, was Mr. Lockwood's stepfather. In addition, Mr. Lockwood was the only person the always-private Johnson ever taught his amazing guitar secrets.

Robert Johnson, born in 1911 in Hazelhurst, Mississippi, perfected his blues guitar playing and songwriting in only a few years. Almost as quickly as he appeared, he died at age twenty-seven in 1938, poisoned by a jealous husband. Johnson left behind only forty-one recordings, totaling twenty-nine different songs.[1] The works include the timeless "Love in Vain," "Sweet Home Chicago," "Rambling on My Mind" and "Me and the Devil Blues." His delicate music combines his tremendous guitar playing, a high-pitched voice, and haunted lyrics of loneliness and despair. His small body of work represents one of the high-water marks of acoustic Mississippi Delta blues.[2] Yet his songs have become enormously influential, recorded by everyone from the Rolling Stones to Eric Clapton. When Columbia Records released *Robert Johnson: The Complete Recordings* in 1990, it sold so many copies that it was awarded a platinum album.[3]

Mr. Lockwood is a short man with a gray beard and almost

purple eyes. He was born on March 27, 1915, in Turkey Scratch, Arkansas. He recounts his Arkansas youth in the heavily accented speech of his southern boyhood, pronouncing words like "four" as "foe." "Where I grew up, there wasn't too much segregation, since there were almost no white people there. My people had our own farms and things. We didn't see whites until we went to town. The few white people there were in business, and we bought stuff from the white folks. It wasn't like you thought. Segregation didn't really bother me. I've been a celebrity all my life, and I've never had no problem with prejudice. I skipped most of that. But I hated seeing it happen to others." He moves his legendary, worn hands frequently when speaking.

Lockwood began his musical career early, starting with the family's organ. "My aunt bought my first guitar when I was about ten or so. She's still living in St. Louis. I didn't think I was going to play it. There was an organ in the house, and I was playing that. My first electric guitar was a pickup on an acoustic. I got my first guitar with built-in pickups from Sears Roebuck in 1939 or so." He continues, "I can't remember the first blues song I ever heard. It was so early that I just don't know. Blues were already there when I came along. That's what people were doing. [Famous bluesmen such as] Blind Lemon Jefferson, Blind Blake.

"I first performed in public when I was about sixteen or so. It was one of those box suppers out in the country, like country people do. It was a little event. It wasn't in no church. There was gambling and drinking and having fun. I used to go out into the plantations in the fall of the year and stay out until we quit gathering the crop. We would stay house to house, and we'd play every night of the week. They were well kept up. Some of the buildings were brand new. People were there to gamble, and there was whiskey and beer. It was for white people to have their fun. Ain't no different than now. But they weren't sophisticated things like they were today."

Like Mr. Lockwood, Robert Johnson took up the guitar as a teenager and attempted to teach himself.[4] He was not accomplished at first and attached himself to noted bluesman Son House in order to learn.[5] Through hours of intense practicing, Johnson quickly developed into an amazing guitarist. He so astonished his fellow musicians with his guitar prowess that he claimed he sold his soul to the devil at a Mississippi crossroads to gain such incredible musical ability. "That story about selling his soul to the devil, that's a load of it," Mr. Lockwood dismisses. "When you are born, you are born in sin, and you are already sold to the devil. If you don't pray like hell, you be going to hell."

Johnson taught Mr. Lockwood his guitar secrets. Mr. Lockwood recounts, "I didn't play the guitar until Robert came into my mother's life. I adored him, since he taught me how to make a living. Robert didn't want to teach nobody. I was already in music when I met him, and that was an advantage. I was learning so fast, I blew his mind. He taught me every time he came home. He never had to show me but twice," he boasts.

Johnson associated with a number of women in his brief life. He was first married to Virginia Travis in February 1929; both she and her baby died during childbirth in April 1930.[6] He married Calletta Craft in May 1931, and she too died a few years later.[7] Johnson then moved in with Estella Coleman, Robert Lockwood's mother. "I don't know how Robert met Mama. He followed Mama home and she couldn't get rid of him," he chuckles. "Mama was fourteen years older than I and ten years older than Robert. He looked like a boy. Robert would leave and go out from town to town to play. He'd come home for a couple of weeks, then go back out. Mama never asked him where he was going or when he'd return. That's why he loved her, I guess," he shrugs. "She knew he was a traveling musician and never gave him no problems. He liked

Mr. Lockwood at the time of the interview
photo by Stuart Lutz

women even better than I did." Inside his living room, Mr. Lockwood points to a portrait of his mother, taken when she was an older women. "That's Mama. She died in the late 1970s right here in this house." Nearby he has a large poster of Robert Johnson, holding his beloved guitar and wearing his fedora at a jaunty angle.

The young Mr. Lockwood traveled and performed with Johnson. "There was one time he carried me to Mississippi. Clarksdale. He put me on one side of the river and he went on the other. Folks crisscrossed that bridge like crazy. They didn't know which one of us was Robert Johnson, and they filled up both our baskets!

"He was making a whole lot of money. I saw him make

At almost ninety, Mr. Lockwood still plays regularly at a Cleveland blues bar

photos by Stuart Lutz

three thousand dollars in the park in two hours. People were filling his hat as fast as he could pull it out. He was playing on street corners, and there were so many people around him that I couldn't see him. He had records on juke boxes, and that's how he could make so much money." Johnson had only two recording sessions in his lifetime: one in San Antonio in November 1936 and one in Dallas in November 1937.[8] One of his songs, "Terraplane Blues," became a regional hit. That song, combined with his endless touring throughout the South, the Midwest, and even the Northeast, increased his fame.[9]

Despite living with Coleman, Johnson still eyed the ladies. On the evening of Saturday, August 13, 1938, he and his friend Sonny Boy Williamson II were playing at a roadhouse near Greenwood, Mississippi. Johnson flirted with the wife of the owner. He was brought some whiskey with a broken seal. Williamson insisted he not drink it, since it could be poisoned; he knocked the bottle out of Johnson's hand. A second pint was brought to him, and Johnson drank it. It was laced with strychnine, weakening Johnson. He caught pneumonia and died on August 16, 1938.[10] His exact burial location is unknown.

"The last time I saw him was 1938," Mr. Lockwood laments. "He came home, then went to Mississippi. The next thing we knew, someone poisoned him. Mama found out, but I don't know who told her. We didn't go to the funeral. I was out of playing for the year after his death because I liked him so much. Robert was my teacher, and if he was alive now, I'd take care of him. I'd be glad to. I wish he were around today to see how far I carried it. There ain't no one but me can play his material. Everyone else screws it up, like Eric Clapton. I like everything he wrote, though I don't play everything he wrote. I can play with a slide, but I don't like it. Three of my favorites are 'Sweet Home Chicago,' 'Love in Vain' and 'Dust My Broom.'"

Once Johnson died, Mr. Lockwood carved his own musical identity, although it was based on Johnson's lessons. In 1941 he recorded two well-known songs, "Take a Little Walk with Me" and "Little Boy Blue." As he tells it: "Me and Sonny Boy [Williamson II] were on the [radio show] King Biscuit Time in 1940. I wasn't there but two years. Me and the people couldn't get along, and I quit. I came on at four in the evening and had a five-piece band. I was in Chicago for twenty years, and I came here [to Cleveland] with Sonny Boy Williamson on my way to New York. And I got stuck. I got married and bought a house and that messed up everything. I was forty-six when I got married. But if I had gone to New York, I wouldn't have all that I have now."

Mr. Lockwood recorded throughout the 1970s and 1980s. In 1980 he was given the first W. C. Handy Award for a traditional blues album, and in 1989, he was inducted into the Blues Hall of Fame. His 1998 release, *I've Got to Find Myself a Woman*, was nominated for a Grammy.[11] He has now been in the blues business for seventy-five years, an amazing statistic considering how many bluesmen die young because of their rough lifestyle.

He discusses his most famous student. "I taught B. B. King. He's from Mississippi and I'm from Arkansas. I played with him for two years. He's the most successful one. He performs three hundred days a year. B. B. makes fifty thousand dollars a day for two hours of work. Lots of folks don't even make fifty thousand dollars in a year!" He shakes his head in amazement.

Mr. Lockwood does not have a single favorite blues song but lists some of his favorites. He opens a battered notebook with his scrawled pencil notes. "Let's see. There's 'Last Night,' 'Stormy Monday,' 'Blues before Sunrise,' 'Misty,' 'Key to the Highway,' 'I Just Want a Little Bit,' and B. B. King's 'Rock Me Baby' and 'Meet Me at the Bottom.' I wrote a lot of songs. Consider 'Take a Little Walk.' Songs just come to me and I write them down. Fortunately, I'm a creative person. My recent ones are 'Hangin' On,' 'I've Got to Find Myself a Woman,' 'Knock on Wood,' and 'Steal Away.' My band, we can play anything and everything. We even do Ray Charles."

In his glassed-in porch, he shows off his framed Doctorate of Humane Letters diploma, recently awarded by the local Case Western Reserve University. There are also small plaques from various blues organizations honoring him with membership. Mr. Lockwood moves to the foyer, where an upright piano is squeezed between numerous guitar cases. He indicates an Honorary Doctorate of Music from Cleveland State University and a picture of First Lady Hillary Clinton presenting him with an award. He chooses this time to discuss a conundrum he faces. "People wanted me to move to a white neighborhood, but someone in the new place wouldn't like it. And people here wouldn't like me leaving," he sighs.

"Remember, blues is about life. It is the foundation of American music. Everything else comes from it. Blues was first, then jazz, then rap. People all over the world like it, and I've been to New Zealand, Australia, Canada, Japan, Europe. Blues ain't never going to go out of style!"

Mr. Lockwood performs every Wednesday night at a downtown Cleveland blues club, fronting the "Robert Lockwood Jr. All Stars." He strolls in the club, his guitar case in his left hand, freeing his right to shake hands with regular patrons whom he recognizes. He is dressed in an oversized white pinstripe suit with beige boots and a tie. He moves very well for someone a few weeks short of ninety.

For a musician who grew up in the traditional acoustic blues environment, Lockwood's current band is surprisingly modern and electric. It includes two saxophonists, a trumpeter, a drummer, an electric guitarist, and a bassist. After letting the band play a few songs without him, including "Route 66," he ascends the stage. He picks up his guitar, a turquoise hollow-body instrument with twelve strings and his name emblazoned on the front. The word "Blues" is written in large letters on the head.

His music is heavily influenced by jazz with his use of saxophones and trumpets, but it is rooted in the traditional twelve-bar blues format. His guitar has a mellow sound to complement his slightly slurred and gruff vocal delivery. He spends nearly his entire performance studying his dexterous left hand, which glides up and down the fret board very quickly and accurately. He does not use a pick, instead plucking the strings with his thumb and two fingers. He alternates between up-tempo numbers and molasses-like ones. In one blues number, one of the saxophonists picks up a flute and plays along. The sound is surreal, but it shows the older Mr. Lockwood is still willing to push his musical barriers within a traditional format. In between his half-hour sets, he mingles with the crowd at the bar.

Toward the end of the evening the band leaves the stage, leaving Mr. Lockwood up there alone. He plays two Robert Johnson songs, the ever-popular "Love in Vain" followed by "Stop Breaking Down." In this way, Mr. Lockwood carries on the blues legacy of the solo performer.

The audience is largely white and middle class, willing to pay twenty dollars per entrée. As the performance continues, it starts flurrying on this Ohio winter evening, and the crowd dwindles. This expensive, snowy scene is many miles from the southern juke joints of Mr. Lockwood's youth.

Robert Lockwood Jr. died on November 21, 2006, at age ninety-one.

NOTES

1. *Robert Johnson: The Complete Recordings* (1990), booklet, 5.

2. Ibid., 7.

3. "Robert Johnson Timeline," Can't You Hear the Wind Howl? The Life and Music of Robert Johnson, http://www.robert johnsonfilm.com/Timeline.html (accessed July 3, 2009).

4. *Robert Johnson: The Complete Recordings*, booklet, 9.

5. Ibid., 11.

6. Ibid., 9.

7. Ibid., 11–13.

8. Ibid., 46.

9. Ibid., 15.

10. Ibid., 16–18.

11. "Robert Lockwood Jr. Is Nominated for a Grammy," Robert Lockwood Jr. Web Site, http://www.robertlockwood.com/grammy.html (accessed July 3, 2009).

HAL PRIESTE
The Last Participant in the 1920 Antwerp Olympics
"Now watch this!"

In 1896 the Frenchman Pierre de Coubertin organized the first modern Olympics, held at their ancient site in Athens. The first few Olympics were a struggle until more countries began sending athletes and the idea became popular. Today the Olympics are a worldwide spectacle, complete with tradition, pageantry, and corporate sponsorships. But the Olympic Games were not always so refined.

Haig M. "Hal" Prieste is both the world's oldest Olympian and the world's oldest Olympic medalist. He is also the last living participant of the 1920 Olympics held in Antwerp. He was born in Fresno, California, on November 23, 1896, to Armenian parents who had fled Turkey earlier that year, but he now lives in a convalescent home in Camden, New Jersey. The LaMaina family has adopted Mr. Prieste, and they travel across New Jersey to visit him every Saturday.

Mr. Prieste is in his room, completely under the bed covers, looking like a squirming ghost. Mrs. LaMaina explains that the 102-year-old is performing his lifelong routine of daily stretches. She uncovers a gaunt man with a hollow face, a wisp of white hair, and dark arcs under his eyes. The LaMainas dress Mr. Prieste in a white shirt and navy blue pants, then lead him to a wheelchair. He is surprisingly short for a world-class athlete, perhaps five foot two. As Mrs. LaMaina pushes him out into the hall, she says, "It's not that he can't walk. It's just that his vision is bad and not long ago, while skipping, he tripped and banged his head."

Since Mr. Prieste's hearing is bad, Dr. LaMaina reviews Mr. Prieste's life and Olympic achievements. "As a baby," he explains, "his father, who was an immigrant, dressed him as a woman for some unknown reason. When Hal was a teenager, he gravitated to Anaheim. There, the famous film director

Max Sennett used to bring his group to the beach, and they hung out with the lifeguards. Max spotted Hal clowning around and asked him to be in his movies. That is where he befriended Charlie Chaplin, [Stan] Laurel and [Oliver] Hardy, and most of the early silent comic greats. I know he was very fond of Chaplin, and said he was a 'fine gentleman.'

"Hal went into the navy during World War I. He discovered that he could swim and dive. On a dare, he jumped off the top of a roller coaster and got a bloody nose, but was proud of himself. After the navy, someone told him that he could probably get into the Olympics, so he saved his money. He went to the local tryouts in Alameda and came in first in diving. He eventually beat the national champion, Clyde Swendsen [who coached the American Olympic gold medal divers from 1924 to 1936], and then the L.A. Athletic Club paid for his trip to New York City. He went there to the New York Athletic Club to train. There, he met Duke Kahanamoku, who was on the swimming team. He was known as 'The Duke' and 'The Big Kahuna.' He won three gold medals and two silvers at the 1912, 1920, and 1924 Olympics."

Today we think of luxurious Olympic villages, but eighty years ago, "Hal stayed in a farmhouse for lodging. For the diving contest, you dove into the canals, which were cold and polluted. Since it was held outdoors, Hal said that it was very windy on that day. But he won the bronze. Hal still has the original medal, and he also has a special medal that was given to every competitor in those Games."

Dr. LaMaina tells a very funny story about pilfering. "The famous Olympic flag, the one with the five rings, was first introduced at the Antwerp Games. When the Duke saw that original flag, he dared Hal to steal it. So Hal just shimmied up the pole and took it. Well, while he was up there, the police saw him, and they gave chase. For five blocks. There's just no way the cops are going to catch an Olympic athlete. And Hal didn't know what to do with it once he returned to the United States. So once he had it, he just kept it. One of the first times we went to his apartment, he says, 'Wait here' and he pulls out the original Olympic flag, which was missing for decades! We didn't believe what it was until he told us the full story. Anyway, he still has it, and he's planning on going to the 2000 Sydney Olympics and present the original flag back to the Games.

"Hal went to the 1996 Games in Atlanta and it was just so wonderful. He got to carry the torch. NBC had dinner there for him in honor of his one-hundredth birthday. They carved a bust of him. He met [Olympic gold medalist diver] Greg Louganis, and he did an autograph signing for the United States Mint. There were over three hundred people in line! And what was really special was that while he was there, he met an old friend of his who he hadn't seen in seventy-six years. The last time they saw each other, he was twenty-four then and she was fourteen. It was very beautiful to see, and they caught up on the years.

"After the Olympics Mr. Prieste learned to surf, and he and Duke Kahanamoku toured doing surfing exhibitions, so Hal went to Hawaii. He then entered show business, and his specialty act was tumbling. At twenty-nine he was a headliner in Times Square, and then worked for Ringling. At forty Mr. Prieste taught himself to ice skate, so he created a comedy routine and skated with the Ice Follies. While in the Follies, he put a broomstick on his head and would skate around that way. He then did a nightclub act in the Borsht Belt and Atlantic City. Mr. Prieste ended up in Philadelphia, where he rooted for their hockey team, the Flyers; the team made him their unofficial mascot, and he would skate with the players during practices. During the intermission between periods, he would skate on the ice with a hockey stick balanced on his head, even though he was in his nineties. On his hundredth birthday, the Flyers honored him and gave him the executive suite."

**Mr. Prieste balancing
a hockey stick on his head**
photo by Stuart Lutz

Mr. Prieste straddling the hockey stick
photo by Stuart Lutz

Mr. Prieste, ever the showman, shows what he can still do. He places his palms on the floor while keeping his knees locked. After a long period of stretching, he rises and says in a loud voice, "Ah! That felt good!" He follows with another deep knee bend.

Mrs. LaMaina hands him his hockey stick. "It's his favorite toy," she explains. Mr. Prieste sits in his chair and balances it on his head for five minutes without touching it. After five minutes, the stick suddenly slips forward. In a flash, Mr. Prieste, whose vision is poor, thrusts out his hands and the stick lands gently in his palms. He then places the stick again on his head and starts doing a variety of stretching exercises with his arms. Sensing he has an audience, he yells, "Now watch this!" and stands up, balancing the stick on his head. He slowly squats down, resting his palms on the floor while continually balancing the stick on his head. Mrs. LaMaina dutifully pulls the wheelchair back to give him extra room.

Mr. Prieste stands with the stick still balanced on his head, and again announces, "Now watch this!" He walks a few feet away, places the blade on the floor, and straddles the stick. He lowers himself, using the stick as a seat, much like riding a horse. Then he goes too far and falls onto his side on the hard linoleum floor. The LaMainas rush to help him, but he waves them off. He rolls over, gets on all fours, and quickly lifts himself. He again picks up the stick and begins the maneuver again as the LaMainas blanch. He succeeds in getting very close to the floor and then stands up again.

Mr. Prieste strides back to his wheelchair and sits in it. Using his standard proclamation—"Now watch this!"—he draws his knees to his chest while precariously balancing on the edge of the vinyl seat. Then he stands and balances on one foot.

For a marvelous twenty minutes, the centenarian Mr. Prieste proves what he is physically capable of accomplishing. The lifelong showman flashes a gleeful smile the entire time as he gives one more performance.

On September 8, 2000, the LaMainas take Mr. Prieste to Sydney, Australia, to attend the Summer Olympic Games, and the rehabilitation home throws a party for him before he leaves. The building's entrance is decorated with colored balloons, streamers, and signs. Some of the residents are outside,

**Mr. Prieste with the
pilfered original Olympic flag**
photo by Stuart Lutz

holding signs that read, "We are proud of our Olympian, Hal Prieste," and others are snacking on cookies and cake. Mr. Prieste is in a conference room, and someone is bending down and shouting something into his ear. The room is packed with television reporters, the LaMainas, and their two grandchildren. The priceless flag, measuring about four feet wide and more than two feet high, is carefully spread on the large table. Its creases are sharp, and the beige linen has yellowed slightly.

Dr. LaMaina says that the flight from Philadelphia to Sydney is twenty-two hours, a grueling journey for someone a quarter of Mr. Prieste's age. He laughs at the thought of Mr. Prieste performing his daily yoga stretches on the plane.

As Dr. LaMaina wheels Mr. Prieste into the lobby, someone turns on proud martial music and the television crews film him. He enters the lobby to huge cheers, and the residents cover him with confetti. He is wheeled into the sunlight and covers his eyes from the glare. After a few minutes, the LaMainas have him securely in the van and they pull away, fulfilling an old Olympian's dream to return an antique banner to its rightful owner. During the Opening Ceremonies, announcer Bob Costas tells the worldwide television audience of Mr. Prieste's high jinks with the original flag.

Hal Prieste died on April 19, 2001, at the age of 104, months after fulfilling his second Olympic dream.

DORIS EATON TRAVIS
The Last of the Original Ziegfeld Follies Performers

*"During the curtain call, we'd come out on stage, and
[President Wilson would] wave to us and we'd wave back to him."*

The Ziegfeld Follies were the most extravagant and legendary revues of the vaudevillian era. The singers, dancers, and performers dressed in beautiful costumes and put on elaborate musical numbers. Florenz Ziegfeld, the originator of the Follies, created the first one in 1907 and produced them until 1925 (though there were also ones in 1927 and 1931). Many famous entertainers of the first half of the twentieth century got their start in the Follies; for many others, their appearances in the Follies increased their fame. The prestigious list of those who worked in the Follies includes W. C. Fields, Will Rogers, Bert Williams, Eddie Cantor, and Marilyn Miller.[1] In the 1930s, three forces teamed to strike a deadly blow to vaudeville and Broadway musicals: the advent of radio, which brought music into every home; the spread of motion pictures; and the Great Depression, which left less money for entertainment than in the 1920s.[2] Doris Eaton Travis is the last Ziegfeld Follies participant alive; she is also the last living member of the Eaton family, and one of the last entertainers from the lost vaudeville era.

The large and successful "Eatons of Broadway" were seen all along the Great White Way in the 1910s and 1920s. There were seven siblings—Evelyn, Robert, Pearl, Mary, Doris, Joseph, and Charlie—although only five were in entertainment. The most famous Eaton, Mary, started in the Follies then appeared as Eddie Cantor's leading lady in 1923's *Kid Boots*. Mary later starred in *The Five O'Clock Girl* and appeared as a cover girl. In a remarkable theatrical occurrence, four Eatons appeared in four different Broadway productions in 1924: Mary starred in *Kid Boots* with Eddie Cantor, Doris in *The Sap* with Raymond Hitchcock, Pearl in *Annie Dear* with Billie Burke, and Charlie in *Peter Pan* with Marilyn Miller.[3] Miller was the queen of Broadway in the 1920s. A beautiful woman, she was made a star by the *Ziegfeld Follies of 1918* and went on to perform in *Sally, Sunny,* and *Smiles.*

Mrs. Travis is about five feet tall and still has the slim build of a dancer. Although she will be 101 at her next birthday, she looks a quarter century younger than that. Her glasses hide her twinkling blue eyes, and she has a full head of white hair. She is very lively and energetic throughout the interview, fidgeting and waving her arms to emphasize points.

She was born on March 14, 1904, in Norfolk, Virginia, but her family moved to Washington, DC, when she was a little girl. "I used to go to dancing school when I was very young," she announces in her crisp, clear speaking voice. "My oldest sister, Evelyn, loved show business. As Mama had seven children, it was up to Evelyn to do the footwork for us. Evelyn saw an ad from a local stock company for a play that needed children, so she took us down to audition. They accepted us, and from then on, for several years, we played all the children's parts. The company had forty-week seasons, with a different play every week. This went on for year after year. The word was out that if you needed a child actor in the Washington area, call Mrs. Eaton because she's got 'em in all sizes, sexes, and ages! She'd put pants on the daughters and dresses on the sons. Mary and I played in many shows over the years. She and I played the leads in a Maurice Maeterlinck play called *The Blue Bird* in 1911. When I was in the local stock company in Washington, I performed for President Woodrow Wilson several times. He loved going to shows on Friday nights. During the curtain call, we'd come out on stage, and he'd wave to us and we'd wave back to him. His daughter also loved showbiz and sent me flowers after I was in a play called *Rackety Packety House.*"

The Shuberts, a family of theatrical producers in New York City, had originally presented the theatrical production of *The Blue Bird* several years earlier. "They had let the Washington stock company present the play for Christmas week. Then the Shuberts decided they would revive *The Blue Bird* as a road company and asked the Washington stock company manager to give them the names of the children who had played the lead roles in the stock company. The Shuberts then sent their agent, Nathaniel Roth, to Washington to see us and talk to our mother about their plans. An agreement was reached and Mama, Pearl, Mary, and I went to New York to rehearse the show. Mary and I played the leading roles. We were on the road with the show for about six months. When we returned, the family decision was made to move to New York. We had proved that we had dancing and dramatic talent, and if we were to continue in show business, New York was the place to be.

"The Shuberts thought Mary was good in ballet and paid for her to go for ballet lessons. Mary started with Theodore Kosloff, one of the great ballet dancers. When he left New York, ballet teacher Ivan Tarasoff took over the school. Mary developed as a ballet dancer and performed as a little white butterfly. Her first appearance in a Broadway production was with Anna Held [the first wife of Florenz Ziegfeld] when she was fifteen. However, the theatrical rules were you had to be sixteen to appear in a musical production, so [Ziegfeld] took her out of the show. Once she turned sixteen, her first big performance was in George M. Cohan's *The Royal Vagabond*."

Mrs. Travis continues to discuss her beginnings in show business. "The Poli stock company had a chain of theaters throughout New England. For two or three years after moving to New York, we played parts in their New England theaters. The general manager of the Poli stock company knew that if you needed child performers, you call Mrs. Eaton. By this time we had relocated to New York City. I missed a lot of school

Mrs. Travis as a young dancer
photo courtesy Doris Eaton Travis

during these years and was going to summer school to finish the eighth grade. Pearl was already in the Ziegfeld Follies. In fact, Mr. Ziegfeld used her to interview new chorus girls beginning in August 1918. Mr. Ziegfeld was preparing a road show to start in October 1918, and he needed to rehearse the new chorus girls. Pearl was assisting with this. I asked Mama if I could go with Pearl to watch the rehearsal. I put on my sister Mary's long dress—I didn't have one at the time—and went down to watch the rehearsals with Pearl. It was the last week of summer school in August. Ned Wayburn, the dance director, came up to Pearl to give her instructions, and I was sitting right next to her. He looked at me and asked who I was. He said that I looked exactly like his wife and asked if I danced. He needed an understudy for [Follies star and dancer

Ann] Pennington. Now, she was not a highly accomplished dancer. Pearl said that I could dance, and Mr. Wayburn said he would like me to be in the chorus. As I was fourteen, Pearl didn't think Mama would allow that at all, but Mr. Wayburn offered that Mama could go with me and he'd pay all our expenses. We talked it over with Mama and she said it was okay. The next day was the last day of school. I passed my classes with an A, gathered my practice clothes, and went to rehearsals. I was in the Follies. Now, I was just in the chorus line, but it was a start.

"The next year—1919—Mr. Ziegfeld prepared for the show. He told Mama that I could be in it. Now, since I was still underage for a month, which was then sixteen, I used a different name. I was Lucille La'Vant that year. I decided to get French, so I used the 'La.' I was the understudy for Marilyn Miller. I went on for her for two weeks in Chicago and Philadelphia after her husband was killed in a car crash.

"In 1920, the third year, Mr. Ziegfeld engaged my sister Mary as the star dancer, and he gave me a shot for a solo dance. In between sketches with comedians, I would dance with Bernard Granville. It was a cute little number. When we returned from the road, my agent wanted me to interview for movies in England. Mr. Glidden, an English director, interviewed us and engaged me for the role. He sent me and Mama on a boat to England. Well, the movie sent its cast to Egypt. What a fantastic trip! Mama loved to travel, and we had a wonderful time there. We rode donkeys, and saw the pyramids and the Sphinx. We crossed the Nile every morning. We were there about two weeks and saw Luxor, Cairo, and Alexandria. Mama traveled with me all the time and was very protective. I'd go, do my job at the theater, then return to the hotel and read. There was really only one close feminine friendship that I had, and that was with Kitty Cosgriff, and I became friends with her when we were both struggling for survival in a stock company on Long Island. She was a lovely Irish lady, but that was the only close friend in show business I had. So even though I was the youngest one, I've enjoyed a lot of the people I've worked with."

Mrs. Travis was the understudy to Marilyn Miller in the Follies. "She was a very pretty young lady, rather the delicate type. She was very cordial to all in the show. My sister Mary and Marilyn were very good friends. We all became good friends with her over the years. The gossips said that she and Mary were at odds, since both were stars, but that wasn't the case at all. I went on as her understudy in the Follies. In fact, three of us understudied her. Mary replaced her in *Sally*, since Mr. Ziegfeld wanted an experienced person. And Pearl understudied Marilyn for *Sunny*. And Charlie appeared with her in *Peter Pan*.

"Mr. Ziegfeld was always very kind and thoughtful to all us Eatons. Pearl started with him first, I was second, then Mary, and finally Charlie as the Dauphin in one of the little sketches. Mr. Ziegfeld was a fatherly figure, and we thoroughly enjoyed our association. Pearl started in his choruses in 1918 and performed on the roof of a nightclub for a couple of years. Mr. Ziegfeld also had an evening show entitled the *Midnight Frolics* that took place on the roof and featured racier numbers. Pearl worked closely with him for a couple of years to select new dancers for the chorus lines. My brother Charlie had a great experience with him when he was about fourteen. He was at the Peekskill Military Academy and he and a bunch of his friends came into New York City for an evening. They were at a nightclub, and Mr. Ziegfeld comes in with two beautiful girls. Charlie told his friend that he knew Mr. Ziegfeld, and of course they didn't believe him. So he walked over, and Mr. Ziegfeld greets him with 'Charlie Eaton! The Dauphin!' He ended up dancing with one of the beautiful girls. When he returned to the table, his friends said, 'Okay, we believe!'

"The last time I saw Mr. Ziegfeld was in the early 1930s after he had been wiped out by the Great Crash of 1929. I hadn't worked for him for several years, and this was after *Showboat*. He hadn't done shows for a couple of years. Anyway, he had an office in the Ziegfeld Theatre, and I heard he was thinking of starting a new show. One morning I went to his office and knocked on the door. I went in, and it was just him at his desk—no secretary or staff. He treated me well. He said, 'I'm going to try to put on another show.' I told him that I was interested in working for him again. He replied, 'I'll let you know if there is. Just keep tabs on it.' It was a brief interview. I remember he looked dejected, very forlorn. I closed the door, and that was the last time I ever saw him. [Ziegfeld died in 1932.]"

Mrs. Travis has fond memories of many of the famous people she met, including Will Rogers, W. C. Fields, and Babe Ruth. "Al Jolson [best remembered for the first movie with sound, *The Jazz Singer*] was a very dedicated performer. I was the leading lady in the show *Big Boy*. I thought he was very pleasant to work with. Periodically, he would call rehearsal and tell the cast they were getting sloppy and he wanted to tighten up the show. He was quite alert to the quality of performance that would go on.

"I was in two or three Follies with W. C. Fields. He was a jolly and good person, not crotchety at all. His girlfriend Bessie Poole was in the chorus with me, and Bessie and I got to be friends. He liked to drive himself when he was on the road, and she'd travel with him. Charlie had a lot of association with Fields. He was in a little skit called *The Birthday of the Dauphin*. Fields was the jester, and [the skit] had Fanny Brice and Raymond Hitchcock. Charlie spent a lot of time with him in his dressing room. Now, there was always this rumor of Fields and little boys that simply was not true. I was speaking not long ago before some theatrical people, and I mentioned that Charlie would hang out with Fields in his room. Everyone gasped and listened to me, like I was going to say something bad or scandalous about Fields. But nothing ever happened with Charlie. They each had a remarkable sense of humor. Charlie just adored him.

"Will Rogers [the legendary comedian killed in a 1935 plane crash] was in the 1918 Follies with me. His act preceded mine. I'd be in the wings, and as he came by, he'd greet me with, 'Hello Doris' or tease me with, 'Tough audience tonight.' He really smiled a lot.

"Bert Williams [a famous light-skinned African American comedian and mime who wore blackface on stage] was also in the 1918 Follies with me. He was a quiet man and very friendly around the theater. He would wait in the wings for the queue. He'd smile at all of us, but I never saw him talking closely with anyone. It was always a 'Hello' or something like that. He just minded his own business.

"I met Babe Ruth when I was in the Hollywood Music Box revue. I have a picture of us, and I'm there kicking a ball. I still have the ball."

Despite all these wonderful stories, Mrs. Travis confesses, "My favorite theatrical memory was in 1998, when I was in the Easter Bonnet, a fund-raiser for AIDS research. It was in the New Amsterdam Theatre, and it was the first time I had been on that stage in seventy-nine years. I did this Marilyn Miller routine, step-for-step, that I had done as her understudy in the 1919 Follies, and the audience went wild. It was the top of my career for me. I love ragtime, and this year I will reconstruct 'Hello, My Honey,' a ragtime number. In 2007 it's the centennial of the Ziegfeld Follies, and I'm holding out for that since I am one of the remaining original Ziegfeld Follies."

When in New York, she still sees Broadway plays. "Last night I saw *Little Women*, and recently saw *Mamma Mia*, *Wicked*, and *Chicago*. But my favorite play is *42nd Street*. In thinking of Broadway today, it is not the Broadway I used to

Mrs. Travis with Babe Ruth
photo courtesy Doris Eaton Travis

know. The aura is gone. It is blanketed today with huge electric signs. And there is so much traffic and activity there. I under-stand that progress couldn't hold onto that era of the twenties forever, and as things go forward you lose a bit of something

Mrs. Travis at the time of the interview
photo by Stuart Lutz

that you once felt. When I walk up Broadway, I miss that. I don't like the microphones the performers use either. Everyone wears one. I think it makes the actors' voices sound tinny and harsh. It loses the lovely quality of the human voice. It would be better to improve the theater's acoustics. Ethel Barrymore was famous for her voice, as were many other actors and actresses. Broadway has improved in one way. When I went to see *Little Women* last night, the scene changing was done superbly. That element of working backstage has improved marvelously. It is a subtle part of the entertainment."

Mrs. Travis tells an interesting story from when her show business career ended at thirty-four. "I couldn't get a job, I was way behind in the rent, and I was desperate," she states. "Then God stepped in and I got a call to take a job as a tap dance teacher at the Arthur Murray Schools. It changed my life. I opened a string of Arthur Murray social dance studios and I was fortunate to get in the dance business. I learned a lot how to handle a business, and it was a big step for me. It forced me to be very active. I was so desperate that I saw the dancing job as my Custer's Last Stand. I kept in mind that it would be a success. And I worked at it seven days a week for ten to twelve hours a day. In 1968 I retired with my husband, Paul, to an Oklahoma ranch, where we raised quarter horses."

Despite her business success, Mrs. Travis did not have a formal education, and she was determined to change that. "My sister Evelyn was always keen on schooling. As the family show business activity increased, our education was affected. I quit school after the eighth grade to concentrate on acting. While on the road, Mama always had books, including English grammar. When I came back to school classes after being on the road, I always got As. As I got into show business more, I met a lot of educated people and I felt inferior to them. I thought that maybe they were a little better than me. It hung with me. When I owned my Arthur Murray dance studios, I tried to resuscitate my education, but it was too much with the business. So the idea of not having an education was always in the back of my mind. When I moved to Norman, Oklahoma, I associated with a lot of professors at the University of Oklahoma. My husband, Paul, had not one, but two degrees from Cornell—and I didn't even have a high school diploma! One day I mentioned that I wished I had a college education. He said that we were only fifteen minutes from the university, and it was time to put up or shut up. I got the high school curriculum; I took tests and mostly got As. Then some friends helped me matriculate into the university. My first semester I took three classes, and I got one C. Now, at this time, I was also bookkeeper for our horse ranch, and that kept me very busy. I was disappointed with the C, and I figured if I got such a low grade, I wasn't learning much. I cut my load to two courses a semester. It took me eleven years, but I graduated with a 3.65 GPA as a history major and was elected Phi Beta Kappa. I graduated in 1992, when I was eighty-eight. It was a wonderful experience, and the students were delightful to me—there was no animosity. I knew I had arrived when the kids asked to see my class notes! I'm about a third of the way to my master's degree. It's a paper on decadence in American history throughout the twentieth century: how music has changed, how social dancing has changed, and how fashion has moved. As I see it, shorter dresses led to more action of bodies in dancing, and the more the dancers used their bodies, the more sensual the dancing became. Today people dance apart and writhe."

Her secret is that she keeps looking ahead. "I always have two or three goals for me, and I work every day. I put a lot of thought in what I am going to do every day. My religion is Christian Science, and I turn to it very deeply. I never smoked or drank, and my mother was a great cook. That's why I'm still going! I still dance a little. Not my cartwheels, splits, or high kicks, but a little soft shoe, some ragtime, and a little social dancing.

"I have a lot of gratitude that I was able to accomplish things. But now I'm sometimes lonely. My husband passed away four years ago, and my brother Charlie, who lived with me for four years, died last August. So I think back to 1918 when I went with Pearl to start in the chorus."

NOTES

1. Gerald Bordman and Thomas S. Hischak, eds., *The Oxford Companion to American Theater* (New York: Oxford University Press, 2004), 679–80.

2. Doris Eaton Travis, *The Days We Danced* (Seattle: Marquand Books, 2003), 7.

3. Ibid., 272.

DOROTHY YOUNG
Harry Houdini's Final Stage Assistant
"Houdini would come out, turn it on, tune it, and I would pop out."

Harry Houdini is the most legendary American magician and escape artist, past or present. Many decades after his premature death on Halloween of 1926, his escapes from handcuffs, sealed milk cartons, straitjackets, and even jail cells remain mythic.

Dorothy Young had barely graduated from high school when she went to work for Houdini as his stage assistant. Mrs. Young's original contract with Houdini forbade her from ever revealing his secrets and tricks, and three-quarters of a century later she remains faithful to that agreement. She is willing, however, to share stories of Houdini's hidden personal warmth and other tales of the greatest illusionist America has ever seen.

Dorothy Young was born in Otisville, New York. Her father was a minister; her mother, a deaconess. "Houdini," she explains, "used to joke that I came from five generations of ministers and he came from five generations of rabbis."

Mrs. Young began working for Houdini at the age of seventeen. "But the story is a bit longer than that," she warns, waving her hand as if to say that her tale began long before she met Houdini. "Because of my father's job, we moved quite a bit and I skipped grades." Mrs. Young freely admits that she wasn't a good student. While attending Beaver College, she was required to attend cultural events, so she went to a concert and saw the famous ballerina Anna Pavlova perform *Swan Lake*. "I can close my eyes and still see her," Mrs. Young reminisces. "Seeing her changed my life. I knew I wanted to be a dancer. My father let me take lessons, and I was a natural." Even now, at the age of ninety-five, her five-foot frame and lithe dancer's body attest to that fact.

After seeing countless Broadway shows, Mrs. Young decided to find a way onto the stage herself. "I bought a newspaper in the city and there was an advertisement that said, 'Girl Dancer Wanted For Broadway Show & Tour.'" She motions with her hands as if framing a marquis. Though she was shy, she mustered her courage and went to the Longacre Theatre. "I got there and the stage was full of girls, and there were two men in the orchestra." Although she didn't know it at the time, one was Houdini himself, and the other was Mr. Smith, Houdini's manager. "I was the last to audition. Since he needed a dancer for the show, I did the Charleston." Mrs. Young smiles as she repeats the vigorous arm motions of the famous Jazz Age dance. "And I was picked. I asked him later why he picked me. He told me that the minute I walked on the stage, he knew I was the one he'd choose. All the others were typical Broadway girls, and he said I was different." She pauses, then chuckles, "And all the others were taller than Houdini!"

Houdini and his wife took Mrs. Young to a lawyer on 43rd Street, where she signed a one-year contract. "Mrs. H.—I always called her Mrs. H., for I wasn't old enough to call her by her first name—took me shopping to choose materials for a costume. This was all fine until I told my parents that I was down on Broadway." Because her father disapproved, she could not be in the show. "After all, I was only seventeen," she said. "I told Houdini 'no' a week before we were to open in Hartford." But the show must go on, and Houdini asked to meet Mrs. Young's parents and reassured them of their daughter's well-being. Houdini promised the Youngs that he would look after their daughter as if she were his own. "My father arranged for me to stay with a widow and her two daughters in New York City the week before we left for Hartford."

And as Mrs. Young spent more time with the Houdinis, she felt like part of the family. "Mrs. H. was like a second mother to me," she remembers fondly, "and once we were in Hart-

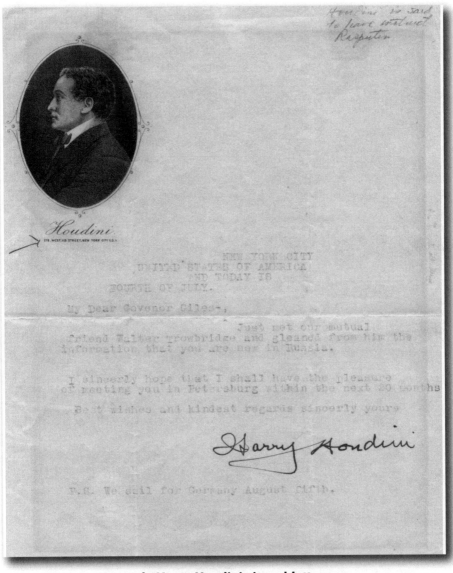

An early Harry Houdini signed letter
photo courtesy Stuart Lutz

Mrs. Young, popping out of the oversized radio, with Harry Houdini
photo courtesy Dorothy Young

Mrs. Young at the time of the interview
photo by Stuart Lutz

ford, Houdini—I always called him Houdini, never 'Mr. Houdini'—came out with a deck of cards and started doing tricks for me, and he told me all about his life."

Performing with the Houdinis was a wonderful experience. "Mrs. H. made all the costumes. Houdini had this unusual tuxedo he would perform in. The sleeves would come off so the audience could see that he was hiding nothing." The magic was left to Houdini, but Mrs. Young took care of the dancing. "There were a couple of times I had to fold up scarves," she says, "but basically I danced. I remember the Houdinis had this very beautiful stage curtain they brought back from a trip to Europe, so I'd come out with Mrs. H. and pull it back. Sometimes she would pretend to be Marie Antoinette and I was her escort. We would start on the opposite sides of the stage, meet in the middle, and pull back the curtain for Houdini's entrance."

During some performances, Mrs. Young worked even more directly with Houdini. "One act I did was to hide inside this oversized radio," she recalls. "Houdini would come out, turn it on, tune it, and I would pop out. He would announce me, lift me up, and then I would do the Charleston. The other number I was in was called 'The Slave Girl.' The stage was empty except for a pole. I was brought out with my hands behind my back and was tied to the pole. The curtain would fall and then I would reappear in a beautiful butterfly costume and do a ballet number."

Mrs. Young enjoyed working with Houdini. Although many people believe Houdini had an irritable personality, Mrs. Young denies this. "Houdini was very kind, compassionate, and faithful. He wasn't temperamental, egotistical, or unfaithful. Never once did he say anything to me about being cute. Those things are just not true, and I'm trying to set the record straight. There was only one time I remember him getting angry. It was up in Buffalo during Prohibition, and Mrs.

H. made a joke about smuggling back some Canadian liquor, and his eyes just snapped. He has these very penetrating eyes." Mrs. Young juts her fingers away from her own eyes to demonstrate. "He knew liquor was very bad publicity during Prohibition. But he was compassionate and not greedy. I never saw him turn down anyone who really needed money."

Mrs. Young can personally vouch for the Houdinis' generosity and kindness. "I must have had a good salary. In Chicago I bought a fur coat. Mrs. H. was just wonderful to me. She was quite a cut-up. She took me to my first Chinese restaurant. We always ate after the show so we would be as thin as possible during it. Once, at a railroad station, we went into a commissary, and she dunked a doughnut. I had never seen that before."

Mrs. Young was not with Houdini when he died on October 31, 1926, after a college student punched the unprepared illusionist in the stomach and burst his appendix. "He died two months after I left the show. The Houdinis wanted me to stay, but I had the chance to be on Broadway, and they understood. It was a chance to further my life. I was working on a Broadway play, *Jarnegan*, so I couldn't get time off to go to the funeral, which was huge, just huge. But I saw Mrs. H. the next day. She was protected by Houdini, but she had a sad life after he died. She visited me in Palm Beach once and we had a wonderful time. But she got to drinking later and . . . it was sad."

Though she enjoyed the year she spent with Houdini, she does not focus on the fact that she is the last link to the greatest magician ever. "You know, I've done so much in my life that I never thought about it until recently, when I realized how big he still is. It was a wonderful experience, and I was like a daughter to them."

Mrs. Young still treasures a photograph of her and Houdini on stage, but most of the physical reminders of those days are gone. "I had a trunk of memorabilia related to Houdini that I left at my sister's, but the Salvation Army hauled it away after my brother-in-law died." She shrugs, as if to say, "C'est la vie." Though the tangible reminders are lost, Mrs. Young will never forget the year she danced for the mythic Harry Houdini.

Afterword

There is an old African proverb that says, "When an old man dies, a library burns to the ground." At the time of this book's publication, about three-quarters of the Last Leaves featured have died. Every time one passes, our national memory dims slightly.

As a historian, I have long thought that an individual's stories—tales filled with bravery, innovation, tragedy, luck, exploration, risk, loss, and humor—are as important as an event's larger significance. While many of us will not actively change the great river of history, few are unaffected by its strong currents. Many of us create our own tributaries, whether by chance or by intention.

Yet today, future Last Leaves walk among us. There are people who have witnessed great occurrences or participated in important technical, military, cultural, and social events. Some of these have already happened, a number of them are occurring now, and many more have yet to take place. And those future Last Leaves will live decades after their events and will recount their personal histories for many years to come.

If you are a young reader of this book, ask your grandparents what it was like to grow up during the Great Depression, in a segregated country, or through the turbulent Vietnam era. If you have children or grandchildren, please tell them your memories and about our country's history: the beautiful, the heroic, and the heartbreaking. All these stories are part of their own future narrative. We all build libraries of our own lives.